STANDING
in the
LIGHT

STANDING
in the
LIGHT

 My Life as a Pantheist

SHARMAN APT RUSSELL

BASIC
BOOKS

A Member of the Perseus Books Group
New York

To old and new friends
in the Gila Valley

CONTENTS

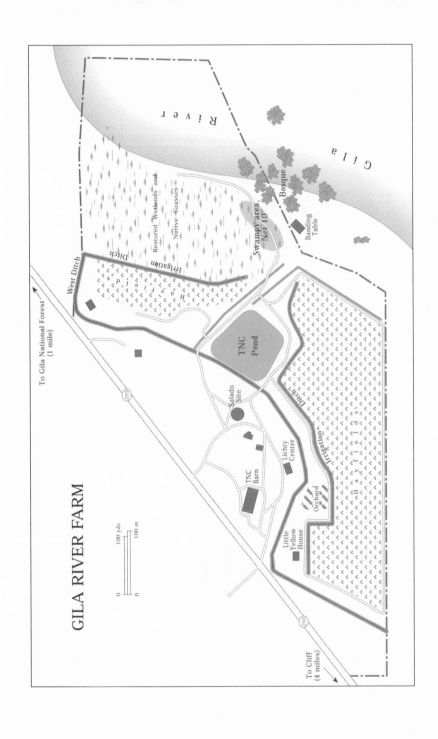

GILA RIVER FARM

To Gila National Forest
(1 mile)

To Cliff
(4 miles)

100 yds
100 m
0
0

River

Gila

River

Bosque

Banding
Table

Swampy area
Net 10

Restored Wetlands and Native Grasses

West Ditch

Irrigation Ditch

H a y f i e l d s

TNC
Pond

Salado
Site

Irrigation Ditch

H a y f i e l d s

TNC
Barn

Lichty
Center

Little
Yellow
House

Orchard

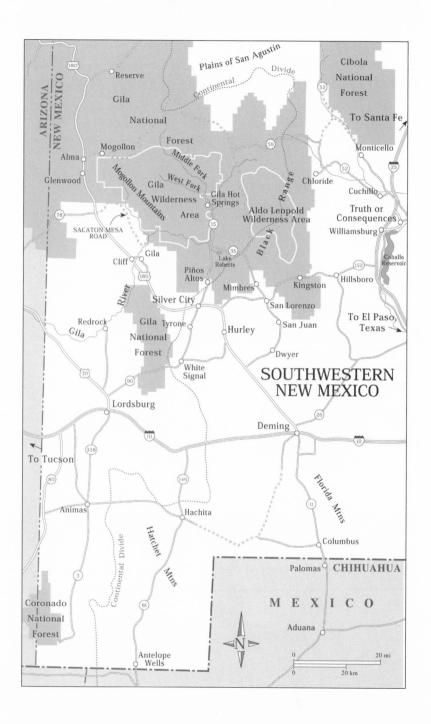

INTRODUCTION

In the second century CE the Roman emperor Marcus Aurelius may have best defined pantheism when he wrote, "Everything is interwoven, and the web is holy." My account uses many more words and covers a year in my life, roughly November 2005 to November 2006. It barrels through the history of pantheistic thought in the West, from the Greek philosophers of the sixth century BCE to the Internet sites twenty-five hundred years later. This overview is personal, not definitive. I am in love with Marcus Aurelius. I ignore Plotinus. I admire Virginia Woolf, whom many would not consider a pantheist at all. As for Eastern philosophies, they come late in my story, in the 1960s and 1970s after their texts had entered the American mainstream and my local bookstore. In this account, science is a good friend—although not perfect; friends are not perfect. Quakerism is central to my experience, and I am grateful to belong to a Quaker Meeting that allows for pantheism as one of its beliefs. My title, *Standing in the Light,* comes from the Quaker phrase "to stand in the Light," a concept with many meanings, encompassing political beliefs as well as spiritual. In my case, it is very much related to the bright New Mexican sky. In my case, pantheism is a word whose back I ride like a man on a horse trying to get somewhere. Or maybe a word more like a house, a place of shelter when it is cold and rainy, a house with big windows and a gorgeous view.

CHAPTER 1

Standing in the Light

I N THE SUMMER of 1996, I sat on my porch steps in the small town of Silver City, New Mexico, trying to decide if I should become a Quaker. I had attended my local Meeting off and on for twelve years but had not yet written my official letter asking for membership. Should I write that letter now? I was forty-two years old, a wife and mother. I felt anchored in my life. I felt the sun on my face. I felt the rough concrete against my legs. I watched an ant move across the sidewalk. Was I ready, for the first time, to join an organized religion? Did I have in fact any *religious* belief, or was I mainly attracted to Quaker culture and history?

The Quakers in my Meeting are also known as unprogrammed Quakers and Universalists. Following the earliest tradition of Friends, we have no scripture, no preacher, no creed. Instead, we practice silence, the act of sitting in a circle, saying nothing, and waiting—waiting for the Light. The Light is a deliberately broad concept. Among Universalist Friends, the Light can take the shape of Christ, the son of a heavenly Father, or the shape of Buddha, a human prince who enlightened himself and preached the Middle Way. Or the Light can take no shape at all and serve only as metaphor, a substitute for the ineffable. In my Meeting, how each Friend defines the Light is a personal choice. We conform to Quakerly ways of opening and closing silence. We share similar ideas about social justice and nonviolence. We wait for the Light. We do not ask much of our members. We do ask this.

In front of me, on my porch step, was a sidewalk, a patch of grass, a broad strip of asphalt, more sidewalk, a stone wall, a pine tree, and, higher above, electrical wires. Cars drove by. A raven gurgled, liquid and insistent. In the blue sky, white clouds floated above brown hills. "Well," I said to myself, "the Light is all this, I suppose, these steps, this concrete, this ant, that raven. The weft and warp. It is," I gestured, "the street."

I did not have the perspicuity to shout, "Pantheism." I would do that a few hours later, looking at a dictionary. Pantheism is the belief that the universe, with all its existing laws and properties, is an interconnected whole that we can rightly consider sacred. At that moment, I had decided to call the wholeness of the universe the Light. I had decided to believe in a holiness that was not confined to any one thing but immanent in everything. God was in the raven and concrete not as a supernatural being but as the miracle of raven-ness and hydrogen molecules and light waves bouncing off a hard surface to enter my soft receptive eye—an image reflected upside down that my brain instantly turned right, my brain humming with insight, adrenaline in the blood, water vapor in the sky, all of it an amazement, all of it numinous. Suddenly, on those porch steps, I was so pleased, so grateful to be part of this existence.

Soon after, I joined my Quaker Meeting, or the Religious Society of Friends, or more simply the Gila Friends, since our membership extends across the watershed of the Gila River in southwestern New Mexico, surrounded by the Gila National Forest and Gila Wilderness in a specific landscape of ponderosa pine, juniper, oak, prickly pear, grama grass, and yucca. It is a landscape of transition, between conifer forest, grassland, and high desert, a southern range for elk, a northern for coatimundi. It is a place where not enough rain falls and then too much, flooding the arroyos. Very few people in our Meeting are originally from this area. Most of us have come here just to be here, our home of choice.

Pantheism is a word easily confused with other words. Pantheon, for example, refers to a collection of many gods. Polytheism is the belief in many gods. When I tell an acquaintance that I am a pantheist, she looks at me askance. Do I believe in tree spirits? No, that is animism, I explain—the belief that individual souls inhabit natural objects and phenomena. Am I a pagan? she wonders. Yes, I say. Paganism is the religion of anyone not specifically a Christian, Muslim, or Jew. But, I add, she is probably thinking of neo-pagans, people from a modern, technological society who are trying to revive the ancient worship of nature. My pantheism does revere nature. But I don't practice any ancient rituals.

Importantly, what pantheism is not is theism—the acceptance of a single, personal god. Pantheism is not atheism either, a disbelief in a sacred or numinous universe. There is some argument here. The well-known atheist and scientist Richard Dawkins calls pantheism "sexed-up atheism." Well, nothing wrong with being sexy. But the pantheist acknowledges a strong religious impulse. The pantheist walks literally, every day, in the Mind and Body of God. Pan*en*theism sounds the most like pantheism but also is not, being the doctrine that God is both immanent in the world and transcendent or outside it, too.

I was born in 1954. Growing up in America in the last half of the twentieth century meant being exposed to almost every belief system listed above. My mother was an agnostic, a widow, and a professional bridge player who raised her two girls in apartment buildings in Phoenix, Arizona. We didn't go to church. In the summers, I was sent to Kansas to live with my father's parents, where being a Methodist was like eating breakfast or buying sneakers, part of the rhythm of life. I recited the Nicene Creed and ate potato salad at the church picnic. Back in Phoenix, I went to temple with Jewish friends and Mass with Catholic friends, like some form of a child anthropologist—but also hungry for something. These were secret worlds. I listened by the door. In college, one of my roommates had an altar to the Hindu god Ganesh. The Hare Krishnas filled the airports then. My older sister practiced Transcendental Meditation. Meanwhile, some Westerners were looking to their druidic past. They wanted to believe in magic, and New Age mythology was a wide net: crystals, covens, tree spirits.

Today I have to wonder why pantheism—a word I only learned in 1996, at the age of forty-two—was the one belief not to winnow out, the wheat separated from the chaff, the gold panned.

There is a time in a reader's life when books are inhaled and absorbed into the body. They become the body of who you are. Between the ages of seventeen and twenty-two, I gulped down writers. I read them fast and whole, something like a snake swallowing its prey, and I read everything they wrote, one book after another, trying to steal their souls or, more nicely, become who they were. Starting with nineteenth-century literature, I read Ralph Waldo Emerson, Henry David Thoreau, and Walt Whitman. Particularly, I read Whitman, in love with the physical world and finding divinity everywhere, for whom "a mouse is miracle enough to stagger sextillion infidels" and a gnat sufficient explanation. I could as easily have read William Wordsworth or Alfred Tennyson.

I read avowed pantheists like D. H. Lawrence and the poet Robinson Jeffers, who wrote, "I believe that the universe is one being, all its parts are different expressions of the same energy. . . . The whole is in all its parts so beautiful, and is felt by me so intensely in earnest, that I am compelled to love it and to think of it as divine." I could as easily have read Frank Lloyd Wright: "I believe in God, only I spell it Nature"; or Albert Einstein: "I am a deeply religious unbeliever. This is a somewhat new kind of religion."

After college, I traveled through India and Southeast Asia, the de rigueur copies of the Bhagavad Gita and Upanishads in my backpack. I was still the anthropologist, still listening by the door. It never occurred to me to become a Hindu or Buddhist. But the ideas echoed nicely. The Hindu god Brahma becomes all things. All the world is Brahmin. Buddha has Reality for his body. The Buddha's body is the world.

Eventually, I went to a graduate writing program in Missoula, Montana. Everything, always, had been about writing. I composed my first story in the fourth grade and never looked back. In my understanding of how I was to live, in my nascent and fumbling sense of how I *could* live, everything had to be transformed into language. Everything had to be transformed. It hardly seems now I had a choice. It seems now that writing was something that happened to me—which is what, I have learned since, many writers think. Of course, it is not true. Of course, we chose.

As it turned out, graduate school was less about writing and more about mountains and cold weather and falling in love. Peter was also in the writing program, a young intellectual from a military family who had spent most of his childhood in Europe and on the East Coast. We were different enough to attract each other but alike enough to stay together. We had mutual dreams. It was in the air. Earth Day. Ecology. Back to the land. We talked about our desire for roots and community. We wanted to connect more directly to life. We were hungry for something.

In the 1980s, Peter and I married, moved to southwestern New Mexico, bought twelve acres in a small valley near the Gila National Forest, and built an adobe house—a house made of mud. Born in city and suburb, we were reading eagerly now about composting toilets and killing gophers and pruning fruit trees. We had a wonderful view of a distant mountain. We had an oppressively large garden, which we irrigated from a nearby acequia, and a small herd of goats. We had two home births— a girl and a boy—and too much homemade cheese in the re-frigerator. Our naïveté that we could live simply and sustain ourselves on this land lasted about two weeks, or perhaps a lit-tle longer. Peter took on a succession of jobs: high school teacher, Nature Conservancy field director, and town planner for Silver City, thirty miles away. I became a teacher of writing skills at the small university in Silver City, a job I still have twenty-five years later.

In the country, we found that our social life revolved around potlucks, and that these gatherings were often Quakerly, since a number of "weighty" Quakers happened to live in our valley, too. Some were involved in the Sanctuary Movement, a net-work of churches committed to helping refugees flee the polit-ical violence in Guatemala and El Salvador. Almost all the Quakers I know are deeply political, believing that the Peace-able Kingdom or Kingdom of God exists here and now and not anywhere else. They want to "stand in the Light" when that kingdom is threatened. Between raising my children, commut-ing into town, teaching, and writing, I was learning about Quaker ideals from people who were trying to live out those ideals. I was learning about silence and the small inner voice that can be heard in silence.

Then we moved to town. Our children were growing up. Peter and I had not quite foreseen that this would happen—that our children would grow up and want to play Little League, join band, or be in a drama club. The local middle and high school required an hour-and-a-half bus ride there and back, and now the days were never long enough for all the things we had to do and all the time spent in a car. In 1996, the same year I finally joined my Quaker Meeting, my husband and I left our small rural valley for Silver City, population ten thousand, with a trade area of thirty thousand. We did this so our daughter, Maria, and son, David, could have a better education and more conventional social life. So we wouldn't have to cross a river to drive thirty miles to work. So I could walk to the university and Peter could walk to his office at city hall. In town, we would be closer to shops and the library. We could go to cultural events, the occasional concert or play. We could have central heating instead of a wood stove. Life would be easier.

My experience on a porch step in a small American town is a version of pantheism first expressed in the seventeenth century. In 1656, the Jewish community of Amsterdam excommunicated the twenty-three-year-old Baruch Spinoza for his "evil opinions" and "abominable heresies." The *cherem,* or banishment, of the young man was unusually harsh:

> Cursed be he by day and cursed be he by night; cursed be he when he lies down and cursed be he when he rises up. Cursed be he when he goes out and cursed be he when he comes in. The Lord will not spare him, but the anger of the Lord and his jealousy shall smote against that man, and all the curses that

are written in this book shall lie upon him, and the Lord shall
blot out his name from under heaven.

Although the Jewish elders did not record the nature of these
heresies, they likely referred to the pantheism that Spinoza
would develop fully in his mature work, *Ethics,* which on publication in 1670 was immediately banned and suppressed
throughout Europe. Spinoza's ideas were not entirely new. Greek
philosophers in the sixth century BCE had also rejected the idea
of supernatural gods in favor of a universe made up of a single
divine substance. Centuries later, the pantheistic Roman Stoics
believed in a divine Unity, which they called God or Fate or
Providence or the Logos. As recently as 1600, the scholar Bruno
Giordano had been burned at the stake by the Roman Inquisition for his notion of an immanent God that could assume many
forms. But Spinoza was the first to describe pantheism in a way
that would appeal to a more modern and scientific sensibility,
offering what he saw as a logical "geometric proof" that God was
and could only be an infinite substance identical with Nature.
Ethics remains Western philosophy's most coherent and complete defense of this idea.

Spinoza concluded that nothing can exist outside God. There
can be no Creation outside the Creator. At one point in *Ethics,*
he lightly scolded, "There are those who imagine God to be like
a man, composed of body and soul and subject to passions; but
it is clear enough from what has already been demonstrated how
far off men who believe this are from the true knowledge of
God." He later conceded that if a triangle could think, it would

also imagine God to be like a triangle. But both triangle and man were wrong.

Spinoza's logic led him to deny personal or individual immortality. Something eternal lived on when a human being died, but it was not that human's personality or "soul." There was no afterlife in the sense of a heaven or hell. There was no relationship with a loving, engaged, personal Father. The Bible said these things because the Bible had been written by people who wanted to believe them. God did not write the Bible. God didn't really care about human beings. God was existence itself.

Spinoza's pantheism harshly rejected both Jewish and Christian tradition. For that time and place, this was very dangerous. People were being imprisoned, tortured, and executed for less. Spinoza knew this and wrote discreetly, sometimes just to friends, sometimes anonymously. His major work, *Ethics,* was kept in a desk drawer and published only after his death by lung disease at the age of forty-four.

The philosopher himself never used the word pantheism. That would be left to one of his disciples, an Irish writer named John Toland who first coined the term in the early 1700s. In honor of his mentor, Toland also called pantheists "Spinozists." Toland had his own problems with church authorities and lived in fear of religious persecution for most of his life. He waited until he had nothing to lose—until he was sick, dying, alcoholic, and penniless—to write and distribute his personal manifesto, which he called *Pantheisticon.*

Toland's description of pantheism relied more on poetry than logic. Grandly, he proclaimed, "The sun is my father, the earth

my mother, the world is my country, and all men are my family."
He defined a pantheist as someone who believed that the only
eternal and divine being was the material universe, which was
infinite with an infinite number of stars and other earths circling
their suns. Thought was a property of the brain. Soul was another. Thought and soul were forms of matter, and death was
the endless transformation of matter. The death of one thing
brought about the birth of something else, contributing "to the
preservation and welfare of the Whole by a continual change of
forms and a marvelous variation which forms an eternal cycle."
Virtue was its own reward.

At odds with the religion and culture of his day, Toland was a
lonely man. In *Pantheisticon*, he indulged himself and imagined a
secret society in which his ideas were celebrated and applauded—
a network of private, underground clubs with pantheistic creeds
and rituals. In such a refuge, educated gentlemen could eat,
drink, joke, and debate philosophy. Toland wrote as if such clubs
existed, and one British Druid order claims it descended from
such a gathering in 1717. A few believers think that Toland
started the Masons, although most historians dispute this.

Whatever the case, the meetings described in the *Pantheisti-
con* would make for a pleasant evening. The president begins by
ejecting any unworthy or dangerous outsiders: "Make sure that
vulgar laymen are far away." The community responds in unison,
"The doors are locked, we are in safety." The president exults,
"All things in the world are One, and One in All in all things."
The community praises, "What is all in all things is God, and
God is eternal, has not been created, and will never die."

Toland died hoping for a future of religious tolerance. He would be delighted today with the World Pantheist Movement, a lively Internet-based organization founded in 1998 with over a thousand members in fifty countries. The WPM's earnest goal is to promote pantheism and support the values of environmental activism and human rights. Their advisers include scientists like James Lovelock, author of the Gaia theory, and cell biologist Ursula Goodenough, a prominent figure in another organization called the Institute of Religion in an Age of Science. Secrecy in such clubs is no longer necessary, and the small membership of these groups may be misleading. Paul Harrison, founder of the World Pantheist Movement, believes that up to 10 percent of people in the religions of Christianity, Hinduism, and Buddhism, as well as many others outside organized religion, have quietly abandoned their belief in a personal god or afterlife even as they retain a strong sense of religiosity. These 200 to 350 million have shifted their focus of reverence from the supernatural to the natural. After parsing the history and meaning of pantheism, the *Stanford Encyclopedia of Philosophy* agrees, "There are probably more grass-root pantheists than Protestants or theists in general."

Like any religion, pantheism disagrees with itself. There is confusion and contradiction. We can define pantheism as the belief that the universe is an interrelated whole that deserves human reverence. Everything is God. But the definition of everything varies.

What Paul Harrison calls scientific pantheism imagines the universe to be made of one substance: matter/energy. The dance of matter/energy is beautiful and holy but also impersonal and nonsentient. As Spinoza first outlined, human consciousness is a product of matter and dies when the body dies.

For a few pantheists, including some Hindus and Buddhists, the reverse is true. The universe is also made of one substance, but that substance is mind, not matter. Matter is an illusion, a product of mind. Everything is God, and God is consciousness.

Other pantheists (also known as dualists) separate the universe into two substances: matter and spirit. Since spirit can exist without matter, the human soul can exist outside the human body—beyond death. There may be a collective World-Soul that manifests itself in different forms, such as gods. A form of soul or spirit may be present in plants, animals, and rocks. This kind of pantheist might also be a polytheist or an animist. He or she might have a magical worldview—supposing, for example, that simply thinking about an object can affect that object and that nothing is bound by merely physical laws. Non-flying things can sometimes fly. Nonthinking things can sometimes think.

I don't believe that. I am a scientific pantheist, credulous in my own way. The culture of science is a distinct one and certainly mine. I believe that the latest discoveries in biology, chemistry, and physics are true, or at least true for the moment, for science is a method, not a destination. I believe we live in the body of the world and that we are compelled to know the world. We are compelled to witness. Thoreau set the bar: "The woman who sits in the house and *sees* is a match for a stirring captain. Those still, piercing eyes, as faithfully exercised on their talent, will keep her even with Alexander or Shakespeare." I believe in that woman. I believe that what we see is real and important and that we have a natural urge to see ever more clearly.

I believe that I live inside larger laws. In the culture of science, the religious impulse can be explained by evolutionary biology. Religion either had some genetically inheritable advantage for the human species or was a by-product of something that did. This is fine with me. The fact that a sense of the numinous may be hardwired does not make the numinous less of a true feeling. Similarly, if I know anything as a parent, I know I would give my life for my child. The fact that maternal love is hardwired does not change that love. Moreover, I would not want to feel differently. I would not want not to love.

I believe that science is about connection and complexity, harmony and surprise. Science is about beauty. The more I see—the more I know—the more beautiful the world seems. Importantly, the way I experience beauty has always been physical. The yellow sunflower hits me with a friendly punch. A mountain view causes a flutter in my chest, a subtle movement, something like an ache. We say that the heart soars, a common description for what we feel before a beautiful natural scene (or a painting or a piece of music). There is a sense of hollowness, a hormonal cascade. There are sensations.

Neurologically, however, I am not built for mysticism. My heart soars at the sight of beauty. Something in my chest flutters. But I never faint or have aural hallucinations. My spiritual responses are not dramatic. Because of this, I have to work hard for my religious view. I have to have faith.

My sense of beauty is also limited, almost always evoked by the natural world. Once I did feel an enormous connection, the heightened pleasure of existence, standing in line at a pharmacy in Wal-Mart. All that color! All those things! And the smiling, complicated faces of people. I recognize that humans are not outside nature and that our accomplishments are often extraordinary. But for the most part, I am moved to an understanding of the divine by the nonhuman, the Beloved-that-is-not-me. In this, I am fairly conventional. A lot of my friends feel the same way.

For a long time after we moved into town, I felt content—even smug. It seemed to me that I could be content almost anywhere, with my family and my writing. I was adaptable. I was self-sufficient. I didn't know myself very well. I didn't know that in moving to the country and choosing to stay there for fifteen years, I had followed an instinct. I had heard a voice. Someone had been yelling in my ear: *This is who you are. This is what you need. Pay attention.*

After we lived in Silver City for about five years, I stopped attending Quaker Meeting. I didn't discuss this with any of my Quaker friends. I kept paying my yearly dues and receiving my monthly newsletter. I just slowly drifted away. I missed one Meeting and then another and then another. I stopped waiting for the Light. Of course, I was very busy, a working mother of two teenagers. That seemed a good enough excuse.

Today, I am crazy with desire—anxious, grouchy, determined—to move back to the country and reclaim myself. By now, Peter and I have sold our first homestead in order to buy new property in another rural area also thirty miles from town. These six acres in the Gila Valley adjoin eighty acres of a Nature Conservancy wildlife refuge on the Gila River. Our land, once again, is near the Gila National Forest, which extends for another three million acres and includes the Gila Wilderness and Aldo Leopold Wilderness. The scattered communities of Gila and Cliff number about five hundred, a settlement dominated by Mormons and the descendents of ranchers, supplemented by retirees and old and new hippies. The Nature Conservancy sponsors the study of the Gila River, and visiting scientists are part of the mix. Our view includes irrigated farmland, the rugged folds of Telephone Mountain, and a more distant view of the foothills of Black Mountain and Antelope Ridge. We have paid more than we can afford for this and understand better that every country house is a satellite to the city. This time we won't pretend to grow our own food or sustain ourselves on the land. We go to the country for reflection and redemption. We go despite the fact that living in town is more ecological. We go with a new set of illusions. We will live here until we die or die trying.

This past summer, my father-in-law gave us money to build on our new property a large single room with a bathroom and kitchen, a place where we can live part time until we manage the move from our jobs in town. The little house was finished in October. An extended porch wraps around walls filled with windows and French doors, as many as I could get for a 360-degree view. We visit the house every weekend and sometimes stay longer, commuting again to work. Every time I look out a window, I hope for the lift of a sandhill crane, a quail or fox, a herd of javelina. Every time, every single time, I am hungry for something.

I cannot say now that I am content. Both my children are in college this fall, and I suffer, I grieve, the loss of my life as a mother. You do something for twenty years, and it feels good, it feels important, and then you are out of the game—fast, like a football player with bad knees. The glory years are over. Good-bye to baby smells, doctor appointments, homework assignments, PTA, deep concerns, daily concerns. Every morning you had a reason to get up. You were always needed. You were never lonely. Good-bye to all that. As parents, we are not supposed to admit this selfish sorrow. Certainly we are not supposed to wallow in it.

I am fifty-one years old, sliding toward death, and I don't much like myself. I have failed at so many things—not the very best writer, not the very best wife or friend, not even the very best parent. I don't much like the world either, which is too full of suffering and disease and war, as the world has always been. I am acutely aware of how my country has betrayed itself, refusing once again to fulfill its potential, to be wise and strong. I am acutely aware of how humanity has betrayed itself, poisoning the earth, heedless of the future we create for our children. As a Quaker, I have lost my sense of the Light. I dislike town. I don't feel special. I am surrounded by miracles—the porch step, the blue sky, black ravens croaking and gurgling—only I don't see the connection. What do they have to do with me?

Still, I feel hopeful. My husband and I have a house in the Gila Valley and a new view of mountains. Living in nature will restore me. This time, I will pay more attention. This time I will take along some friends, books I haven't read for many years, some things I have forgotten. I will take along my science, my neglected pantheism, my neglected Quakerism. If I know anything, I know that I do not want to live in a universe devoid of community, mystery, and awe. I do not want to be alone in my brain, my timid and lazy personality, unconnected to the rest of the world. I cast my lot with Spinoza, Thoreau, and Einstein. I want to live every minute in a holy universe, so pleased and grateful to be part of this existence.

Of pantheism, I will ask the questions we must ask any religion: How can I lead a better and more joyful life? How can I come to terms with my death and suffering? How can I come to terms with all death and suffering? How should we live as humans on the earth? How can we be at home here?

This time, during my days and nights in the Gila Valley, rooting my life back into the natural world, this time I will go deeper.

CHAPTER 2

The Early Greeks

FROM INSIDE THE house, I am using binoculars to watch the greater sandhill cranes fifty feet away. This family group—a female, male, and adolescent—arrived here a few weeks ago in early November. They are digging through a flooded field of clover for insects and grubs. The greater sandhill crane is about four feet high, not as tall as an emu (six feet) or an ostrich (eight feet) but impressive enough to make you pause. Birds shouldn't be this big. Birds are modest brown blurs flitting from branch to branch. Birds don't reach up to your chest with wings stretching out in a vampiric cloak and a dagger-sharp bill that could gut a coyote. The two adults in my field have slate gray plumage brightened by a white chin, cheek, and upper throat. The juvenile's head is tawny with a mottled body of brown and gray. Suddenly the female gets excited, perhaps by a snake in the grass, and the patch of naked red skin on her forehead turns brighter red, engorged with blood. I think I can actually see this through my binoculars.

She raises her wings, and the red patch is hidden. She jumps slightly, an awkward hop. I wonder if she is about to dance. The juvenile bird moves back, as if scared or warned.

Cranes have a long adolescence, not breeding until they are at least four years old. They mate for life, or at least for the life of that particular mate. Although few in the wild live for more than twenty-five years, a male Siberian crane in captivity was believed to be eighty-three when he died. The game old bird still fathered chicks into his late seventies. Theoretically, the female I am watching now could have been coming to this field every year for half my lifetime. Nothing much has changed from her point of view. The Gila River shifted course. Some cottonwood trees fell down. This year, a big box appeared on the land, a woman inside watching.

This family group is part of a larger flock of one hundred to two hundred greater sandhill cranes that come to the Gila Valley every November to spend the winter. These birds nest and breed in the northern Rockies of Idaho. When the weather turns cold and the young are strong enough to travel, they migrate south. They like the fields of the Nature Conservancy's Gila River Farm next door, and my field, and the fields owned by the Phelps Dodge Corporation to the south. During the day, they feed on green shoots, roots, and bugs in the winter pastures. At night, they prefer to stand and roost in shallow water, and so they fly off, perhaps to a large stock tank on the nearby Moon Ranch or maybe to pools further down the river.

To my disappointment, the female does not dance but folds in her wings and holds still. Cranes can look oddly human, with their long legs, erect stance, and series of well-considered actions: one foot placed carefully in front of the other, a lowering of the neck, a jab at the ground, a raising of the head, a stately movement forward. Ten birds in a field look like so many peasant farmers slowly going about their tasks. Fifty birds remind me of a convention. There is an air of gossip and professional opportunity, a constant and subtle flow, exchanges over territory and status, significant preening, a single wing stretch, a double wing stretch, an alert stare. If alarmed, the entire convention will spread wings and flap away—their gurgles, knocks, and rattles filling the air. Family members, in particular, keep a constant vocal contact, staying together in the confusion of takeoff. Any allusion to humanity is dispelled, for the sound of cranes is distinctly inhuman, weird and prehistoric.

I hear that sound daily now as small groups like this fly here and there, looking for a better field or just a change of pace. Ornithologists describe the call of the sandhill crane as a buglelike *garroooo-a-a-a* or, more simply, *gar-oo-oo,* which is absurd. It doesn't sound like that at all. It doesn't sound like anything I would be able to describe. The word throaty comes to mind, but that seems obvious. Still, something tracheal, vibrational, jazzy is going on, like the Latin American instrument guiro used in bossa nova music and played by sliding a wooden stick across the grooves in a carved gourd. In his discussion of the crane, the ecologist Aldo Leopold sidestepped the issue and wrote instead, "When we hear his call we hear no mere bird. We hear the trumpet in the orchestra of evolution," referring to the sandhill cranes' having been around for nine million years, our oldest known living bird species.

Aldo Leopold, also known as the "father of wildlife management," is a local hero who helped establish the nearby Gila Wilderness in 1924, the country's first designated wilderness area. In his seminal book, *Sand County Almanac,* he looked beyond the management of natural resources to something more profound: relationship. The land is a community. We are part of that community. As such, we have responsibilities as well as privileges. Moreover, we learn things from the land, wordless lessons about our own nature and the nature of the world. "The physics of beauty is one department of natural science still in the Dark Ages," Leopold wrote. "Not even the manipulators of bent space have tried to solve its equations." In the north woods where Leopold hiked and hunted, the autumn landscape was "the land, plus a red maple, plus a ruffed grouse. In terms of conventional physics, the grouse represents only a millionth of either the mass or the energy of an acre. Yet subtract the grouse and the whole thing is dead."

Subtract the greater sandhill crane and the Gila Valley—with its coyotes, foxes, bears, mountain lions, bobcats, javelina, deer, cows, horses, dogs, cats, skunks, beavers, raccoons, porcupines, coatimundis, rabbits, hares, gophers, mice, packrats, wrens, sparrows, thrashers, woodpeckers, flycatchers, owls, hawks, and innumerable insects—would seem empty.

In the field outside my yellow house, the female changes her mind about something, lifts her wings again, and still does not dance. Instead she takes a running start. With wings fully extended, she springs upward, flapping strongly, the upstroke more rapid than the down as she gains altitude. The male and juvenile follow. This family and their flock will stay in the Gila

Valley about four months, defining our winter. In late February, they will fly north again, stopping for nearly two months in southern Colorado before ending up, if lucky, at the same nesting site in Idaho that they chose last year. Home for the sandhill crane is an extended range of over two thousand miles. Home is a loop, a cycle, a rhythmic motion back and forth.

The early Greeks had a fondness for cranes, which they captured and domesticated. The Greek word for cranes, *geranos,* comes from the myth of Gerania, doomed to wage war against these birds as punishment for neglecting the gods. Apollo liked to turn into a crane, and Hermes invented the Greek alphabet after watching flocks of cranes fly—the chevron pattern undulating as the lead crane moved back and another crane came forward. In a story from the sixth century BCE, the lyric poet Ibycus was attacked by bandits and fatally wounded. Dying, he saw some cranes pass overhead and told his murderers that the birds would avenge him. In the Corinth marketplace, one of the robbers saw the cranes again and cried out as a joke, "Behold, the avengers of Ibycus!" Overheard, the man was questioned and confessed, and "the cranes of Ibycus" became a Greek proverb, signifying the discovery of a crime through divine intervention.

The sixth century BCE also saw the rise of the philosopher-scientist and the beginning of Western science. This was a paradigm shift, a new way of thinking. These men were concerned with the physical structure of the world and rejected mythology as an explanation. They didn't believe in Apollo or Hermes or the cranes of Ibycus. We know them mostly from the writings of later historians, including Aristotle, who described them as *physici,* interested in finding logical principles within nature, as opposed to *theologi,* satisfied with the rule of supernatural beings.

Three of the earliest *physici*—Thales, Anaximander, and Anaximenes—all came from Miletus, a city-state on the coast of what is now Turkey. They could be called the first known pantheists. Like the scientific pantheists of today, they believed that the universe was made of a single, unifying substance. They believed that this primary substance was material and yet somehow divine in its inherent power, glory, and eternal nature. They may have also believed in a divine impersonal soul that permeated all of matter.

The multitalented Thales was an astronomer, engineer, and statesman. His contemporaries thought he could predict eclipses, a skill that gave him considerable cachet among the seafaring Greeks, always interested in what the heavens were doing. Thales had, in fact, made a lucky guess concerning the dramatic eclipse of 585 BCE, which interrupted a battle between two warring neighbors near Miletus. Impressed, the Greeks began to take his ideas more seriously. Perhaps there was something to this paradigm shift, this notion of studying the natural world, applying reason, and coming up with information that could be used by practical men. Although Thales surely had predecessors, he is sometimes described as the first scientist, possibly because he was the first to be socially accepted, admired, and remembered for his work.

Thales was interested in all kinds of knowledge, including the origin and structure of the universe. In his pursuit of one unifying substance, he determined that the world consisted of water. Probably he had more to say on this subject but left behind no written record. Perhaps he meant that everything originally came from water. Or perhaps that everything, ultimately, was composed of water—in the way that gaseous vapor and solid ice were once liquid. Water was the building block of all matter. In any case, the answer Thales came up with is not so important as the question he asked: not *who* made the universe but *what* it was made of.

Thales seemed to combine his scientific interests with a religious belief in a life force that infused everything, causing even stones (magnets) to move toward each other. Although he is quoted as saying, "The world is full of gods," a likely interpretation is that he saw a universe interpenetrated with a natural energy powerful and pervasive enough to be considered divine.

Anaximander may have been a pupil of Thales who went beyond his teacher with the imaginative leap that the unifying substance of the world was not anything we could actually see. Like other *physici,* Anaximander emphasized the importance and reliability of the human senses, but he added the idea that science must also infer the existence of things our senses could not detect. He called his invisible stuff *apeiron,* "the principle and element of existing things," and he also considered it powerful, eternal, and divine. His story of the cosmos had cold masses and hot masses separating out of the *apeiron* to form the earth and other celestial bodies. The earth was circled by the stars and moon and stood at the center of the universe, where it was held in place by the forces of equilibrium. Anaximander believed strongly in the role of opposites—hot versus cold and wet versus dry—which helped drive the evolution of the universe and which he metaphorically described in terms of conflict and resolution.

His account of human origin is the first on record to be reasoned theory, not myth. Animal life on earth began with a separating out from slime or moist matter heated by the sun. The first men and women were fishlike creatures, or possibly they grew from embryo to puberty inside fishlike creatures from which they emerged, able now to survive on land. From the premise of a single, impersonal, infinite *apeiron*, Anaximander developed more theories that led to the material world he lived in. He threw into his scheme everything he knew of geometry, physics, biology, and zoology, and if he didn't know much, and if much of what he knew was wrong, the effort is still astonishing.

The third *physicus* from Miletus was Anaximenes, who concluded that the single substance of the world was air, which could take on many forms through familiar processes like condensation and unfamiliar ones like "thickening" into fire, earth, and stones. Just as the substance holding together the universe was air, the soul holding together the human body was air. Air was measureless, infinite, and always in motion. Air, in some way, was divine. Anaximenes became the last of the Milesian philosophers to look for the origin of the universe and the stuff of which we are made. In 494 BCE, at the end of his career, the city-state of Miletus was destroyed by the Persians. Rebuilt fifteen years later, Miletus flourished now as a center famous for the quality of its wool.

Today the early Greek most associated with pantheism is Heraclitus, who lived thirty miles north of Miletus and was young when Anaximenes was old. Heraclitus does not quite fit the definition of a *physicus,* since he made no contribution to any of the new fields of science such as physics or astronomy. He was more interested in the inner world of the human mind than the outer world of natural phenomena, and his pithy sayings include "I went in search of myself" and "Man's character is his fate." Like the *physici,* however, he stressed the importance of the human senses and of reasoning: "Whatever comes from sight, hearing, learning from experience: this I prefer."

Heraclitus believed that the universe had underlying principles or laws, which he called the Logos. These underlying principles could be expressed as a two-part idea: All things are one and all things are in a constant state of change. The task of a human being was to seek wisdom through understanding the Logos. As a teacher of the Logos, Heraclitus was a riddler and literary stylist. To get across the concept of Oneness—which he might variously describe as fire, God, the Logos, or Zeus—he wrote, "God is day night, winter summer, war peace, satiety hunger." To explain his idea that everything in nature was always in motion, he noted, "One can not step twice into the same river." For Heraclitus, constant change meant constant conflict. Thus he proclaimed, "War is father of all and king of all." At the same time, he believed in an ultimate and sacred Unity that reconciled all opposites and strife: "The same thing exists in us living and dead and waking and sleeping and young and old; for these things having changed round are those, and those having changed round are these."

The epigrams of Heraclitus require some pondering. But if you have ever read any philosophy at all, you will only feel grateful to this man for the brevity of his language. In his own lifetime and for centuries afterward, his enigmatic style was rarely well received. In addition, he provoked the anger of the Greeks by mocking traditional views and icons, saying, for example, that the beloved poet Homer should be beaten with a staff. For this arrogance, his biographers would punish him with a humiliating death in a dung heap.

In a history of pantheism, many threads begin with Heraclitus and return to him. His work would strongly influence the later Stoics, who took the notion of Logos and made it their own. In turn, the ideas of Baruch Spinoza can seem strikingly Stoical. Much of the wisdom of Heraclitus resembles philosophical Taoism, a form of pantheism that arose in China during the fifth to third centuries BCE. Similarly, the concept of a Unity that encompasses all opposites and change is echoed in modern physics, in which the universe is a process of change based on the underlying oneness of the quantum field.

I find these echoes both exciting and disturbing. On one hand, part of me persists in thinking that the modern world began just a short while ago and that ideas are formed in a linear fashion. Yet the familiarity of men like Heraclitus and Anaximander hints at something outside history and linear progression. Perhaps ideas are more intuitive. Perhaps they are real and leap at us like tigers.

That seemed to be the case with the Greek *physicus* Democritus, whose beliefs would become the basis for our understanding of atoms. Without any evidence at all, Democritus conceived of an infinite, impersonal universe unified and made up of interconnected and eternal substances he called *atomos*. These tiny, indivisible particles careened about in empty space until they collided and bonded and became those things that are familiar to us: dirt, ants, Grandma. Similarly shaped atoms tended to attract each other, perhaps with little hooks to help them attach. Everything was made of atoms, constantly bombarded by other atoms, and constantly leaking atoms. We could hear and see and smell as a result of thin streams of these atoms entering our body to be processed by the collection of atoms that was our body and mind. When we died, our atoms dispersed and went on to bond with something else. It was all about the motion of extremely small, invisible particles.

As one wag said, "There is almost no view so crazy that you can't find some Greek philosopher who held it."

Within half a century, the Greek philosopher Epicurus would enlarge on the theory of *atomos* by suggesting that atoms occasionally swerved, making an unpredictable sideways jump. This unpredictable swerve helped atoms bump into each other and brought into nature a certain randomness, changing a mechanistic universe to something full of chance and opportunity. In such a universe, which was infinite and full of infinite worlds, complex forms naturally arose. As one follower of Epicurus explained, given enough time and space, atoms moved and met and joined in all possible combinations. Eventually these became the "earth and sea and sky and the generation of living creatures." To explain the well-ordered designs of nature, Epicureans took up the theory of natural selection: Good biological designs tended to survive and reproduce, and bad ones did not.

Some twenty-three hundred years ago, these men were creating a picture of the world that impressively resembles my own. As far as we know, neither Democritus nor Epicurus expressed a religious conviction that the universe they described was divine. But their ideas, expanded and refined in the coming centuries, would become a pillar of thought for what we now call scientific pantheism.

Democritus (460–370 BCE) and the better-known Socrates (469–399 BCE) lived in the same time period, although they did not have much to say to each other. Democritus is labeled a pre-Socratic, as are the pantheistic Heraclitus, Thales, Anaximander, and Anaximenes. The term pre-Socratic sounds diminutive, a kind of opening act before the Real Philosopher takes the stage. In fact, the intentions of the pre-Socratics were simply different. They were interested in the nature of the world; Socrates was interested in how men should live in the world. They were interested in what we would consider science; Socrates was interested in ethics.

The brilliance and authority of Socrates caused the discussion within philosophy to shift to his side. In 399 BCE, Socrates was condemned to death, most likely for his role as a critic of the current ruling class. His martyrdom increased his reputation as a man who lived in pursuit of truth and virtue. Plato was a pupil of Socrates who expanded on his ideas and added a new theory of purer and ideal Forms that existed behind the perceived world. In Plato's metaphysics, matter was a shadow of something more real. Plato's student was Aristotle, the teacher of Alexander the Great and a tireless investigator of all things from biology to logic. Like Socrates and Plato, Aristotle was enormously influential. There is general agreement that these three men laid down the foundation for almost all of Western culture and philosophy.

They were not, however, pantheists. I have an agenda, and so we will not linger.

From my house in the Gila Valley, in the early winter sunsets of November and December, I watch the long-legged, long-necked sandhill cranes fly across the field like slow-motion arrows. The mated pairs especially do not want to lose each other in the darkening air as they navigate to where they will roost for the night, standing in shallow water, one leg raised. They rattle eerily. They call to each other, *garroooo-a-a-a gurgle-gurgle-khrrrr-khrrrr-khrrrr.*

The sun sets to my right. The light behind the cottonwood trees is pink and yellow, pearly like the inside of certain shells. A few clouds gloom the east, blue-black rolls with a stern demeanor. South, in front of me, is the panorama above Bear Mountain and Telephone Mountain and the more distant rumpled foothills of Black Mountain. The color blue deepens to cerulean, a hint of turquoise. A cloud flares orange. I think of nineteenth-century paintings, gilt-framed, in certain museums. The light fades. The planet Venus remains, unblinking, unfailing, a good friend.

I have come to live here in the country for this sky. The Greeks were intensely interested in the weather, the movement of sun and moon, the changing stars. I am also interested, but not for any practical reason. I do not have a ship to navigate or an eclipse to predict. Mainly I need to look at the sky in order to believe there is a reason for getting up each morning, making the bed, going to work. I think it is that important, to see something grand and beautiful every day, to feel some part of me relax and loosen into that space.

31

This sky, like all the skies I have ever seen, holds no grief or suffering, no emotions except the ones I create, the pleasure of personifying clouds—those stern furrowed brows to the east, the childlike innocence of puffy white cotton balls, the majesty of flat-bottomed ships. Similarly, the philosophy of Thales and Anaximander and Heraclitus holds no grief or human drama, no tears or laughter. We do not know if these men ever had brothers or sisters, married, had children, loved these children, lost someone they loved, anguished, or doubted. It seems only that they thought about the one divine substance of the world, sauntered along the beach, poked at something in a pool, and came up with a theory: The world is made of water. The world is made of air.

Of course, that is not how things really work. That is not how we live our lives. My own life was shaped by the death of my father, a Kansas farm boy who went off at seventeen to World War II, joined the air force, and became a test pilot. In a profession that takes bravery for granted, he was known for being brave. In 1956, he tested the X-2 rocket plane and set a speed record, climbing high into the stratosphere, high above the clouds, moving three times the speed of sound. In his descent, the plane went out of control, and he died in the crash. I was two years old. My sister was five. My father was thirty-two. Almost immediately, my mother had to leave the air force base and make her way as a single parent. She never remarried, never really recovered.

I was too young to know my father. But my sister remembers a dream shortly after his death. He came into her room, sat on her bed, and told her everything would be OK. My sister felt comforted, a dream that would last all her life. I found comfort, too, in my father's decency and heroism. My grandmother described him as a good son on the Kansas farm, doing his chores, shooting ducks with my granddad, stringing popcorn for the Christmas tree. In the air force, he once saved a man's life by smashing open the canopy of a burning plane. The man lived but lost both feet. When my father became a test pilot, he was the one all the manufacturers wanted to try out their planes, for he always brought them back; he never abandoned ship. Even so, my mother said, Mel Apt was just a normal, fun-loving adult, the sort who drank martinis and wore a lampshade on his head at late-night parties.

In my childhood, growing up in the suburbs of Phoenix, Arizona, single-parent households were not common. I felt different, and I dramatized my father's absence. When President Kennedy was assassinated in 1963, I wept more than the other fourth-graders. Later, reading about my father in family scrapbooks—articles from magazines like *Reader's Digest* and *Aviation News*—I internalized him, the Hero, the purer and more ideal Form. In essence, he came and sat on my bed. He told me he loved me and would always love me. Everything would be OK.

At the same time, I should be ready for death. The phone would ring in the middle of the night, the woman from the hospital speaking too softly. This death would come at the most inconvenient time, say, when I had two small children. I might never recover. I might grieve and grieve for what could not be. This kind of loss could break me. God was a sniper in the sky. God was like one of those soldiers in Bosnia. Look, a red kerchief. Bang.

From that date, 1956, until now, fifty years later, nothing very bad has happened in my life. This amazes me—that no one I love has died. No one I love has a degenerative disease or has been in a terrible car accident. No one I love has drowned. It really seems remarkable. Obviously, this run of luck cannot continue. Eventually a truck will turn left without signaling. I will get breast cancer. My husband will have a stroke. If this seems morbid, it is also true. We all die.

Although the pre-Socratic pantheists had little to say about death, two other schools of early Greek philosophy—Epicureanism and Stoicism—did.

Born in the middle of the fourth century BCE, Epicurus imagined an impersonal universe of colliding and dispersing atoms as an interconnected Unity, eternal and infinite. We do not know if he saw that Unity as sacred. But his ideas of how to behave as a human being in the world, particularly concerning our understanding and acceptance of death, are ones that later pantheists would repeat and find comforting.

Epicurus began teaching some eighty years after Socrates. Like many philosophers of this time, he was concerned about the problem of how men could be happy. For Epicurus, happiness was not about satisfying one desire after another, an unending and unfulfilling task. Happiness was about tranquillity, "freedom from pain in the body and from disturbance in the soul." In the commune he established in Athens, the pursuit of tranquillity meant a simple life with a simple diet and little indulgence. A man should not go hungry, nor should he overeat—since that would cause pain in the long run. A man should not be too warm or too cold, nor should he live in unnecessary luxury. Epicurus shunned the stress of politics and commerce and focused on being virtuous—for a pleasant life was synonymous with a prudent, honorable, and just life, even as a life of prudence, honor, and justice would inevitably be pleasant. The philosopher was a model of moderation, and it is a linguistic irony that his name evolved into the word epicure, formerly a pejorative for someone who excessively enjoys food and now a reference to anyone who shows particular discernment in food or wine.

For the most part, Epicurus was a practical man who thought we should trust our senses. Otherwise, life would get too confusing and untranquil. Yet we also needed to exercise judgment. Our perception of the world could be distorted. The gods were a good example. Epicurus acknowledged that the gods might exist, since so many people had seen and talked about them for so long. But immortal beings such as Apollo or Hermes were not what we imagined them to be. Most likely, they resembled ghosts or ethereal forms that entered our senses in thin streams of atoms that we processed imperfectly into stories and dreams. In all probability, the gods were simply blissful fellow creatures with some unusual characteristics. They had no interest in us—and no power over us.

Epicurus wanted to free people from superstition and anxiety. Happiness began with being physically comfortable. Next, we needed to be psychologically at ease. Particularly, we should not be afraid of death. Tales of an unhappy afterlife were scaremongering. Neither the mind nor the soul survived death. The atoms simply dispersed. There was nothing left to suffer. Only sensation caused suffering, and death was an end to sensation. Since we would never experience death, why should we fear it?

Epicurus concluded, "There is nothing terrible in life for the man who has truly comprehended that there is nothing terrible in not living."

You may be thinking what I am thinking: This makes sense from the perspective of the dead. But to lose a wife or husband or child to death is often painful and full of sensation. In the remaining writings we have, Epicurus says little about this subject. He does, however, speak of physical suffering, which could be extended to the emotional: "Great pains quickly put an end to life; long-enduring pains are not severe." In short, by definition, unendurable pain is not endured. We die or recover. Chronic pain can be endured, and with the help of philosophy, moments of happiness will begin to dominate.

Epicurus found happiness in a stripped-down world of atoms in which the human task was to be comfortable and avoid pain. If reverence was hardly mentioned by the philosopher, some of his disciples would feel differently. Two hundred years later, the Roman Lucretius—a staunch Epicurean—was periodically seized by "a divine pleasure and awe" whenever he found himself in the beauty of nature. For Lucretius, this universe of colliding and dispersing particles had managed to become numinous. The earthly forms of plants, animals, and landscapes were especially "joyous," "lovable," and deserving of worship.

Among the early Greeks, Epicureanism and Stoicism were competing ideas about how to live in the world. Stoicism did not have a single charismatic leader like Epicurus but developed under a number of philosophers. Stoicism was also more clearly pantheistic.

The Stoic and the Epicurean shared some important beliefs. Both promoted virtue as central to a good life and downplayed conventional success such as fame and fortune. Both prized tranquillity. Both thought the world was composed of one substance and rejected Plato's idea of two (one material and one immaterial, those pure and ideal Forms that included the human soul). Both were materialists who denied the existence of an afterlife.

The differences between the two were also significant. For his one material substance, the Epicurean saw atoms swerving randomly without purpose. The Stoic believed in a matter interpenetrated with energy—pneuma, or fiery breath—a divine animating force that directed the universe and could be described as God, Providence, Fate, or the Logos—borrowing from Heraclitus. Because the Logos was rational, beneficent, and perfect, so was the world we lived in. Everything was working just as it was supposed to work. Everything was fated, even our pain and suffering, which was not really a bad thing (there could be nothing bad in a divine rational universe) but just what was. No harm could be done a man except the harm he did himself by not following the Logos—by acting without virtue.

Virtue meant living in harmony with nature and fate. It included duty to the human community. Humans had a special place in this Universe-as-God, since our inner Logos reflected the larger Logos. Plants and animals had been created for us, and the human task was to be grateful, cheerful, and productive. While an Epicurean withdrew from the world to his commune and garden, the Stoic believed in public service. While an Epicurean avoided pain and sought pleasure, a Stoic accepted either without undue emotion. A Stoic was also interested in reason and in knowing the Logos better, since that understanding would help him accommodate to his fate. Accordingly, the Greek Stoics developed dense, complicated systems of logic and natural science that are virtually unreadable.

Like Epicurus, the Stoics were concerned about the problem of death. They took their solution one step further. Death was not only something we should not fear. Death was a comfort. Death reminded us of our fleeting personal existence and the unimportance of worldly success. Death was another thing to be grateful for. Suicide was always a good option if life ever got too seemingly unpleasant, although for obvious reasons (such as public service) suicide should not be encouraged. Still, one Stoic philosopher asked rhetorically: What is the highway to freedom? And answered: Any vein in your body.

The Stoics also had an answer for personal loss or grief. The key was to understand your role in a fated universe. Expectations should be kept low. Nothing in your life was really your own. You should not say of something, "I lost it," but "I gave it back." Did your child die? He was given back. Did your wife die? She was given back. Were your possessions destroyed or stolen? They were given back. Everything was on loan. Everything was temporary.

Most pantheists today would feel an affinity with Epicurus and the Stoics, although we might argue some of the details. We also try not to fear death and to accept death as a natural process.

In the magazine *Pan,* published by the World Pantheist Movement, a father wrote about the loss of his twenty-one-year-old daughter. The ritual of grieving was important. The parents insisted on a green funeral, burying their child in a wooden casket where she would naturally decompose and return to the earth. The Unitarian minister was carefully referred to as a pan*en*theist (believing that God is immanent in the world but also a presence outside the world) who spoke of how this young woman would eventually become the dogwood flowers, the dew on the flowers, and the caterpillar drinking the dew. Next the mourners walked through some woods near the grave site, startling a doe and fawn, enjoying the sun and wind, what the father described as the divinity of nature.

This Texas couple felt they could not "come out as Pans just yet." They worried that people would not understand the belief that their daughter had lived a full life in her short life. In grief sessions, they kept quiet when others railed against the injustice of God or consoled themselves with the promise of heaven. "Fortunately, most of our friends don't feel the need to 'comfort' us with their religion," the father wrote, "although many acquaintances insist on making that effort." When this parent visits his child's grave, he listens for the harsh call of a jay or rumble of a bullfrog. He sees his daughter in the spider web and circling hawk. He feels her presence in the sunset "painted by west Texas grass fires."

There are other ways for a pantheist to grieve. In a *New York Times* interview with novelist Carlos Fuentes, the author spoke of the death of his two adult children: "You go on. You go on. You bring the person you love inside you. That is how you cope. You make him or her live within you. The whole experience I had with my children is in me. It is nowhere else I can see. . . . The experience of having them within myself is what matters."

You bring the person inside you. I understand completely. No one did it better than I did as a child, writing my own mythology, the Hero Father, the man soaring into the clouds and falling from them, too, never a disappointment, never a cross word between us.

I look at these skies in the Gila Valley. I stand on my porch before this brilliant blue turning deeper cerulean, trails of water vapor flaring orange and pink, and the roll of stratocumulus traveling north to drop snow in the Mogollon Mountains. I stand in this grace, space, and light, and I do not think consciously of my father dressed as I have always known him in the eight-by-twelve black-and-white-photos from Bell Aircraft: a short, balding man wearing a flight jacket, posed before a rocket plane.

I do, however, feel a connection. I know he loved clouds. In one of our few home movies, a rare vacation, my father panned over my mother and the two little girls she held by the hand to focus on a storm drifting over the Grand Canyon. He was drawn instinctively to that beauty. He was drawn to the sky and wanted to watch, over and over, what it looked like in 1955.

It looks much the same today. It has no human sorrow or drama, no history, no meaning except what we give it. We tell ourselves stories about the world and about death because stories are how we think and play, and thinking and playing are who we are, the animal with language. My science is not a denial of that. My pantheism is not a denial of human emotion or of how these emotions entangle metaphorically with all those atoms colliding and dispersing and reuniting. "There are gods in everything," Thales said. The philosopher-scientist did not abandon the story of his time but referred to it affectionately. Apollo is in the crane. Our beloved daughter is in the spider web. My father is in the sky.

Cranes have always attracted stories. In the Southwest, the Zunis have a Crane clan to which the Creator gave the medicine seed of hail and snow, since cranes come during the first winter storms. The Navajos use a crane effigy to cure illnesses, and the Hopis place a crane-winged staff at the entrance to the chamber that represents their emergence from the earth. Cranes are linked to both health and the underworld—much as they are linked in the Greek god Hermes, who leads the dead to the underworld and whose staff of snakes topped by crane wings became the symbol for the medical profession.

In Silver City, the Religious Society of Gila Friends makes paper cranes to celebrate Hiroshima Day, a commemoration of the United States' first use of the nuclear bomb. The Japanese have long revered the crane as a symbol of immortality, and this modern crane story is about a sick little girl named Sakado who wanted to make a thousand origami cranes but died first of radiation poisoning.

I have no particular story about cranes, although seeing and hearing them makes me happy. That is true of many wild animals. I grew up in apartment buildings with Siamese cats and a highly chlorinated swimming pool. Cranes are outside my normal experience, outside my personal joys and sorrows, memories, anxieties and confusion. In my world, cranes are not about immortality or disease or death. When I watch them, I am not participating more in being human; I am participating less. Perhaps this is the cause of my happiness.

I am still waiting to see a crane dance. First, the bird lowers its head while lifting and spreading its wings. The head rises, the wings stroke down, and the crane jumps up. Sometimes the crane throws a stick into the air. Now if another crane is nearby, it might start jumping, too, facing the first crane, or both cranes might stand and jump together side by side. According to ornithologists, this behavior can spread through an entire group of cranes until everyone is dancing, jumping up and down, wings and heads rising and falling. The point of all this is unclear. Synchronous dancing is common among birds forming or having just formed pair bonds. But my husband, Peter, and our biologist friends Mike and Carol have seen the greater sandhill cranes dance here in the Gila Valley during winter—when these cranes are finished with nesting and breeding. Dancing, then, is not just about mating. In a group, dancing can also lead to fighting or flying and seems related to excitement, stimulation, and a release of energy.

A crane dancing alone would seem so intent, like a woman doing yoga or a man performing a ritual to his god. A group of cranes dancing would be a wonderful sight, all that graceful and ungainly movement. A group of cranes dancing would make me feel special, as though handed a gift I didn't deserve but had always coveted. I feel certain I would be seized by a divine pleasure and awe. It is a good reason to keep my binoculars handy.

CHAPTER 3

Ruler of Everything

A FRIEND OF MINE recently expressed amazement that her beautiful daughter, then in medical school, wanted to become a pathologist. Where could she have gotten such an idea? I replied with some amazement of my own, "You don't watch much TV, do you?" The rest of us know that the world is awash in beautiful female pathologists, every day and night of the week, in various *CSI* and *Law and Order* shows, and in their multiple spin-offs and unending reruns. Add all the programs about real-life surgeries, autopsies, and crime scenes, and it is fair to say that we television watchers are obsessed with looking death in the eye and that we have grown obsessively matter-of-fact. Blood, mucus, shattered bone. Nothing disturbs us. Nothing is secret or forbidden. We like to see things travel in the body—all those interior shots, the way bullets explode skin and rattle the brain pan. We see nothing wrong with decomposing and being eaten by bugs. That's just life. We have skipped past the pain and suffering to its natural conclusion. We could all be pathologists now, lifting the sheet without undue emotion, taking a poke into an ear or mouth.

In other ways, too, we have become Stoics. We know that people do horrible things to each other. We watch that on television and in the movies as a kind of exorcism, or perhaps a manual of what-to-do-in-case, or perhaps just to feel some adrenaline. We look into the face of evil, the many faces, and begin our analysis. We see cause and effect. The child abuser was first abused. The serial killer is chemically damaged. We dissect Pol Pot, the Rwanda massacres, the latest famine.

And we feel a weariness, much like that of Marcus Aurelius, the Roman emperor and Stoic who in 170 CE wrote in his diary, later called the *Meditations,* "Evil: the same old thing. No matter what happens, keep this in mind: It's the same old thing, from one end of the world to the other. It fills the history books, ancient and modern, and the cities, and the houses too. Nothing new at all. Familiar, transient."

Who wrote as though he were just an ordinary man, someone you and I could talk to about our problems: "When you wake up in the morning, tell yourself: The people I deal with today will be meddling, ungrateful, arrogant, dishonest, jealous, and surly." These people were not evil, however, only ignorant, with a nature related to the emperor's own, "not of the same blood or birth," of course, but sharing the same Logos that permeates everything.

Who believed like a good pantheist and Stoic that evil was just a term for something misunderstood or misnamed or unim-

portant. How could there be evil if the universe was both divine
and perfect?

Who believed that physical pain and suffering were also
unimportant. In the end, nothing could hurt you—the real you,
your character and virtue. Nothing enslaved you but your desire
for things you could not control.

This January afternoon I am walking with my twenty-one-year-
old daughter from our yellow house in the Gila Valley to the Nature Conservancy pond a quarter mile away. Both Maria and my
son, David, are students at the University of New Mexico in Albuquerque. Their winter break has come and gone, and tomorrow they go back to what we now accept as their real lives.

As Maria and I walk this country road, we are in the middle
of our own *CSI* show for insects. After a few corpses we barely
notice, Maria stops to examine the pinacate beetle being
dragged by ants. At the Gila River Farm, the gravelly mounds
of ants are everywhere, every few feet, the busy movements
ubiquitous, tiny legs marching, tiny mandibles clamped
around a seed or someone else's body part. The pinacate beetle is also called darkling beetle or stinkbug, and it is an insect
I like—modestly charismatic with its shiny black carapace and
endearing way of stopping at any sign of threat, putting its
head to the ground, lifting its tail vertically, and posing like an
acrobat. This signals an attacker that the beetle is about to un-
leash a bad scent. It is the scariest headstand in the world. In
this case, the strategy didn't work, and the black carapace is already half disassembled. My daughter comments that she

didn't think harvester ants ate meat. I wonder if these *are* harvester ants. They *look* like harvester ants, she says. I decide not to get into an argument about something I don't know. I don't know, I say, and we walk on, pausing again before a dead squirrel, also being investigated by ants. I fancy I saw this squirrel alive yesterday and wonder what happened.

We both know that nature is brutal. Take butterflies. Out of a hundred butterfly eggs, maybe one will survive to hatch, grow, form a chrysalis, change into something completely different, spread her beautiful wet wings, and fly. The rest are eaten or parasitized, part of ecology's gigantic food mill. Often a parasitic wasp will inject her eggs into a living caterpillar, where the tiny wasps hatch and grow and eat the animal from the inside out. I think I saw a caterpillar on this road, too, one of the few moth or butterfly species in which the caterpillars live by hibernating through the winter. If this caterpillar is someplace I can see him, moving about unnaturally, then he is likely, already, full of wasp larvae.

The Nature Conservancy pond is an oval about two acres large and full of birds. Maria and I stand back so as not to disturb anyone. We count green-necked mallards, white-headed buffleheads, coots, and wood ducks. An egret sits in one of the walnut trees circling the pond, and the water reflects back that image, white egret and bare-branched tree slightly rippling. To the north, a few miles away, mountains rise over two thousand feet, and their red-striated cliffs are also reflected, the rippling rock sheared by the passage of a coot.

Coots are unpleasant parents. Commonly, they hatch as many as nine eggs, with nine fluffy little coots following mother and father in the water. But feeding that many coots is difficult. By the third day, when a chick opens her mouth and begs, she is pecked hard as punishment. Some chicks get more punishment than others, stop begging, and starve. Systematically, the parents kill the weakest of their children until only two are left. Suddenly I remember having actually seen this scene, watching in David Attenborough's film *The Life of Birds* how the mother coot stabbed and pecked, and the fluffy baby dropped her head and sank lower in the pond and floated lifelessly. It made me feel a little sick. It made me feel weary.

The blue winter sky is a crystalline bowl fit snug over the Gila Valley. The air is crisp, cold enough for a jacket but not so cold as to be a hardship. The coots glide through reflections of mountains and trees. I look at them with a jaundiced eye.

My daughter will graduate from college this year, go out into the world, make mistakes, walk dark streets where people do terrible things to each other. Evil *is* new to her. I am arguing now with the Roman emperor Marcus Aurelius. Evil is real and important. Pain and suffering are important. And I am afraid for her.

Maria watches the mallards and buffleheads move effortlessly across the water on the pond. She doesn't speak, calm and quiet, which is her nature. She gives the scene one more minute of her time. She wrinkles her forehead. She is thinking about something. What? I have no idea. Let's go back, she says at last. She has clothes to pack, things to do.

Marcus Aurelius ruled the Roman Empire for almost twenty years in the second century CE, a period that would later be called the Golden Age for its relative prosperity. Born into an aristocratic and wealthy Roman family, the boy lost his father when he was three years old. By the age of eleven, this serious and dutiful child was already being groomed for high office. In 136 CE, the childless emperor Hadrian adopted Marcus's maternal uncle as his heir, with the provision that the uncle adopt Marcus as his heir in turn. At this time, too, Marcus met Apollonius the Stoic, with whom he would eventually study and whom he would thank for having taught him to "pay attention to nothing, no matter how fleetingly, except the *logos*."

According to a biography written many years later, Marcus was unhappy with his new role as the future emperor. When asked why, the teenager spoke of the corruptible nature of power and burden of responsibility. He dreamed he had shoulders of ivory. How could they support such a weight? A bust of that time shows a beardless boy with firm chin, wide-apart eyes, a solemn expression, and abundant curly hair. He was said to have loved hunting, wrestling, and ball games. But he was also studious and a bit odd, in the habit of reading at the gladiatorial spectacles instead of watching them. He would never be physically strong. Even when young, he complained of chest and stomach pain. As an adult, he took opium, possibly for ulcers.

In 138 CE, Emperor Hadrian died; the uncle became Emperor Pius, and Marcus (with another adopted younger brother) the heir-apparent. Marcus Aurelius later wrote of his debt to Pius and the lessons his new father taught him about compassion, hard work, and indifference to pomp. It was from Pius that Marcus learned not to be arrogant and to live simply at court, without bodyguards, expensive clothes, or ostentatious furniture—"the whole charade."

The future emperor seemed to be growing up in a surprisingly warm and affectionate household. Letters between Marcus Aurelius and his tutor, Fronto, are intimate and detailed, a lively, literary correspondence. In a typical note to Fronto, Marcus mentions his mother and the wife of Fronto, Gratia, as well as Fronto's baby daughter. The heir-apparent is now in his early twenties. He is self-conscious, self-deprecating, eager to please, and a little smug:

> We are well. I slept somewhat late owing to my slight cold, which seems now to have subsided. So from five a.m. till nine I spent the time partly in reading some of Cato's *Agriculture* and partly in writing not quite such wretched stuff, by heavens, as yesterday. . . . Then we went to luncheon. What do you think I ate? A little bit of bread, although I saw others devouring beans, onions, and herrings full of roe. We then worked hard at grape-gathering and had a good sweat and were merry and, as the poet says, *still left some clusters hanging high as gleanings of the vintage.* After six o'clock we came home. I did but little work and that to no purpose. Then I had a long chat with my little mother as she sat on the bed. My talk was this. What do you think my Fronto is now doing? Then she: And what do you think my Gratia is doing? Then I: And what do you think our little sparrow, the wee Gratia, is doing? While we were chattering in this way and disputing which of us two loved the one or other of you two the better, the gong sounded. . . . After coming back here,

before I turn over and snore, I get my task done and give my dearest of masters an account of the day's doings, and if I could miss him more, I would not grudge wasting away a little more. Farewell, my Fronto, wherever you are, most honey-sweet, my love, my delight. How is it between you and me? I love you and you are away.

Such tender exchanges would continue until the tutor's death twenty-six years later. In almost every aspect of life, Marcus Aurelius seemed to be a man in touch with his feelings—a devoted son to his mother, grateful to his adopted father, an excessively loving and demonstrative friend. At twenty-four, he married, and his wife immediately started bearing children, one after another, and on occasion two at a time. In further letters to Fronto, Marcus fussed over them. Concerning his first child, a daughter, "Thank the Gods we seem to have some hope of recovery. The diarrhea is stopped, the feverish attacks got rid of; but the emaciation is extreme and there is still some cough." Within two years, he had twin sons, who died as infants, and then another daughter, "We are still experiencing summer heat. But since our little girls—we mustn't boast—are quite well, we think that we are enjoying the healthiest of weather and the balmy temperature of spring." Too soon the oldest girl would also be dead, and another newborn son. It is easy to imagine the anxious father, listening for a cough, delighting in a laugh, tickling his youngest child, exulting and then weeping.

Yet at some point, despite his emotional nature, Marcus Aurelius became a Stoic. Rome had conquered Greece centuries earlier, adopting much of its culture, including its schools of philosophy. In an ecumenical age, Stoicism was one belief among many. Foreign gods filled the marketplace, even as everyone worshipped the Roman gods—as much to demonstrate their alliance with the state as anything else. Some scholars, like the tutor Fronto, scorned all religion and philosophy as inferior to literary study. Powerful and well educated, Marcus Aurelius had a choice, and he chose—like many of the Roman elite—a Stoic pantheism that emphasized virtue combined with duty and service.

As an amateur philosopher, Marcus Aurelius did not pursue much original thought but repeated that of earlier Stoics, as well as men like Democritus, Epicurus, and Heraclitus. His pantheism could be expressed in a single sentence: "Everything is interwoven, and the web is holy." The universe was a unified body, what some Stoics saw as a living organism. All its parts formed a whole; all its parts were divine. Nature was guided by the rational principle, the Logos. Our job was to live in harmony with nature, which our inner virtue, or Logos, naturally reflected. Inner virtue was all that mattered. Unruly emotions were to be avoided, although Marcus Aurelius made a nice distinction when he asked "to be free of passion, but not love." At the same time, our interconnectedness meant that "in a sense, people are our proper occupation."

In some areas, the emperor was agnostic. Did the gods exist, too? What happened after death? He didn't know and, stoically, tried not to worry about it.

He had a lot of other things to worry about. The reputation of Marcus Aurelius as a philosopher-king and poster boy for

Stoicism—grateful for his existence, accepting his fate—is enhanced by the fact that his fate included so many problems and occasions to put philosophy into practice. At age thirty-nine, he became ruler of a kingdom whose borders were dangerously extended to include Britain in the west, Germany in the north, Syria in the east, and North Africa in the south. Both the previous emperors, Hadrian and Pius, had neglected their military responsibilities, and though the center of Rome held, its edges were crumbling. In 161 CE, the Parthians invaded in the east, and Roman legions had to be sent from as far away as the Danube, weakening the empire's defense against the Germanic tribes. That same year, in the city of Rome, the River Tiber flooded, setting off a widespread famine. It would take five years to subdue the Parthians, and when the troops returned home, they brought with them plague, probably smallpox. At this point, the northern borders erupted, with heavy fighting on the Hungarian Plain. More barbarians attacked the Balkans. The Grecian provinces of Thrace and Macedonia were invaded. The city of Athens was spared only by luck. Finally, the enemy entered Italy itself, something that had not happened for hundreds of years. A contemporary account notes, "Among the barbarian dead were found even the bodies of women wearing armor." This was telling. The barbarians did not want plunder so much as a new home.

Meanwhile, in his personal life, the children of Marcus Aurelius kept dying—a four-year-old son, a seven-year-old son, another infant—so that he seemed to illumine the Stoic caution that as you kissed your child at night, you should say in your heart, "Tomorrow, perhaps, you will be taken from me." Altogether, only five of the emperor's fourteen children would survive. His adopted brother and coruler also died. His wife was rumored to be unfaithful (When did she find the time?) with a fondness for dancers and gladiators. His health was bad. Often, he had trouble sleeping and eating.

Yet he could not rest. From 169 to 176 CE, the emperor was mostly in the battlefield commanding his troops, fighting the barbarians, defending his borders, and making the administrative decisions of an empire. During this time, he began to write *Meditations,* a book of spiritual reflection that still sells in bookstores today.

I read Marcus Aurelius on Sacaton Mesa, a twenty-minute walk from my yellow house on the Gila River Farm. A dirt road climbs to the top of this plateau and stretches for twelve miles, with a 360-degree view. Once an ancient lake bed, Sacaton Mesa now defines and overlooks the Gila Valley. Directly north are the red-striated cliffs and peaks of the Mogollon Mountains, solid, commanding, irregular, with gray rock formations that erupt like giant's teeth from the lower slopes of juniper and yellow grass. To the east, Bear Mountain and Telephone Mountain stand like sentinels above the Gila River. The rumpled foothills of Black Mountain and Antelope Ridge run south. Low massive shapes like sleeping animals lie further west.

The mesa itself is desert, a rolling plain covered with prickly pear and snakeweed, a small bush that typically replaces blue grama grass and dominates ranges overgrazed by cows. Last fall, after the summer rains, the leaves of the snakeweed were a luminous lime green, a brilliantly colored sea of plants lapping at the base of the Mogollon Mountains. Now, in winter, they are olive green, slowly turning brown. Yucca stalks punctuate the landscape like exclamation points, rising six feet high from a spiky rosette of leaves.

Ever since I was a child, I have cultivated the ability to walk and read at the same time. It is a simple matter of peripheral vision and the confidence that this is the right thing to do. I walk and read now on Sacaton Mesa's long dirt road, passed rarely by a rancher's truck. When I hear the sound of an engine, I put down my reading to save both the rancher and myself the embarrassment of thinking me dangerously eccentric. Every few pages I look up to an enormous space filled with sky, mountains, and desert. This is perfection. I have a good book, and I have a good view.

Meditations is divided into twelve sections, some only a few pages long, many of the entries a paragraph or single sentence. They are the thoughts of a man who could snatch only minutes between ruling on a judicial case, meeting with diplomats, or attacking the enemy. These things called for public decisiveness. The ruminative *Meditations* were an antidote to that life, supremely private, at times uncertain, melancholic, pessimistic, then rallying. They expressed a vaguely hopeful pantheistic creed: "One world, made up of all things. One divinity, present in them all. One substance and one law—the *logos* that all rational beings share." They were also exhortations to the rational self. Be more rational. Work harder. Don't show off. Focus on what is important. Be grateful for what you have. Fight for equanimity. Fight your flaws. Stop being afraid of death. Stop being afraid of pain. Stop being afraid of sorrow. Stop whining.

The tone is familiar. Reading Marcus Aurelius is like reading the diary of an earnest seventeen-year-old bent on self-improvement. It is so hard to be good—so hard to be a Stoic! The emperor scolded himself incessantly: "Yes, keep on degrading yourself, soul. But soon your chance at dignity will be gone. Everyone gets one life. Yours is almost used up."

By now, Marcus Aurelius was in his early fifties, perhaps my age exactly. I also find myself thinking and feeling like a seventeen-year-old, a spiral return to the anxieties of adolescence. No doubt, hormones are involved, a chemical rearrangement both for the teenager and for the man or woman nearing menopause. What is this new life ahead of me—old age rather than adulthood—and what does it mean that I am here now surrounded by the beauty of snakeweed and yucca? What does it mean that we all must die and we all must suffer? Nothing I have learned has prepared me for this mystery, and in any case I keep forgetting. What did you say again?

Everyone gets one life. That's a chilling thought, even more chilling when you have already lived over half yours. Soon my chance at dignity will be gone. It is not simply that I have not accomplished all I wanted to accomplish. It is that I still want to accomplish these things. I want fame and fortune. I want to write a *New York Times* Notable Book and then be on the *Times* best-seller list. I want more friends—invitations to parties, fun times. I want to be popular. I want to be admired. I know these things have nothing to do with my inner virtue. They won't really make me happy. Like Marcus Aurelius, I know how I degrade myself.

Like Marcus Aurelius, I have deeper disappointments. My generation came of age protesting the Vietnam War, promoting civil rights and social justice. We would end racism and poverty in America. We would end world hunger. We would make the world a better place, and I would be a part of that. None of this happened.

Like Marcus Aurelius, what I really want is to be wise and serene. Stop whining. Stop being distracted. Accept what I have. Accept who I am.

I read a few more pages of *Meditations* and look up, immeasurably pleased, at the view of mountains and sky. The Roman emperor has written, "Nothing is so conducive to spiritual growth as the capacity for logical and accurate analysis of everything that happens to us." Yes, exactly. This has always been my favorite approach to a problem. How can I analyze myself now into wisdom? How can I reach serenity through logic?

Like all Stoics, Marcus Aurelius admired logic and reason as reflections of the larger Logos of a rational universe. He believed the most logical and reasonable thing he could do as a Stoic was not to desire what he could not control. The list of things he could not control was long and included his body, other people, his reputation, and his property. What he did control was his inner virtue, which could also be described as his will to be in harmony with nature. When he welcomed with affection whatever happened to him in life, he acknowledged a beneficent universe and understood his role in that universe. The fact that this role was fated seemed to negate free will. Yet desiring only the Logos could be seen as an act of free will—as well as a kind of freedom from pettiness, ambition, lust, and greed.

Reason could be used to examine every troublesome event that arose in daily life. The emperor agreed with Epicurus that our human impressions of the world came through the senses and were generally accurate. But emotions could also distort information with a false value judgment. I might perceive something as bad: an insult, a theft, a death. But a closer look using the intellectual power of the Logos allowed me to analyze the situation with more dispassion.

"What is it," Marcus Aurelius asked himself, "this thing that now forces itself on my notice? What is it made up of? How long was it designed to last? And what qualities do I need to bring to bear on it—tranquility, courage, honesty, trustworthiness, straightforwardness, independence or what?" Was this thing from God or fate? Was it a coincidence? Was it chance? Was it due to the ignorance of another human being? If so, treat that person as nature required—with compassion and justice.

Reason required a cold, clear perspective. Marcus Aurelius had to keep reminding himself, just as I do: You are not the center of the universe. This event is not really about you. You have to stay focused. The nature of the world is flux and change. Why would you expect anything else?

Reason often led a Stoic to take action, for that was also the nature of the world. Being human meant participating in human affairs, not withdrawing from them. We were social animals, fundamentally cooperative and unselfish. Sometimes, true, a Stoic had to kill or hurt people in self-defense or for some larger good. Certainly the Roman armies led by Marcus Aurelius caused considerable pain and suffering as the emperor did what he felt he had to do to protect and expand his empire. Yet in *Meditations* he warned repeatedly against showing anger or unmanly rage. It was "courtesy and kindness" that defined his real self. He was here to serve others.

Marcus Aurelius would repeat these ideas over and over in his notes from the battlefield. They were difficult ideas to absorb. They seemed to get stuck somewhere. Being a wordy animal as well as a rational one, the emperor thought: Perhaps if I say it differently? If I use a metaphor? If I use a different metaphor? If I say it tomorrow, and the day after? *Meditations* is a repetitive book, a technique of writing that reinforces and rekindles, variations on a theme: how to be better.

Marcus Aurelius, Marcus Aurelius. On Sacaton Mesa, I clutch your work to my chest like a seventeen-year-old girl. We are soul mates. You examine yourself ruthlessly and chase your own tail. You think you can be perfect but know you cannot. You celebrate the beauty in nature, the ripeness of figs and bending stalks of wheat, yet you are often bleak beyond despair. You want to serve others—but you do not really like people. Sometimes, you have a wit that makes me laugh out loud: "The best revenge is not to be like that." More often, you sadden yourself. You are saddened by the world.

I understand your contradictions. And the connection is exhilarating. How can we be so alike? How can someone like you—ruler of Rome, the most powerful human being in your time—be anything like me, a middle-aged woman, ruler of nothing? How can I possibly feel a kinship across this expanse of centuries, gender, culture, and status?

Some of this, I know, has to do with language. I happen to be reading an excellent translation by Gregory Hays, a man not afraid to extract from the original Greek (the language Aurelius wrote in instead of Latin) colloquialisms like "from the bottom of my heart" and "Don't gussy up your thoughts."

But mostly, Marcus Aurelius, I can see you so clearly because you have stripped yourself so bare. You talk only of the essentials. You don't gussy up your thoughts. From reading *Meditations,* I would not know that you command hundreds of thousands of soldiers or that you lost miserably your first encounter with the barbarians or that the war keeps dragging on and on with too many small but exhausting battles. I would not know that in the year 172 CE you were said to have magically summoned a thunderbolt to destroy an enemy's siege weapon, an event commemorated on the Aurelian column in the Piazza Colonna at Rome. I would not know that your own people slander and mock your wife; that your son and heir, Commodus, troubles you deeply; that your old friend, the Roman governor of Syria, plots rebellion and has just proclaimed himself the true emperor of Rome. In response, you have the right and the power to kill his entire family—sister, parents, wife, and child. Of course, you do not.

You are not interested in talking about your personal troubles or your power, even though they are the background to every page. I watch *CSI.* You stand with the physician Galen and watch the autopsies of your soldiers. You accept the heads of prisoners (also recorded on the Aurelian column) with that same world-weary expression. Writing your spiritual reflections, you can't help but use the images of gangrene, suppuration, and abscess. A severed hand is what we do to ourselves when we separate from nature by rebelling against fate. Lancets should be kept close by. The word gore comes up often. From you, the Pollyanna chirp of Stoicism—Ain't life grand!—is free of ignorance or hypocrisy. You have seen too much gore to be naive.

This February, as winter slides into a period of cold gray days, I take you with me everywhere. In Silver City, during the middle of the week, when Peter and I are not in the Gila Valley, I read you as I walk to the local cemetery. I can start at my house and in fifteen minutes be at the edge of town. To my left, the mostly Protestant graves seem dull in shades of brown and gray. To my right, the Catholic cemetery is alive and shocking with bright color—red and orange plastic flowers, American flags, blue statues of the Virgin. Instead of cement, one grave has astro turf and lawn ornaments. A bunny, a squirrel, a pink flamingo. Over another patch of dirt sits a bed frame. Rest in peace. On the graves of children, some families put toys under a small tree decorated for Christmas. This month I see Valentine presents, banners spelling *MOM,* and balloons with hearts. Once I found a letter blowing in the wind: Dear grandma, I miss you very, very much. . . .

This all seems natural to me. I was also a child in a cemetery and spent Sunday afternoons sitting on my father's grave, watch-

ing my Methodist grandmother put white chrysanthemums in a
Folgers can covered with tin foil. The cut flowers were from her
Kansas garden, where they were grown as a useful crop for fu-
nerals, weddings, anniversaries, hospital visits, and church. It is
obvious to me now that my grandmother was a Stoic: practical,
hardworking, distrustful of emotion. She accepted her son's
death. She accepted her life as a good one despite its hardships.
She knew her place in the world, a farmer's wife, with all the
prejudices of the Midwest. At the same time, she was part of
something larger and beneficent.

It is also natural to read Marcus Aurelius surrounded by the
dead, for death was often on his mind. He believed his own
would come sooner rather than later, a reflection of his poor
health. He worried about what people would think of him, his
imperial legacy, and he devised spiritual and mental exercises to
put things in perspective: Remember the ancient courts and
rulers—all gone, ashes and dust. Remember that Alexander the
Great and his mule driver both died, and the same thing happened to them both—dissolved into the life force or dissolved
into atoms. We are all One and we all go back to the One.
(More than once, the emperor contemplated suicide but rejected it as unnecessary.)

In 175 CE, after seven years in the north fighting the barbarians, the emperor decided to go home. First, he visited the
East—where the Syrian governor had threatened rebellion—to
confirm his rule over these territories. His wife and son accompanied him. En route, the forty-five-year-old empress died, possibly in her fifteenth pregnancy. Back in Rome, Marcus

Aurelius mourned his wife's death and then prepared a celebration of his return. In a scene of paternal devotion, he did not ride in the triumphal chariot but ran beside it while his teenage son controlled the horses. Soon after, Commodus was elevated to coruler, the succession assured. In 178 CE, father and son went north again to conquer more land for the empire. In the spring of 180, Marcus Aurelius fell ill at the age of fifty-nine and died.

I grieve. He was so young. I am in love with this man. If I could travel back in time, I would go to his tent on the River Danube near present-day Vienna and try to cheer him up. I would tell him he mustn't be so hard on himself. Everything is interwoven, and the web is holy. I would stroke his cheek, pat his brow. Somehow I think Peter would understand.

No one is perfect. Despite his virtues, Marcus Aurelius reflected the prejudices of a brutal age. The life expectancy of a Roman citizen was about twenty-five years, most people dying of poor nutrition, disease, or violence. Slaves were abused as a matter of course and required a professional—the *tortur*—to punish them when the master got tired. Unwanted infants, especially girls, were commonly exposed at the local garbage dump. In some areas, the emperor tried to help, strengthening the rights of orphan children. But he could do only so much, and he did only so much. If we define evil as the extreme needless suffering that human beings inflict on each other (and on other living creatures), then Marcus Aurelius tolerated a great deal of evil.

He also unleashed evil on the world. For surely he must have known that his son Commodus was unstable and should never have been named heir to an empire that included one-fifth of the world's population. Perhaps the emperor was blinded by fatherly love, or perhaps he felt he had no choice. In any case, the results were disastrous. Commodus was a cruel and neglectful ruler who became obsessed with killing people and animals in the gladiatorial arena. Within two years of his reign, the eldest daughter of Marcus Aurelius would try to assassinate her twenty-one-year-old brother, a crime for which she was executed. This was the little girl—running about the room in high spirits and good health—of whom the fond father had written to Fronto. This was the new family scene, murderous and vengeful.

By 192 CE Commodus referred to himself as a god, *Hercules Romanus*, and was increasingly absorbed in a bizarre fantasy life. In one public performance, he dressed a group of crippled men in snake costumes and beat them to death with a club. By now he had already ordered the massacre of numerous Roman officials and their families, and no one knew who would be next. At a fourteen-day spectacle in which Commodus killed hundreds of leopards, lions, deer, and other animals, the senator Cassius Dio recorded how the emperor approached him carrying the head of an ostrich and a bloody sword. Commodus said nothing but grinned meaningfully. Dio believed that "many of us would have been killed on the spot for laughing at him—for it was laughter rather than fear that took hold of us—if I had not chewed some laurel leaves that I took from my garland and persuaded those sitting next to me to do likewise." Moving their jaws steadily, the men concealed their nervous amusement.

Commodus died after he drank poisoned wine—and after an assassin was sent in to strangle him. The next emperor lasted three months, followed by four years of civil war, more civil unrest, more assassinations, and a collapse of central authority as the military tried to seize control. Between 235 and 284 CE, twenty emperors rose and fell, along with another thirty pretenders. Taxes increased. Commerce declined. The poor suffered the most. In the end, the Golden Age of Marcus Aurelius would be admired mainly in contrast to what came next.

One group that had never much appreciated the Stoic emperor were the Christians. Early in his rule, Marcus Aurelius had allowed officials to use criminals condemned to death as part of the gladiatorial games. At this time, to declare oneself a Christian—to refuse to offer sacrifice to the Roman gods and obedience to the Roman state—was a capital offense. In an infamous case, when bodies were needed for a public entertainment, officials duly rounded up some Christians, offered them the chance to recant their faith, were conveniently refused, and tried and condemned them. Animals tore apart the old men and boys. The woman Blandina hung on a stake the entire day.

Christianity thrived on such martyrdom. And Christianity offered an eternal life of comfort and bliss that nothing else—certainly not Stoicism—could compete with. For those Romans born to die early of disease or violence, born a slave flogged by the *tortur,* born a woman married at the age of twelve, born a la-

borer half dead from work and little food, Christianity provided
an intimate relationship with a loving Father, a community of
fellow Christians on earth, and a heaven and hell afterward. In
that heaven and hell, all wrongs would be righted: the *tortur*
punished and the slave freed. Divine justice would prevail, and
that justice was not abstract or impersonal.

By 313 CE, Emperor Constantine was legalizing Christianity throughout the Roman Empire. An estimated tenth of the
population had already converted. Sixty-four years later, Christianity became the official religion, and suddenly the world was
full of an evil newly defined and newly dangerous. It existed in
people who did not believe what the church believed. It existed
supernaturally in Satan, the fallen angel who had rebelled
against God.

For the first Christians, evil must have been puzzling. Why
would an all-powerful and omnipresent God allow evil in the
world? The early clergy were intellectuals who had no problem
turning to Greek philosophy for help. Some of their answers
could be found in a revision of Stoicism. What a man might perceive as bad or evil might really be God's will, and thus a hidden
good. Also, bad things didn't really matter; what mattered was
our response to them, our inner virtue—for which, as a Christian, we would later be rewarded. Importantly, the temptation of
evil allowed us free will. We were responsible for our actions
even in a universe ruled by God. Eventually, the Christian St.
Augustine would argue that evil was not actually included in the
Creation but experienced only when a man separated himself
from God. Similarly, the Stoics had believed that evil occurred

when we failed to follow the Logos within us; evil was omission rather than an active presence.

Christianity could borrow so much from Stoicism because the two religions already had so much in common. Both believed in a divine Providence interested in humanity and requiring certain moral behavior. The Stoic version of Providence was an impersonal, pervasive intelligence that was matter interpenetrated with pneuma. The Christian version was a loving, personal, transcendent Creator who existed outside matter. In both viewpoints, man was made in God's image; the Logos in us reflected the Logos of the universe. Thus all men were brothers or, as Marcus Aurelius would have it, citizens in a great city.

Rather, for Christians, all men who believed in Christ were brothers, and there was actually a lot more to it than that. The devil was in the details. The church in Rome had very specific ideas about what Christians or anyone else should believe, and they enforced their religious view as the only one possible. After a fairly decent run, from the sixth century BCE to the fourth century CE, pantheism in the West was about to disappear, or virtually so, for some twelve hundred years.

Because I do not like being cold and am already sleepy by ten o'clock, I have to force myself outside at night. I take blankets. I whine. Then I am on a lawn chair in the Gila Valley looking up at a blaze of stars, the entire sky filled with glittering points of light, nothing here but darkness and light, stars and me.

At first, the Milky Way looks like a long thin cloud. But this milky whiteness is really an extradensity of stars, that cloudiness the edge of an arm in the spiraled disk that is our galaxy. I know that our sun and earth formed in one of these arms and that I am now looking across space at another arm, both of us far from the galaxy's center, which is a turbulent maelstrom with a massive black hole. What I know about the night sky is actually more confusing than helpful. The heart reels. The head spins. The tiny part of the universe I can see is so big and chaotic that I immediately seek order. In so much beauty, I have to admire something small.

My favorite constellation is the Big Dipper because it is easy to find. But in February the Big Dipper would be behind me, on the north side of the house. Too cold to move the lawn chair, I look instead for the belt of Orion or the Pleiades, a star cluster named for the seven daughters of Atlas, who was condemned by Zeus to hold up the heavens on his broad shoulders.

Oh, the beauty of stars! I exclaim.

But my thoughts wander to the problem of evil. Like the Stoics, I do not believe in evil as a supernatural force outside nature. I do not believe that any part of nature is evil. I could even say that I do not believe evil exists in a divine universe.

Yet I have no problem using the word evil to describe the pain that human beings deliberately and gratuitously cause each other. Let's take a worst-case scenario. Your child is tortured and killed *just like on all those television shows, and all those movies and best-selling thrillers.* Someone's child is tortured and dies screaming.

At this point, any belief I have in reason is long gone. At the extreme edge of human suffering, Stoicism breaks down. For surely it would be inhuman now to be stoical—to say that this pain was unimportant or to call my response a false value judgment. In some profound way, Stoicism would not be virtuous but a betrayal of who we are.

I hope to never, personally, see the face of evil. If I do, I will not—I am certain—behave like a Stoic. I will not accept my fate with cheerful affection or remotely want to. Instead, I expect to wail and protest, curl up and die, or buy a gun. Maybe I will abandon all my pantheistic beliefs and become a Christian just so I can have some divine justice—so someone will go to hell and someone be saved in heaven. I expect to behave shamelessly. Regarding evil, shamelessness might be the most reasonable response.

For the moment, I do not believe in the Christian heaven. I cannot imagine an afterlife designed for just a few people. I cannot imagine where this place would be or what I would do there. Nor do I believe in the Stoic's intelligent and benign Providence. Looking up at the Milky Way, I do not think the stars care for me or my husband or son or daughter, for any of my family and friends. I do not think humans are at the center of fate or even fated.

Still, we are here. I am here. Everything is interwoven, and the web is holy. Surprisingly, still, that makes sense.

I imagine the Roman emperor Marcus Aurelius awake and restless, also leaving his tent on the battlefield and going out to look at the night sky, more brilliant and beautiful in the darker, unpolluted world of two thousand years ago. I know he thought about the vastness of space and described Europe and Asia as distant recesses, minuscule and insignificant. He thought of time as a turbulent river. The present was a fleeting split second. Yet he also believed that the present was all we had—and all we needed: "If you've seen the present then you've seen everything— as it's been since the beginning, as it will be forever. The same substance, the same form. All of it."

Looking up at the stars. It is another good spiritual and mental exercise. But there are limits to how much vastness a human being can stand. Perhaps Marcus Aurelius thought next about his wife. Or the war. Or the governor of Syria. Then he went back inside his tent and took his dose of opium, desperate for a good night's sleep.

Above me, the same stars glitter and one begins to move. Most likely, it is an airplane, a group of people sitting obediently in their seats as they travel through the air in a large heavy object. Perhaps it is something even stranger than that. Aliens. Gods. An interstellar event.

Sometimes you just have to shake your head. You have to stop analyzing. How can the part know the sum? Sometimes you have to let the questions go. Let go of evil. Let go of fear. Let go even of self-improvement. Be kind. Be grateful. Stretch your legs under the warm blanket. For this moment, my family is safe, the night is peaceful, and I am staring up at the Milky Way, another arm of our spiraled galaxy. The present contains everything, all I have, all I need.

CHAPTER 4

The Gila River

IN SOUTHERN NEW MEXICO, some six thousand feet high in the Gila Wilderness among ponderosa pine and spruce, the west, middle, and east forks of the Gila River combine to flow south. They descend through drier and drier country, prickly pear and yucca and mesquite, until the water emerges from the mountains and canyons of the Gila National Forest. Here the riverbank is lined with cottonwood and willow, a linear oasis, emerald green in spring and summer, gold in fall, gray this early March. When I stand on a hill and look down, the water glistens silver, a kind of mythic serpent rising from the earth, following its desire in dreamy curves. Squint—and I can almost see the creature lift its head.

Just past the national forest line, a few miles above my house, the river is diverted into two irrigation ditches that run on each side of the Gila Valley. In dry months, most of the Gila River is in these ditches, which water the valley's large, sweeping fields of pasture. The West Ditch is the one I pass over as part of my driveway.

Our property of six acres adjoins the Nature Conservancy's Gila River Farm, some eighty acres of irrigated fields and river bottom. In 1999 the Nature Conservancy bought this farm with the goal of preserving its riparian area for endangered species like the southwestern willow flycatcher. They also wanted to experiment with a mix of agriculture and wildlife, and they use the West Ditch to irrigate hay, fill up ponds for ducks, and create new wetlands for the sandhill crane. To help pay for their wildlife refuge, the Conservancy sold some of the farmland to people like Peter and me, with plenty of regulations that we cannot subdivide or build too high or have horses or cows or use pesticides or shoot guns or play with fireworks. Our cats have to stay inside. Our behavior should be impeccable.

The Nature Conservancy land is open to the public, and Peter and I walk these eighty acres as though they were part of our private estate. (The Conservancy owns more property up and down the river, some one thousand acres in all.) Our nearest neighbor on the farm is the Lichty Ecological Research Center, a four-bedroom, two-bath adobe built by the previous owners. The center is now used for environmental meetings and to house visiting scientists. Peter and I are regular guests here, too, perhaps to watch a slide show on desert plants or eat dinner with a group of biologists. The science being done in the Gila Valley is important to us—another way to enter the land.

In some cases, we actively participate. We are in a bird-banding group which is part of a national program that looks at the breeding patterns of North American birds. We help pull up exotic weeds on the farm—Johnson grass and star thistle—so the native grasses can return. We report sightings of rare animals and fancy ourselves amateur naturalists. Mostly, however, we are cheerleaders, keeping track of the latest project and rustling a pom-pom. The science being done in the Gila Valley is so new as to be a first date. Hydrologists are just now studying this last major free-flowing river in New Mexico. Surveys of existing species are just now starting. This is a different intimacy from the traditional relationship of farming or mining or ranching, different from the Native American villagers who lived here thousands of years ago or the Apaches, Hispanics, and Anglos who came later. New questions are being asked—new courtesies, negotiations, and terms of endearment. Peter and I are voyeurs.

This morning, still cold in March, we go over to the Lichty Ecological Research Center to see Vicenc, a thirty-year-old Spanish hydrologist who has arrived recently on a two-year Fulbright to study the primary productivity of the Gila River. Primary producers are those green plants and algae that convert carbon dioxide, water, and sunlight into carbohydrates and oxygen. Vicenc is interested in scale, how primary productivity changes from the broad channel of the river to its tributaries, the increasingly smaller streams and creeks. He wants to know how these areas respond to flooding, which is a natural part of this system, and how they will be affected by global warming. To record the amount of oxygen in water at any given place, he has left a battery-operated device at nine monitoring sites up and down the valley. At each site, he also analyzes the water's chemical composition, looks at sediments, and catches insects.

Vicenc is from northern Spain or Catalonia—which he will quickly tell you is not Spain since many people in that region want to secede and form their own country. He often hikes five hours to one of his river sites and five hours back, carrying a hundred pounds of batteries and supplies. He seems to like doing this and suggests, mischievously, that we come with him. He asks us now to walk the half mile to the Conservancy's river bottom land so that we can show him exactly what happened last year—when the river flooded dramatically.

Floods are like fire. People tend to think of them as destructive. The river thinks of them as creative, drivers of productivity. Floods bring soil and seeds and organic matter. Log jams create new habitats: new oxbows, new sloughs, new bars, new ponds. Different plants, different animals. More oxygen, more carbohydrates. Change and flux. A flood on the Gila River is not common. But it is not rare either, especially in August after the summer rains or in early spring following a wet winter.

The latter is exactly what happened last winter, in 2005, when enough warm weather and rain melted the snowpack in the mountains and the serpent morphed into a mouth wide and foaming. As the river burst down through the canyons, it exploded the dams used to divert water into the irrigation ditches and spread out until it had covered the fields of the Nature Conservancy's Gila River Farm, until it nudged the bridge that bisects the valley, until it had changed its course, changed its desire, leaving behind new oxbows and sloughs, new bars and ponds, tumbling cottonwoods and sailing them south, scouring away the good and bad, creating and destroying, creating and destroying. I found myself murmuring, "War is father of all and king of all." Peter said something about Hindu gods, especially Kali, the multiarmed earth goddess, destroyer and creator, fanged and often accompanied by snakes. Ranchers and farmers looked glum, thinking of their fences and ditches. Our biologist friends Mike and Carol looked joyful and ran around marveling, "Look at that! Look at that!" They felt the echo of power. They saw its shape in what was left behind.

Vicenc wants Peter to tell him about the flood, the irrigation system in the Gila Valley, and the boundaries of the different properties along the river—particularly those owned by the Nature Conservancy. Peter knows all this, since for nine years he was the Nature Conservancy's field director in southwestern New Mexico, before he became the city planner for Silver City. We take the loop around the Nature Conservancy pond as my husband goes over some history.

In the 1880s, the Gila River was a large, deep, fast-flowing stream with heavily wooded banks as well as some marshy areas. After the start of large-scale farming and the floods of the 1940s, the U.S. Army Corps of Engineers built levees along the major flow and check dams in the tributaries. Unfortunately these levees channeled the force of the water during the more severe floods of the later twentieth century—the levees eventually washing away, along with much of the riparian, or streamside, habitat. Today some stretches of the river are broad, barren, and cobbled, with steep, cut banks still crumbling. Vegetation has a hard time reestablishing itself in these badly eroded areas. Other parts of the river, however, are recovering quickly now that the levees are gone and the river can flood naturally.

This history is not irrelevant. Just recently, a new legal settlement means that money for water projects in the Gila Valley is now available. Some important people want to use that money to divert water from the river and control flooding.

We reach the riparian forest of cottonwoods, ash, walnuts, willows, and sycamores. This is a healthy part of the Gila River. As always, I am struck by how messy it looks. Many of the trees are in the process of falling down, and the underbrush is more cluttered than pretty, filled with the litter of past floods—broken branches, upended logs, tangled roots—as well as new bushes, saplings, and flowering plants like four-o'clock and jimsonweed, space that has suddenly opened up and space that has slowly filled in. When I first saw this jumble, I felt jumbled, too. So many patterns and angles, so much asymmetry. I felt like tidying up, straightening a few of the horizontal cottonwoods, clearing out some of the debris. Now I am more relaxed or, at least, resigned. Disorder. Disarray. This is what water does moving through its favorite bosque.

Peter leads us along a rise with a well-established trail that ends abruptly in a cut bank. Six feet below, the Gila River curves against the base of this miniature cliff and then broadens out until it disappears around a bend to our right. My husband points in that direction, to a spot some three hundred yards away. Before the flood, this trail continued nicely and the course of the river was way over there. Vicenc asks questions. Peter answers. Soon they are deep in river-speak.

I notice new orange flagging in a stand of willow and a large contraption under a black walnut tree. So the graduate students are back. I admire their persistence.

The flood last winter also undid the work of these students, who had been visiting the Lichty Ecological Research Center and setting out pitfall traps to measure biodiversity (just count what insects and small creatures fall in) as well as plastic tubs to measure biomass in terms of leaf litter (just look inside and weigh what's there). One student was tapping water from juniper and cottonwood trees to check isotopes (different forms of an element that decays radioactively at different rates), which allowed her to determine what depth the water came from and helped her see if a juniper tree was taking deeper groundwater than a neighboring cottonwood. Another student was looking at tree roots by putting tubes into the soil and sending down a small video camera. Most of these experiments had been ripped away. The graduate students were philosophical, and the one studying tree roots seemed quite pleased, since the flood exposed massive systems twenty feet long, something she would never have seen in her tiny tubes.

Now the pitfall traps are in place again, and the plastic tubs, and the monitoring wells, all the clever instruments these scientists bring as part of their dialogue with the river. Most of them also bring a new humility, forced to go slow, at the river's pace, or sometimes fast, at the river's pace.

Other studies have just started. This March, a biology professor from Western New Mexico University in Silver City is doing an ambitious survey of the flora and fauna of the Gila watershed: plants, reptiles, and birds. Mammals are not in the grant yet. Next year, the professor says.

In that survey, beginning with reptiles, the herpetologists will eventually find North American spadefoots, Couch's spadefoots, plains spadefoots, Mexican spadefoots, Great Plains toads, Arizona toads, red-spotted toads, woodhouse toads, canyon tree frogs, mountain tree frogs, boreal chorus frogs, American bullfrogs, Chiricahua leopard frogs, mole salamanders, tiger salamanders, American box turtles, ornate box turtles, American mud turtles, spiny softshell turtles, collard lizards, eastern collard lizards, great earless lizards, common lesser earless lizards, Texas horned lizards, greater short-horned lizards, round-tailed horned lizards, Clark's spiny lizard, southwestern fence lizards, Yarrow's spiny lizards, desert spiny lizards, crevice spiny lizards, ornate tree lizards, common side-blotched lizards, banded geckos, western banded geckos, Chihuahuan spotted whiptails, Gila spotted whiptails, little striped whiptails, New Mexico whiptails, Sonoran spotted whiptails, tiger whiptails, desert grassland whiptails, great skinks, Great Plains skinks, western alligator lizards, Madrean alligator lizards, gila monsters, New Mexico threadsnakes, western threadsnakes, ring-necked snakes, Chihuahuan hook-nosed snakes, western hog-nosed snakes, nightsnakes, common kingsnakes, Sonoran mountain kingsnakes, milksnakes, coach whips, striped whipsnakes, gophersnakes, long-nosed snakes, eastern patch-nosed snakes, Smith's black-headed snakes, plains black-headed snakes, black-necked garter snakes, terrestrial garter snakes, Mexican garter snakes, checkered garter snakes, narrow-headed garter snakes, western lyresnakes, Sonoran coral snakes, western diamond-backed rattlesnakes, black-tailed rattlesnakes, western rattlensnakes, Mohave rattlesnakes, prairie rattlesnakes, and desert pygmy rattlensnakes.

You get the idea. The list for fish is much shorter but still unique among Southwestern rivers for having all the native species found here when the first Anglos arrived. The list for plants and birds would tax your patience.

Vicenc is gesturing in a way I perceive as very European. Peter is also moving his hands strangely, some visual graphic concerning the movement of groundwater. They seem about to flap their arms and fly away and then—suddenly—we are returning to the Lichty Ecological Research Center. Conversations with Vicenc can be this disjointed as he misses something we have said in English and we miss something he has said in his soft, sibilant Spanish accent. I get the impression that he has to meet up with another friend, perhaps another scientist, or maybe he thinks we do. Briskly we walk back, circling the pond.

I will never get to know Vicenc very well, never get past his courteous shyness and the technical explanations of his work. I never learn what he does with his data, either. He has shown me the charts and graphs, and I nod when he explains how global warming may change the chemistry of the Gila River so as to be harmful to certain sensitive species. I nod when he says that stretches of the river may dry up altogether, something that already happens in summer when most of the water is diverted into the irrigation ditches. I also know that Vicenc is comparing the Gila River to a river in Switzerland, although I am not sure why.

Mainly I am stuck on that original concept—all those primary producers, green plants and algae, converting sunlight, carbon dioxide, and water into carbohydrates and oxygen. Light hits the pigment chlorophyll, a complex molecule with many loosely attached electrons. Some electrons become separated, and light energy gets transferred to these electrons, which are now "excited" and which pass on their energy to other molecules. Eventually these molecules will be converted to new molecules. Eventually our own bodies will change them again into movement and thought, wars and oil paintings. We all depend on this act of grace. We all come from light. We are transformed by light. Most of us learned about photosynthesis in grade school. It is a subject we might have better studied in church.

Next weekend I am back here along the river bottom to meet with Mike and Carol and their three-year-old son, Dominic, who live down the road, some of our nearest neighbors. Mike is the Nature Conservancy's naturalist at the Bear Mountain Lodge in Silver City. Carol was also a naturalist at the lodge but now bicycles around the Gila Valley with her son sitting grandly behind her like a sultan and his rickshaw driver. Mike and Carol are a handsome couple in their mid-forties, and I like them enormously, not the least because they know so much about birds.

Every spring and summer, they run a bird-banding station at the Gila River Farm, part of a national program with over five hundred stations trying to assess what bird species are breeding where. I am part of this banding crew, which makes me feel absurdly important. For ten Sundays from May to August, we will set up ten nets and catch birds. We band the birds and write down their species, age, and sex. We blow on their chests to reveal their sexual parts and brood patch. We weigh them and measure their wings. Mike and Carol do most of the work, with Carol the go-to person for molt wear: which feathers are missing, which feathers are coming in. This coming May, we will also take two tail feathers that researchers elsewhere can check for isotopes, as well as swabs of fluid from the bird's genitals so researchers elsewhere can look for avian flu. I've been tagging along for two seasons now and am still only a net runner, anxiously untangling a Bewick's wren or waiting for Mike to get the blue grosbeak that has a vicious bite. When all the data are collected from thousands of birds in the Southwest and thousands more across North America, patterns will begin to emerge—what is surviving and what is not.

Every year we put the long banding table in the same place, under a large cottonwood tree beside the trail that now ends at the cut bank and glistening bend of the Gila River. We meet at this cottonwood today, trying to decide where to put the nets this spring. According to protocol, all ten nets should be in the same place each year. But after last winter's flood, half the original net sites are in the river. We need new sites, and we talk about that. Dominic distracts us by acting like a three-year-old. Much like Dominic, not quite on point, I am enthused about hosting a dinner party, getting all the banding crew together to kick off the season. We discuss the best date for my party, and for those ten Sundays in the summer. It is a little early for this kind of planning, but we feel anticipatory. These March days will get warmer, the trees will leaf out, the birds will sing, and we will be at the banding table again.

I am especially anticipatory. Bird-banding mornings are my own little nature study, as I try to identify the call of a fly-catcher, tramp from net to net on the changing river bottom, and note which trees have finally fallen down, the print of a mountain lion, and the new patch of four-o'clock with its magenta flowers opening clocklike in the late afternoon. Is the beaver back? Is that a sphinx moth—a hallucinatory blur in the air, then a focused image pink and white and black, banded and checkered like an Escher print? The moth poises before an evening primrose, its heavy body miraculously aloft. Look at that! Look at that!

I marvel at the sphinx moth. I marvel at the four-o'clock, *Mirabilis multiflora,* whose parts can be made into a tea to treat colic and eye infection. I marvel at this, too: all the plants around me connected to the human body. Yarrow clots blood. Mullein root increases the tone of the bladder. Cottonwood and willow reduce pain. My bladder is related to mullein root. My body reflects the chemistry of willow. I marvel at the complexity.

But is all this holy? Does it form a web of life we can consider sacred? Or are these things just very interesting?

I decide to ask Mike and Carol what they think. This is a little delicate. We have been friends for a few years, and now we are neighbors in the Gila Valley. We laugh and talk easily. We exchange books and tools. But there are gaps in what we know about each other. Our spiritual beliefs are one of these gaps.

Carol surprises me. Before she became a biologist, she says, she studied music and once spoke in tongues as a young adult in a Pentecostal church, loving God and the warmth of that community. Now she has the same emotions—love and awe and warmth—as strongly and as wonderfully in nature, in the divinity of the universe. Her image of God has shifted. Her experiences have not. She cites one example. On a recent walk, she found herself confronted with a great horned owl who stared at her eye level, predatory and somehow numinous. The feeling was so strong she had to look away. In humility, she had to look away.

Mike claims he is less emotional than his wife. It is just his nature, he says. He is impressed by the scientific ideas of deep time and evolution and by the fact that life came out of matter. He gestures at his son, Dominic, who is leaning against Carol's leg and begging to go home. "Isn't it amazing," Mike asks, "that love itself came out of matter?"

Mike is a big fan of the nature writer Henry David Thoreau and can quote long passages. Once, as we walked together along the bird-banding trail to Net Nine, Mike quoted this one:

What is it to be admitted to a museum, to see a myriad of particular things, compared with being shown some star's surface, some hard matter in its home! I stand in awe of my body, this matter to which I am bound has become so strange to me. I fear not spirits, ghosts, of which I am one, but I fear bodies. I tremble to meet them. What is this Titan that has possession of me? Talk of mysteries! Think of our life in nature—daily to be shown matter, to come in contact with it—rocks, trees, wind on our cheeks! the *solid* earth! The *actual* world! the *common sense!* Contact! Contact! Who are we? Where are we?

I look at Mike now, so clearly in love with the physical world. The *actual* world! The *solid* earth! Not emotional at all.

I look around me. Trees askew, sandy arroyo, rocks in the sand, plants growing. A stretch of river bottom in southwestern New Mexico. I can call this sacred, or I can not. Most religions have it right: God cannot seem to exist without us. We are made in his image, our Logos reflecting the larger Logos, our belief in the divine defining the divine.

I am involved in a word choice. Sacred means "holy" or "revered." In some dictionaries, the antonym is unholy or blasphemous. For my purpose, the antonym to sacred would be ordinary or meaningless. The middle ground between sacred and secular is fascinating. Very nice! Very entertaining. Primary producers. Blue grosbeaks. Coots. Good job, David Attenborough! Great factoids.

How do I want to describe the world? How do I want to feel about the world?

West of the Nature Conservancy pond is a small archaeological site, a few rooms once populated by the Salado people around 1300 CE. Up and down the Gila Valley are more ancient sites dating from the time of the early Roman Empire to the first Apache settlements in the sixteenth century, a flow of people migrating, hunting, farming, conquering, and being conquered. Mostly they stayed by the course of the river. Mostly their adobe and rock homes are now bulldozed lumps and troughs where pot hunters looked too hard for buried treasure—something old to sell for a good price. Potsherds still litter these sites, especially after a storm and rivulets of rainwater have uncovered new pieces of painted clay.

For much of my life, I have visited places like this, scouted for a sherd, and picked it up—a piece of cooking ware or the zigzag design of black on white. I have felt something flow down through my body from head to heart to arm to earth. The woman who made this pot links with me, some hundred thousand years ago, when we were hominids together in Africa. The woman who stands here today traveled through Europe and sailed to the New World as soon as she could build a boat, fished in New England, farmed in the Midwest, ranched in Colorado, and mined in Arizona. The woman who made this pot came by a different route. It is not really that we meet again but that we have never truly been separate.

Once, visiting the Salado site, I felt a larger and different kind of connection flowing down through a sherd of clay to soil where billions of bacteria live in one fertile ounce, where grama grass and four-o'clock convert sunlight into energy, where the grasshopper mouse waits in his burrow anxious to come out and hunt pinacate beetles, scorpions, and lizards, throwing back his head and howling his shrill, wolflike whistle song. I felt something flow down into the earth and then flow back up through a body with ten times as many cells as there are stars in the Milky Way. Ninety percent of these cells are microbial, not human. I call this superorganism myself, six hundred bacterial species in my mouth alone swimming the mountains and canyons of teeth. I flowed out through the skull, accelerating faster. Sweat from my forehead evaporated, rose, joined with other molecules, and became a cumulus cloud. I traveled east and south, following desire to tangle in the fur of a coatimundi, a long-tailed, long-snouted, white-masked relative of the raccoon. This particular bachelor male was being driven away from the matriarchal band where he had mated with the females. Now they were pregnant, and he had to leave, his tail straight up. He chittered and grumped. I left him, too, still flowing eastward, to Silver City, New York, around the globe, everywhere, everything.

How do we define the religious experience?

People speak of being outside themselves. They touch something bigger, something more than being Sharman, thinking about Sharman's problems, Sharman's insecurities, and Sharman's vanities. They break through the limits of their life, these particular talents and faults, this father, that mother, this race, that country, this gender, that body. The time they betrayed a friend. The ragged edge of a cuticle. Who would really want immortality as oneself? It seems so little and so depressing.

People speak of relationship. Perhaps they talk to Him, or Her, and they get an answer. Perhaps they spread out, connected to everything, part of everyone. They speak to the bacteria and grasshopper mouse. The important thing is that they are not alone.

People speak of feelings. Awe. Joy. Peace. Perhaps they are afraid. Perhaps they are uplifted. Hormones cascade, neurons fire. The chest hollows. The body gets involved.

Was my experience at the Salado archaeological site a religious one? Sometimes I think so. But not always.

I believe, without doubt, in an interconnected universe. Any faith I have in a *sacred* interconnected universe is hard-won. I have to cultivate belief. I have to get up early and bird-band. I have to visit ancient sites, wait for floods, be with other believers, form the neural pathways, keep a notebook—even at war, even fighting the barbarians—where I jot down reminders, reinforcing and rekindling. I have to be on the alert for the numinous experience. I have to welcome reverence. I have to search and struggle. I have to doubt.

Which is, I think, the way religion has always worked.

A herd of javelina live on the Gila River Farm. Also called peccaries, javelinas are the native piglike animals of the New World, about two feet high, weighing between forty and sixty pounds, with a large wedge-shaped head, compact body, short legs, and small cloven feet. Their coarse hair is peppered black and gray. Their upper tusks point down. Their lower tusks point up. Their muzzles, like any farm hog's, end in a disk of rounded cartilage—but javelinas are clearly wild, not domesticated. They exude wariness, alert to coyotes and bobcats and humans, vulnerable to accidents and respiratory infections. Social animals, they live in bands with a dominant male and dominant female and a mix of adults, adolescents, and young.

They eat whatever they can find, a prickly pear cactus or tomatoes from a garden, being mostly vegetarian but not turning down the occasional grub or snake. Although Peter and I do not see them often, their hoofprints are everywhere, in front of our house, up by the irrigation ditch, and all around the pond and river.

One evening as I walk over to a dinner with Vicenc at the Lichty Ecological Research Center, I smell that distinct odor—not quite skunk, but not pleasant either, the scent javelinas emit when they feel threatened. Now I spot them, a group of about eight half hidden in the bushes and grama grass. Javelinas have poor eyesight, but they can smell me, too, and they become agitated. They mill and clack their teeth. Some give out a huffing, woofing sound. Half decide to cross the dirt road. Three gallop over, crashing over the irrigation ditch into the fields. One more follows and turns to stare. Somehow I know he is an adolescent male. The black mane on his back is erect as he tries to make himself look larger and more intimidating. Although I cannot see it, the scent gland near his rump is open and leaking musk. He woofs. He huffs.

Then as javelina sometimes do, he panics and flees in the wrong direction, straight at me, all the while snorting in javelina language, "A human! A human! Run! Run away!" The raised hairs give him a punk look, and he is actually leaping, covering three feet in a single bound. We are on a collision course until I think to step aside. He swerves at the same moment. We miss each other by a wide margin. I know that javelina attacks can be dangerous and painful, and I have been nervous myself when faced with a mother and her young. But this guy is just too comical. He just makes me laugh.

A few days later, I am walking uphill on the road to the national forest line. I can see below the snake of the Gila River looping in dreamy silver curves. The gray and brown cottonwoods show a blush of green, the first budding of leaves. This winter has been so warm that Peter and I are worried that the trees are leafing out too soon and will snap in a spring freeze. We feel protective, wondering if nature is not making a mistake.

Too soon or not, the cottonwood trees are luminous in the sunlight, with that particular color of new growth. Where the asphalt road turns to dirt, a pickup truck rattles by and unexpectedly stops. Two young men want to know if I have seen any javelina. They are hunters, and the season closes today, March 31. In poorer South American countries, javelina are an important source of meat. Here in New Mexico, people hunt them mainly for entertainment, barring that token recipe for javelina stew and the urgent warning to remove the musk gland. I suppose this keeps the animals wary and controls their population. The hunters smile. I smile and say no. They rattle away. Of course, the Nature Conservancy does not allow hunting on the Gila River Farm. The piglike animals who live there are not dumb.

The very next morning, Peter motions me over to a window. A herd of javelina are moving around the house. Although javelina usually give birth in the summer, they are able to breed anytime, and we can see two lumps trotting under the heels of their mother. She will aggressively defend them from any perceived danger, including other herd members. A smaller adult follows her. This adolescent is probably the nanny, a sexually immature female who can also secrete milk and nurse the babies. As far as scientists know, the ability of this young female to nurse is unique among wild mammals, something only javelina do.

At the closest point to our house, the group quicken their trot. The sky is brightening, losing its yellow and orange glow, turning a more ordinary white and blue. The javelina nudge each other over the wooden bridge that spans the irrigation ditch. I have just seen the beginning of someone else's day, and I contemplate the choices ahead: where to eat, where to hide, where to stop and let the babies rest.

Looking out the window, I am pleased to see these animals, although they make me think twice about having a garden. At this moment, I do not have the wherewithal for a numinous experience. And it takes wherewithal. I know that. It takes humility and gratitude and awareness, what I might consider the best in me, not the normal me. It takes more effort than I have on my first cup of coffee.

Still, I feel good, inside the circle. I feel a little bigger than myself.

CHAPTER 5

A Renaissance Magician

I N   T H E   L A S T   H A L F of the sixteenth century, the Italian scholar Giordano Bruno developed a freewheeling pantheism that embraced, promoted, and weirdly mixed a dozen different themes, from nascent science to ancient mysticism, social justice to free love. He publicly admired the mathematician Copernicus and the new and seemingly bizarre theory that the earth revolved around the sun. Like other Renaissance scholars, Bruno had also discovered the ancient Greeks, men like Heraclitus, who taught him that life was flux and change, and Democritus and Epicurus, from whom he adopted atomism and the idea of an infinite universe with infinite other earths and suns—possibly, even, other intelligences like our own. Bruno wrote prodigiously: plays, poems, allegories, lectures. He championed freedom of speech and thought. He praised reason but also insisted on higher truths that could not be understood by the intellect alone.

One of these higher truths was the concept of the universe as a divine Unity, an immanent God who could assume both corporal and incorporeal form. Bruno believed in souls, in their transmigration from the body, and in their eternal life as part of the larger universal soul. He believed in magic and fancied himself a magus, or magician, a poet and wordsmith capable of evoking the hidden powers and sympathies in nature. His pantheism was animistic, with an astrobiological twist, for he declared that celestial bodies also had souls and were analogous to living beings. Above all, he admired the ancient Egyptian cults that had worshipped nature, for "animals and plants are living effects of Nature," he wrote, which is "nothing else but God in things."

It sounds like fun. Except that this *was* the last half of the sixteenth century, Bruno had taken the vows of a Dominican monk, and the Roman Catholic Church considered these ideas abhorrent, dangerous, and heretical. At the age of fifty-two, the writer and philosopher found himself tied to a stake as part of a public execution in Rome's Campo di Fiori, a plaza named after flowers. Giordano Bruno was not the only pantheist to die for his beliefs. But he was certainly the most voluble. Today his statue faces the Vatican in Rome in the same plaza where he was killed, and Web sites immortalize him as a martyr to science and symbol of defiance against intolerance. He would not be displeased.

Growing up in a small town near Naples, Italy, Bruno often looked out at a great, gloomy mountain in the distance. He would later write, "In my childhood, I thought that nothing existed beyond Vesuvius"—then and now, one of the most dangerous volcanoes in the world. His father was a soldier, his mother from the "lower gentry." At seventeen, he became a monk in the monastery of S. Domenico, later a priest and doctor of theology. His intellect and talents were soon noticed. In 1571, Pope Pius V brought him to Rome to study *ars memoriae,* the art of memorization, a subject in which Bruno excelled. At the same time, he was proving to be a rather troublesome friar, scornful of his superiors and critical of established beliefs. Returned to the monastery, at the age of twenty-eight he was discovered reading subversive books in the outhouse. Charged in 1576 with heresy and insubordination by the Neapolitan Inquisition, Bruno fled back to Rome to learn that the Roman Inquisition was also drawing up accusations against him. He fled this time to Switzerland, abandoned his monk's habit, and began a life of travel.

Hardly a safe haven, Europe was in the middle of thirty years of bloody warfare stemming from the rise of Protestantism, which challenged the dominance of the Catholic Church. In Geneva, the now-excommunicated monk hoped to find some refuge among the Calvinists, a Protestant sect that controlled the city. Instead, after Bruno disagreed with the authorities on a variety of religious matters, he was thrown into jail and forced to publicly apologize. In 1579, he moved on to a troubled France, where only seven years earlier French Catholics had hunted down and killed thousands of French Protestants (perhaps as many as a hundred thousand) in the course of a few months. Despite the social turmoil—and despite the offensiveness of Bruno's ideas to Catholics and Protestants alike—the scholar managed to make a life for himself in Paris by focusing on one of his first loves, the study and teaching of memorization.

Mnemonic devices had been used by orators from Roman times through the Middle Ages. Imagine a building, attach images to its parts that correspond to the parts of your speech, and then mentally walk through that building, "seeing" the images and information they signify. A good memory was highly prized in a world without books or with limited access to them. But Bruno was not interested simply in giving a good speech. He believed that increasing the powers of memory simultaneously increased the powers of the mind and enlarged the psyche. Moreover, when a student of the magical arts used certain archetypal images as part of his mnemonic system, then he could tap into the greater mind and psyche of the universe. Such potent and numinous images could open doors. They reflected the divine Oneness of all things.

Bruno's published works on memory were a complex system of graphic word pictures. Many of these involved the sun and moon. Some were original and startling—"a dark man, of immense stature, with burning eyes, angry face, and clothed in a white garment" and "Saturn: a man with a stag's head, on a dragon, with an owl which is eating a snake in his right hand"—while others referred back to Egyptian mythology, Greek mythology, the Zodiac, the Jewish kabbalah, and the legends of sorcerers like Merlin and Circe. These magical pictures were placed in various imaginary wheels divided into parts and corresponding to other wheels, which could be memorized and "imprinted on" by the obedient student. Give yourself up to such a system, Bruno wrote, and "you may gain possession of a figurative art which will assist, not only the memory, but all the powers of the soul in a wonderful way."

Possess such a system, and "you will arrive from the confused plurality of things to the underlying unity."

For Bruno, the relationship of memory, imagination, and godlike power—the relationship of the human mind to the larger universe—was linked to an occult tradition going back thousands of years. This tradition had been preserved in the Hermetic writings, a set of books thought to be the work of Hermes Trismegistus, a mythical and highly revered Egyptian sage believed to have lived right after Moses. The lost wisdom of this sage had been "rediscovered" in the fifteenth century. In Bruno's time, these texts were seen as a sacred entrance into a golden past—when men were better and purer and closer to the mysteries of life. (In fact, historians would later discover that the books were written by Greek authors from 100 to 300 CE.) In one of these treatises was the Egyptian Reflection of the Universe in the Mind, something that Bruno took to heart:

> Unless you make yourself equal to God, you cannot understand God; for the like is not intelligible save to the like. Make yourself grow to a greatness beyond measure, by a bound free yourself from the body; raise yourself above all time, become Eternity; then you will understand God. Believe that nothing is impossible for you, think yourself immortal and capable of understanding all, all arts, all sciences, the nature of every living being. Mount higher than the highest height; descend lower than the lowest depth. Draw into yourself all sensations of everything created, fire and water, dry and moist, imagining that you are everywhere, on earth, in the sea, in the sky, that you are not yet born,

in the maternal womb, adolescent, old, dead, beyond death. If you embrace in your thoughts all things at once, times, places, substances, qualities, quantities, you may understand God.

Combining his mnemonic system with the Hermetic experience of "reflecting the universe in the mind," Bruno became a kind of Renaissance magician activating images that would help him achieve a knowledge of the divine, as well as a semidivine personality. He was not alone in his efforts. Magic was still very much part of the Renaissance world—and not, necessarily, a bad or un-Christian part. A hundred years earlier, one theologian wrote, "There is no department of knowledge that gives us more certainty of Christ's divinity than magic and cabala." An important distinction was made between good magicians, who used natural magic, and bad magicians, who relied on demonic magic. A good magician aimed to discover the secret powers of nature, the hidden sympathies and resonances, which he could manipulate and control for good ends. Some good magicians were an early form of the scientist—with alchemy the precursor to chemistry and astrology to astronomy. A bad magician, of course, might try instead to call up a demon or use his power for evil, which was a serious concern.

In France, as Bruno's magical, marvelous system of memory became more popular, the French king himself took interest. Henry III had already studied the history of magic, and he became one of Bruno's patrons. In 1583, the political and religious violence in Paris increased, and Bruno left for England with letters of recommendation from Henry III to the French ambassador. (The king himself would be assassinated six years later by

Catholics angry at his attempt to work for peace with the Protestants.) In London, as a guest of the French ambassador, Bruno composed some of his most important works or dialogues—a mix of allegorical story and playwriting.

One of these works was dedicated, mischievously, to the doctors of the University of Oxford. Bruno had tried lecturing at Oxford, where faculty were fined five shillings for each disagreement with the "laws" of Aristotle. By now, the writings of Aristotle had been reinterpreted by the church to fit the Christian worldview. They were enshrined as uncontestable dogma, including the belief that the sun revolved around the earth. Bruno immediately disagreed with these laws, particularly the Aristotelian idea that the universe was closed rather than infinite and that the earth was the center of this closed universe. Instead, Bruno lectured on the newest ideas in astronomy and his own scheme of a divine universe that had no boundary and that contained an infinite number of earthlike worlds revolving around sunlike stars.

The Oxford faculty received this lecture, in Bruno's words, with "a constellation of the most pedantic, obstinate ignorance and presumption, mixed with a kind of rustic incivility which would try the patience of Job."

Equally, one observer wrote how Bruno, the visiting scholar, "undertooke among very many other matters to set on foote the opinion of Copernicus, that the earth did goe round, and the heavens stand still; wheras in truth it was his owne head which rather did run round, & his braines did not stand stil."

It was a fair description. Bruno's brains did not stand still as he continued to write and publish feverishly, to charm the

French ambassador, to chat up Queen Elizabeth whenever possible, and to outrage almost everyone else. He had various love affairs, admitting once that he bedded as many women as possible, with no "desire to become a eunuch." He was not above plagiarizing the work of other scholars and claiming it as his own. Nor was he humble. He admired Copernicus but also dismissed him as a mere mathematician, describing the astronomer's work as "the dawn that must precede the rising of the sun," the sun being Bruno's own philosophy.

That philosophy was a mystical, animist pantheism that could be called syncretic, eclectic, half-stolen, or half-digested. It is not so much that you love or hate the man, so much as you don't know what to think. Mounting to the highest height and descending to the lowest depth, Bruno tried his best to understand God by making himself equal to him, embracing in his thoughts all things at once, growing to a greatness beyond measure, drawing into himself all arts, all sciences, and the nature of every living being, on earth, in the sea, in the sky, fire and water, dry and moist, young and old, living and dead. He tried his best to believe that nothing was impossible.

In 1585, the French ambassador left England and returned to France. Bruno went, too. He stayed in Paris for less than a year, trying but failing to have his excommunication from the Catholic Church annulled. He had time to fall in love with a new version of the compass, and he published four dialogues that attempted to appropriate the device as his own by labeling its inventor a "triumphant idiot" who could not—unlike Giordano Bruno—grasp the significance of this important work. In another graceless incident, he gave a public lecture describing his concept of an infinite universe with multiple worlds. At the end, he shouted triumphantly for someone to defend Aristotle. When someone did, Bruno tried to leave, was attacked by the students, and escaped only on the promise he would return the next day to continue the debate. Prudently, he left town instead.

He went on to Germany, tangled with the Calvinists again, and escaped to Prague, where he did not find employment. Excommunicated by the Protestants, too, he continued to write but could not find a way to make a living. Next, in 1590, he traveled to Frankfurt, then Zurich, and back to Frankfurt.

His mnemonics retained their striking images, "a crowned man of an august presence most gentle of aspect, riding on a camel, dressed in a garment the colour of all flowers, leading with his right hand a naked girl," or yet another "naked girl rising from the foam of the sea, who on reaching dry land wipes off the humour with her palm." As one scholar has noted, for this artist, "The fable, the poetic image, and metaphor are no longer vain ornaments but become vehicles of thought." As Bruno himself wrote, "To think is to speculate with images."

In the fall of 1591, Bruno moved to Venice, responding to the invitation of a wealthy gentleman who wished to be taught the secrets of memory. In hindsight, we have to wonder why the scholar returned to Italy, where he knew he would be exposed to the Inquisition. Probably he was penniless, and certainly he was arrogant, with the inflated belief that his charm and intellectual gifts made him invulnerable. He was also naive and fostered the hope of reconciliation, that someday he would convince the church to see him as an important philosopher and thinker—not a threat. He may have had a sense of mission, for the politics of Europe had shifted and Bruno anticipated new reform within the Catholic hierarchy. More simply, he may have been homesick. His father may still have been alive. He may have missed the language, the music, the food. Once in Venice, at least, he did not go immediately to his patron's house but lived independently until March 1592.

On his part, the wealthy gentleman, named Mocenigo—the villain in this plot—may have always been a spy for the Venetian Inquisition or, as likely, became alienated from his teacher as the months passed. By May, relations between the two had clearly soured. When Bruno planned a return to Germany to supervise the printing of his latest work, Mocenigo opposed the journey. On the night before Bruno's departure, the patron locked his tutor in a room and summoned the authorities. That night Bruno was taken to the prison of the Holy Office.

Bruno's trial by the Venetian Inquisition lasted over two months. Mocenigo was a star witness. He accused Bruno of describing the Catholic faith as blasphemous and "against the majesty of God" by confining God to the Father, Son, and Holy Ghost. He testified that Bruno held many erroneous views on the Trinity, on the divinity of Christ, and on the Holy Mass. Bruno did not believe that sins were punished in hell and even denied the virginity of Mary. He practiced magical arts and called Christ a magician. He said that the universe was infinite with infinite worlds. He said that all monks were "asses" and the church "asinine."

Mocenigo further stated that Bruno had frequently complained that the original Christians converted through gentleness and good works, but now the church resorted to violence and force. Bruno had asserted a new golden rule: "To not do unto others that which we would not have done unto us." Bruno had argued that the current state of ignorance, corruption, and hatred could not continue but that a new society had to emerge, one that practiced tolerance and encouraged freedom.

For the most part, all these accusations were perfectly true. They repeated what Giordano Bruno had written in his books and presumably spoken out loud to Mocenigo. On trial for his life, the scholar now denied almost every charge and either apologized for or recanted what he could not deny.

He justified his ideas about an infinite universe by explaining that he had been speaking philosophically and that such philosophical thoughts had no relation to the tenets of faith. They were the idle products of reason, not "substantial truth." He tried to realign some of his theories with Christian dogma. His soul of the universe, for example, was really another name for the Holy Ghost. In other instances, he explained, he had been repeating the ideas of heretics like Democritus and Lucretius and Epicurus. They were not *his* ideas. Bruno did admit doubt concerning the nature of the Trinity, but these were internal dilemmas, not public denials of church doctrine. He also admitted that at times he had been in error: He should never have condoned the sin of fornication. He admitted that in sixteen years he had been to a confessor only twice but that he intended someday to live as a good Christian. He admitted he was curious about the magical arts, but nothing more. In fact, he held books on necromancy "in contempt."

Bruno also reversed his most basic belief in pantheism and an immanent God, declaring, "I have believed and maintained without doubt all that which every faithful Christian must believe and maintain concerning the first person [the Father]."

Strategically, at a few crucial points, he simply sputtered and contradicted his accuser. Of course, Mary was a virgin! Of course, the bread and wine of Mass became the body and blood of Christ! Of course, sinners were damned!

At the end of the trial, the former monk humbled himself completely, kneeling before the judges as he begged for mercy: "All the heresies that I have entertained, and the doubts that I have had regarding the Catholic faith and matters determined by the Holy Church, I now detest and abhor; and I am repentant for having done, held, declared, believed, or having meditated upon any matter that was not Catholic."

Who can blame him? I would have been on my knees from the start, simpering, "Don't mangle my fingers. Don't use the rack. Don't burn me alive." I admire Bruno's gamesmanship, the weeks of talking and cajoling, twisting and turning, which required all his charm and intellectual gifts. As he pleaded for his life, he probably thought it would be spared and perhaps even that he would be set free. He had some cause for hope. The Venetian Inquisition was relatively mild and in the sixteenth century had sentenced to death only 5 heretics in 1,565 trials.

At this point, unfortunately, Rome stepped in. Bruno had made too many enemies and been too generous with his opinions. The pope himself demanded the writer's extradition. Although Venetian authorities did not usually comply with such requests, this time—under political pressure—they did. In February 1593, the forty-five-year-old Bruno was transferred to the Castel Sant'Angelo, the prison of the Roman Inquisition.

Eight years passed. Even in jail, Bruno had a hard time keeping quiet, and fellow inmates began to accuse him of making new heretical statements. In further interrogations, the Roman Inquisition went over these offenses, as well as those from the Venetian trial. The fourteenth deposition returned to Bruno's ideas of an infinite universe with many worlds, and the fifteenth to his interest in magical arts. The philosopher continued to deny everything except for the odd minor transgression. In 1594, he wrote an eighty-page response. There were more charges, more interrogations, more long replies. The Roman Inquisition probably felt that its case was weak, since the defendant denied his heresy and the new witnesses against him were prisoners. Legally, this opened the door to torture, used when evidence was inconclusive and extreme measures needed to discover the truth.

In January 1599, officials presented Bruno with a shortened list of eight charges, and he finally submitted. He would agree that these views were heretical and recant them. In return, he would not be executed. In February, at another interrogation, Bruno remained submissive. In April, he produced a written statement of his retraction. In August, that statement was considered satisfactory except for two points, one involving the Trinity and one the analogy of body and soul as being like a ship and pilot.

In September, the Inquisition reversed its position and decided that the legal case against Bruno was still weak. The Pope ordered a further retraction by Bruno and a reexamination of all previous interrogations.

The next day, Bruno said again he would do whatever the church wanted him to do. He also had prepared another written statement.

In that statement, Bruno recanted his recant. Perhaps he realized he was never really going to be forgiven or forgotten. Perhaps his renewed insistence that he had done nothing wrong— that he had nothing to repent—was a response to torture or perhaps a way to avoid torture. In any case, the philosopher refused any more acts of submission. He had a forty-day period in which to change his mind. He remained firm.

On February 17, 1600, Giordano Bruno was marched from prison to the Campo di Fiori, where he would be burned alive. He was stripped naked. In one report, his tongue was tied in order to stop him from speaking. According to a more detailed account, tying the tongue meant thrusting a metal spike horizontally through the cheeks and another spike vertically through the lips, forming a bloody cross that effectively blocked speech. Once the fire started, Bruno was not offered the mercy of strangulation. He is best remembered today for this moment.

Certainly the astronomer Galileo, who also subscribed to the theories of Democritus and Copernicus, remembered it thirty-three years later when he took his place before the Inquisition and denied his beliefs.

Ah, evil, Marcus Aurelius would have sighed. The same old thing. The same old thing, from one end of the world to the other. Nothing new at all.

Peter and I always seem to be working. I teach writing skills full time as a professor at Western New Mexico University and part time at a low-residency master-of-fine-arts program at Antioch University in Los Angeles. I am also an elected member of the local school board and direct a school-based food pantry program for children who go hungry on the weekends. Peter's job as the city planner for Silver City is from eight to five with evening meetings. We like what we do but we may do too much of it. The Gila house is a refuge where I also grade papers and take books to read as part of my latest writing project. I am not at all unhappy about this, nor do I feel too busy. Occasionally, though, I notice a clock ticking inside me, a speeded up metabolism related solely to work and getting things done. Next. Will the next in line please step up? I have a business—a life—to run. It's ticking along very well, very efficiently, very fast. NEXT.

We schedule in hikes. One spring afternoon we go with our neighbors in the Gila Valley, April and Merritt, to the east side of the Apache Box. This involves an hour's drive through an exceptionally beautiful grassy valley, up a seemingly endless dirt road, past Brushy Mountain, and finally a two-hour bushwhack through national forest land to stand on a precipice overlooking a deep canyon. The view intrigues. The canyon plunges five hundred feet and then sidewinds. We cannot see the bottom, only the jut of overlapping cliffs like an optical illusion. For Peter, it is a challenge. A reasonable curiosity. What's down there?

We agree to come back in two weeks and walk through the Apache Box from the west side. That approach means driving a much longer way into Arizona and then through the Iron Knot

Ranch, now a Tibetan Buddhist Retreat Center. The center was established under the guidance of H. E. Chagdud Tulka Rinpoche and is founded on the belief that the true nature of all things is compassionate and wise and that we are prevented from realizing our true nature by a superficial but pervasive ignorance. The resident lama from the center sometimes speaks in Silver City on this subject, and although Peter and I have talked about going to these lectures, we never find the time.

For us, this two-day trip is a rare vacation, a car camp. April and Merritt invite other friends from the Gila Valley, Gail and Emanuel. Nothing is more pleasing to me than to be with Gail again, who was my midwife twenty-two years ago when I gave birth to my daughter, Maria, and who was my midwife nineteen years ago when I gave birth to my son, David. He was a big baby, almost ten pounds, and the labor intense. I remember crying out Gail's name in outrage, as though this large head crowning was somehow her fault. Since then, we have met at cervical exams at her office and potlucks at the Lichty Ecological Research Center, where we talk easily about children and politics. April and Merritt and Gail and Emanuel are close friends, and Peter and I the outsiders, new to the Gila Valley. I am aware of this, but it doesn't make me anxious. Gail is a funny person, and we are funny together, and at some point in this trip, we are both laughing hard and I touch her arm and say, "I've missed you." And she says, "I've missed you, too."

On Saturday morning, driving to our campsite near the Apache Box, we pass faded prayer flags flapping from the scrub oaks by the dirt road. Here and there, large mounds of rock are topped by sticks of newer flags striped blue, white, red, green, and yellow. These fillips of humanity are not intrusive or jarring but seem to soften the backdrop of rocky mountains dry as bone and just a bit hostile, the bones of Arizona, my home state. Soon we see a half dozen buildings and small trailers scattering the desert with its own scatter of mesquite and stunted juniper trees. April and Merritt have been to the Tibetan Buddhist Retreat Center before, and we decide to stop and visit. Immediately, we are greeted by a young man happy to show us around.

We go up a small hill to see the new prayer wheels. Now we are stunned and try not to show it. Tibetan prayer wheels are devices for spreading a spiritual blessing. Traditionally, rolls of thin paper are imprinted with copies of mantra, or prayer, wound around an axle in some kind of container, and spun round and round. Tibetan Buddhists believe that turning a prayer wheel and spinning these words will disseminate that prayer and make the world a better place. Such mantras invoke the attention of compassionate, enlightened beings. They invoke our own nature of compassion. At the retreat center at Iron Knot Ranch, inside a large, warehouselike room, men are now installing seventeen twelve-foot-high white cylinders like monstrous water heaters, which contain the words *Om mani padme hum* in Tibetan script. The papers have been printed and shipped from Minnesota. The cylinders, weighing many tons, were hauled up by truck. One of these prayer wheels will be turned by hand, using a large wooden device in the center of the room. The other sixteen will turn mechanically, solar-powered, day and night.

The building that holds these seventeen prayer wheels has the air of an industrial shop as three men struggle to move one of the cylinders onto its base. I have seen this scene many times. Men struggling to move something heavy in such a way that nothing breaks and no one gets hurt. The men discuss leverage and physics. They are proud, intent, a little nervous. Gail, April, Peter, and I look at each other and look away. There is something about the scale and technology that seems inappropriate. But what do we know? This is Tibetan Buddhism in the twenty-first century.

Merritt and Emanuel take a few more pictures with their digital cameras, and then we walk over to the temple, an open-air ramada with a central altar rising to the ceiling. From every side, the altar glows with color. Red, green, yellow, blue. A smiling bodhisattva, a mocking demon, spirit faces, curlicues, flowers, lions, monkeys. Walk around the altar and say your prayers. Focus on the images.

The retreat's Web site later explains, "One of the traditional methods for removing hindrances to the recognition of our true nature is the creation of representations of enlightened body, speech, and mind." The temple, with its demons and bodhisattvas, is a representation. The prayer flags fluttering from the scrub oak trees are a representation. The huge cylindrical prayer wheels will be painted with more representations. The prayer wheels themselves are representations—the more, the heavier, the faster, the better. These representations radiate healing in every direction. "No matter who adds oil to the lamp," the Web site assures me, "everyone benefits from the light."

Giordano Bruno would have felt right at home. The Tibetan Buddhist Retreat Center is full of hidden sympathies, secrets to our true nature that a good magician can use for the good. Here the metaphor of turning the wheel of dharma is made real. Stories have power. Images actualize the divine. There are things we cannot understand by reason alone. Like most older religions, Tibetan Buddhism has a magical worldview, one it shares with the medieval alchemist and American shaman, with the woman studying Tantra and the neo-pagan resurrecting druidism. Pantheism is also at home here, perhaps mixed with a belief in animism (nonhuman things and phenomena can be imbued with a humanlike intelligence or spirit) and polytheism (the divine nature of the universe manifests in many forms, including gods and goddesses).

Before we leave, a young woman comes up to me with a gift. She has a vial of water infused with the spiritual power of her master. I do not really understand. Perhaps the fluid contains saliva from her master or perhaps it is a liquid he has blessed. She offers me a taste. Water to my lips. Something good, she promises, will come of this. Of course, I say, although Peter declines.

For a while, after we drive to our campsite and sit outside eating our lunch, April, Gail, Emanuel, Peter, Merritt, and I cannot stop talking. We reminisce about our own experiences with Eastern religions, the sixties and seventies, all that wonderful information pouring in, the books and lectures and visiting gurus. I remember the devotees in orange robes dancing through the streets of Berkeley. I remember the Golden Temple Restaurant, where I often ate lunch, the vegetarian rice and *masala dosas*. Peter remembers meditating in Thailand. His Buddhist nun looked so serene. Eventually, the conversation devolves. Emanuel says to me, "I would never have put that stuff to my lips!" He is remembering those parties where young men handed out LSD. I scoff but do an internal check. "No," I say. "It was a gift, a blessing."

Then we put away our food and begin walking.

It is the end of April and hot. These are the gravelly desert slopes I know so well from spending most of my life in the Southwest. I have trudged up slopes like these countless times. One slip and a prickly pear jams into your knee. Watch for rattlesnakes. Feel the sun on your neck, the pull in your calf muscle. And say, "Sorry about that," to the person below if you unwittingly start a rock slide.

Paradoxically, we must climb to reach the bottom of the canyon. Our goal is a dark notch in the cliff above, a dry waterfall where seasonal rains come tumbling down and a few trees have rooted to catch the flow. More people drown in the desert than die of thirst. The large boulders here are evidence of that, proof of a rushing stream mostly absent and then suddenly not. As the boulders get bigger, the way around them becomes problematic. In places, Merritt or Peter or Emmanuel goes ahead and helps the rest of us with an outstretched hand. We wonder if we can do this. In fact, this might not be a climbing route for humans. Mountain lions, yes. Teenagers, perhaps. Merritt, after all, will be seventy this summer. April had knee surgery last month. It would be easy now to sprain an ankle or worse, and that would certainly ruin the weekend. We are all thinking this, although no one says anything.

At some point, we separate. April, Merritt, and Gail traverse to a ridge that looks into the canyon. Perhaps they will see another way in. Peter, Emanuel, and I continue bouldering—just around the corner, just a few minutes more in this suddenly cooler, shadowed air—until the ground begins to level off and walls of stone rise steeply above us. In this narrow space, the large fallen rocks are pink and orange, melded together in a precarious pattern. We marvel. We take pictures. We can't stop pushing forward even though we know, once again, that we are being a little stupid. I do the math. Together the six of us combine some two hundred years of adult hiking experience. How many times have we thought the same thing? Don't separate from your friends. Go back now. Don't jump down. You'll sprain your ankle.

Soon the entrance widens and we are walking on the canyon bottom. The sun is explosive, a waterfall of light. We continue to marvel as we find a path that winds through a meadow with tall yellow grass, late spring flowers of thistle and daisy, green ash trees and more juniper. The walls of stone rise higher, a thousand feet on either side of a canyon bottom less than three hundred feet across. We have been led here by the gods through a hidden passageway to a hidden world. We crawled, we faced danger, and we emerged into beauty: sunlight, grass, and trees.

The path brushes an abandoned mine and becomes a rutted road, and the road starts to climb, and we can see that it goes to the very ridge where our friends are waiting. We could have driven to this spot in the right vehicle. Not so hidden, then. But still magical. Peter, Emanuel, and I follow the road, find April, Merritt, and Gail, and the six of us return to the meadow, where we keep pointing out new features, a beautifully shaped oak or covey of quail. We feel proprietary, even prideful. Later we hike back to camp, eat dinner, and sleep under the stars.

The next day, driving home, Peter wants to take a dirt road that he feels sure will lead us back to Silver City, a different way back, which is a goal in itself to a certain kind of person. We drive for hours on the forgotten mining roads of eastern Arizona until we are thoroughly lost—until we see two golden eagles fly parallel to the car, twenty feet from the window, closer than I have ever seen an eagle in the wild. Everyone in our vehicle is astonished and gladdened.

But no one believes this is a sign. No one on this trip really believes in gods or magic. From the west side, the Apache Box was everything we had hoped for, a lovely place and a story, too. We are grateful for both. Eventually we reach a highway and find our way home.

As a scientific pantheist, I feel the need to analyze. How is science different from a magical worldview?

To explain a phenomenon, scientists propose a hypothesis, test that hypothesis, try to disprove it, record their data, and integrate this information into a larger understanding of how things work. They construct models that describe nature. These models are based on past observations and can be used to predict future observations. The best models are ones that lead to the most testable predictions. In these efforts, scientists try to be objective. They invite scrutiny.

Magic is harder to pin down. Magic can be defined as "any art that invokes supernatural powers." But in her book on neo-paganism, *Drawing Down the Moon*, NPR correspondent and Wiccan priestess Margot Adler also describes magic as "the mobilization of confidence, will, and emotion" combined with "the use of imaginative faculties." She tells a story about a group of modern-day witches in Colorado, members of a polytheistic nature religion. One day, the leader of the group asked for volunteers to gather fish from a drying riverbed. The fish would soon die and could be used instead as fertilizer for the garden. The fish are slippery and elusive, and the volunteers feel they have been given an impossible task. Then the leader reminds them that "magic is simply the art of getting results." He tells them to visualize themselves as bears slapping their paws together in the water. Perhaps he tells them that they *are* bears. They are hungry bears. Perhaps the bear-god is involved. Within an hour, the group have filled their buckets to the top. This magic did not require the supernatural but an understanding of human psychology and the natural environment.

Magic is also the construction of models that describe nature (which may include the supernatural). These models are also based on past observations and can be used to predict future observations. But the models of magic are not necessarily logical or objective. They align more with need and desire, imagery and poetry. They align with rapture and living communion. They are not meant to be tested or disproved. They get results only when embraced.

Recently, the philosopher David Abram expressed a uniquely modern view of magic when he described it as having an ecological function. Magic is a way for the shaman or magician to keep a balanced relationship between the human and nonhuman world. Magic is a heightened sense of connection. Magic is our awareness that we came from the earth, were shaped by the earth, and exist in constant dialogue with the earth. In *The Spell of the Sensuous,* Abram wrote that magic is the experience "of existing in a world made up of multiple intelligences, the intuition that every form one perceives—from the swallow swooping overhead to the fly on a blade of grass and indeed the blade of grass itself—is an *experiencing* form, an entity with its own predilections and sensations, albeit sensations that are very different from our own."

Where I live in the Gila Valley, a number of people cultivate a magical worldview. They have a harvest ritual, dances to the goddess, a Day of the Dead party. They drum at night across the river from my house, a tribal thumping. They are a mix of old hippies and new, and they easily mix their magic with science. Some are versed in Jungian psychology and may refer to a particular god as an archetype. They believe in the power of story and myth. They also believe in evolution, computers, and car repair. They may believe that science has not yet discovered their version of the world. (And that could be, one scientifically minded friend says. Bring it on! he says—meaning the material proof of fairies or tree spirits.) Or they may believe that science can never pierce the veils of their world. They might also be pragmatists who simply find the magical worldview more useful—more productive and more fun.

I suspect that many of them are dualist pantheists who see the universe as a divine Oneness made up of two substances, spirit and matter. They are Western animists and polytheists breaking with the last two thousand years of theist tradition to join with hundreds of millions of Hindus and Buddhists, tribal people in Africa, indigenous people around the world. They are syncretic and artistic, making it up as they go along.

Sometimes I think they do a bad job. They engage in all the fallacies I warn my writing students against. *Secundum quid,* or hasty generalization: a conclusion based on insufficient evidence. *Post hoc, ergo propter hoc,* or false cause: the belief that because one event happens after another, the first was the cause of the second. *Petitio principii,* or begging the question: a form of circular reasoning that assumes the truth of the argument in the premise rather than the conclusion. *Ad numeram,* or bandwagon: an argument that relies on going along with what other people believe. *Ad verecundiam,* or false authority: the use of an unqualified authority to support a claim. *Cum hoc, ergo propter hoc:* the belief that because two things happen simultaneously, they are causally related. *Ad antiquitam:* the belief that something old must be right because it is old. *Ad hominem:* a personal attack on someone because he disagrees with you.

These people don't write good compositions. They aren't logical. They aren't scientific. They refuse to look at the facts. They believe in tree spirits. I roll my eyes at them. They roll their eyes at me.

At some point, I should confess: Magic plays a huge role in my life as a writer. I would give up much before I would give up magic or magical thinking, which takes up hours and hours of my time, days and months and years, and gives me such enormous pleasure. This admission requires some backtracking. I am eight years old and writing feverishly for my adored fourth-grade teacher. My first story is about a pencil who goes to a dance. The books I read are almost all fantasies: children opening the door to a secret world, magicians discovering their true nature, animals with souls, plants with souls, planets with souls.

Margot Adler also connects her interest in magic to what she read as a child and further says that most neo-pagans are avid readers, part of an elite group, about 20 percent of people in America. Over and over again, she finds that a neo-pagan became a neo-pagan by picking up a book. Although I continue to read children's literature and some adult fantasy, more important, I write these stories, too. I live in them. All my fiction has a magical worldview. To date, these stories include five children's books and two adult novels, the majority of which are unpublished. I am always talking to animals, and they are always talking back. I dive into the earth and sink through bones. I sit in a circle with the spinning head of a bear. Much like Giordano Bruno, I use these images to reach for something beyond reason. I try to reflect the universe in my mind.

I am not so different from one of my New Age friends who says she likes to play with the idea that her dead sister talks to her or that her totem animal, the coyote, sends her dreams at night. I simply compartmentalize more. I call my magic metaphor. Then I put it in a box and shut the lid.

After my climb up and into Apache Box, I have decided to become less judgmental. Who am I to scoff at mechanical prayer wheels? To say where dreams come from or deny the power of Coyote?

And what do I really want, after all? I want rapture and living communion. I want to play like a child. Above all, like everyone else, I want to find my compassionate heart.

CHAPTER 6

Baruch Spinoza

I N MAY, WE START bird banding. Mike goes out at 5 a.m.
to the cottonwood bosque, or riparian forest, on the Gila
River Farm and sets up ten nets. Each net is strung between two
poles, thirty-six feet long and nine feet tall, the bottom of the
net high enough so a bird won't dangle and rest on the ground.
Some nets are in shady underbrush, others in dappled light near
the riverbank. Since the winter flood of 2005, we have moved
Nets Five to Nine to new sites across the new river channel. In
addition, Carol thinks the location of last year's Net Ten was
too sunny—too hot for the birds. Now we put Net Ten in a
mosquito-filled swampy area that will become our least favorite
place to go.

The birds fly into the mesh, entangling their wings, head, and
feet. They stay trapped until a net runner comes to disentangle
them and slip them into a cloth bag. If the bird has an obvious
brood patch, the net runner will put a red clothespin on the bag,

indicating that this is a parent taking care of its young and should get priority over other birds. If there are more birds than bird banders, the cloth bags are hung on a clothesline near the banding table, where they wiggle and shake impatiently. Each bird in turn will be taken out of the bag in the "bander's grip," its back cupped in the palm of the hand and its head held firmly between second and third finger. Using something like pliers, the bander puts a band around the bird's leg and notes its species, age, sex, weight, wing length, appearance of breeding patch or cloacal protuberance (where sperm is stored), molting pattern on the wings, and unusual details such as injury or disease. Two tail feathers are pulled out for the isotope study. Swabs are taken for the avian flu study. Ideally, this should all take less than fifty minutes from the time of entanglement to release, so as not to unduly stress the bird. Nets are checked every twenty minutes.

Peter, Sarah, and I do net runs and help record data. Eleanor is our official recorder and puts it all in the big book. Carol, Mike, and Patricia bird-band and do everything else, whatever is needed. Nena takes care of Dominic, Carol and Mike's three-year-old son. We start at 6 a.m. and go on to noon. Protocol dictates that we stop whenever the temperature rises above 85 degrees in the shade, which may happen later in the day. We will do this for ten nonconsecutive days during the nesting and breeding season, until mid-August. So will over 499 other stations across the United States in the MAPS, or Monitoring Avian Productivity and Survivorship program, with southern stations starting earlier and banding for ten days and northern, colder stations starting later and banding for as few as six.

MAPS was organized in 1989 when scientists noticed a significant decline in populations of North American bird species, both resident and migratory. We were not only losing birds; the decline was accelerating. Nearly twenty years later, we can use information from MAPS to help pinpoint which species, where, when, and why. One study showed, for example, that tree nesters like eastern wood pewees and Acadian flycatchers are having less breeding success than cavity nesters like downy woodpeckers and black-capped chickadees—probably because of higher parasitism by the brown-headed cowbird. Cowbirds originally followed buffalo on the Great Plains, and now they follow cows, which are everywhere. In a typical scene—caught on videotape—a cowbird pushed off the eggs in a Bell's vireo's nest and within forty seconds laid her own while the parents screamed and fluttered and pecked at the intruder. Finally, the cowbird left. The vireos presumably felt victorious and set about the business of raising young cowbirds. Based on what we now know about eastern wood pewees and Acadian flycatchers, we can try to help their declining populations by providing them with a less fragmented habitat (cowbirds are an "edge species" and tend to like fragmentation) or by killing the cowbirds. We can also predict how future changes, such as global warming, will affect these and other birds.

This season, Carol and Mike do not expect to see much breeding activity in the Gila Valley. Last year we banded some three hundred birds. But this winter and spring were dry, and as a long-term drought continues, there are not enough seeds and insects to feed babies. In drought, birds often delay breeding or do not breed at all. Or they breed and their hatchlings starve to death.

May 7 is a practice training in the field. The long bird-banding table is set up on the flattened sand of a wash that runs into the nearby Gila River. A cottonwood tree shades the table, with more cottonwoods, sycamores, ash, walnut, and willows close by, forming this streamside forest. About a hundred miles from the Mexican border, we are also at the tail end of the Rocky Mountains, with temperatures that can freeze at night until mid-May and still heat up for a warm afternoon. In the early morning, we shiver in sweaters and pants. Later we will be throwing off our clothes.

Mike has already put out the nets. We catch a few birds, a red-capped Lucy's warbler and yellow-breasted Wilson's warbler. We process them to get back in the habit, perfect our technique, and learn again how to work as a team. It is important to bird-band right. We don't want to injure any birds. We don't want the data we collect to be wrong, and we don't want to record the data wrongly because this would be embarrassing and less useful for Mike and Carol. They are the real scientists. The rest of us are amateurs who need a lot of guidance. Sometimes Carol gets a little wrinkle across her forehead. I know this wrinkle is keeping us on track. She is trying to be careful.

In 1656, the twenty-three-year-old Baruch Spinoza, a Portuguese Jew in Amsterdam, was excommunicated from his community and cursed to the end of his days, cursed day and night, waking and sleeping, going in and going out. Specifically, the congregation asked the Lord to smite the young man and blot out his name from under heaven. The exact nature of Spinoza's "abominable heresies" and "evil opinions" is not known. But the testimony of an Augustinian monk reporting before the Spanish Inquisition three years later stated that Spinoza was punished for "having reached the point of atheism." The monk also declared that Spinoza believed "that God exists only philosophically . . . and that souls died with their bodies."

Spinoza was not an atheist—but something quite different, something unique and somewhat new. His pantheism was part of a growing spirit of inquiry and self-examination, of looking inward for spiritual answers rather than outward. Soon after his banishment, he was invited to meet with a Quaker leader who wrote back home to England, "There is a jew in Amsterdam that by the Jews is Cast out (as he himself and others sayeth) because he owneth no other teacher but the light." The letter reveals a natural affinity between Spinoza and Quakerism, for Quakers were also part of this new spirit of inquiry, with their Quakerly emphasis on the small inner voice and their rejection of creeds or scriptural authority. "I spoke to him, and he was pretty tender," the Quaker leader reflected, tender being a word used to describe a growing closeness to the spirit of God and the inner voice that whispered of God. For Quakers, that inner conviction was all that mattered. For Spinoza, too, so the Quaker wrote, "to read of moses and the prophets without was nothing to him except he came to know it within."

Quakerism was a young religion. Only ten years before, its founder and chief promoter, the twenty-two-year-old George Fox, had experienced a divine Light in his soul while walking through the dew of an English field. This inner Light, available to anyone and everyone at any time, became the primary tenet of Quakerism. God was in each of us. We required no priest or text to know God. Early Quakers saw themselves as reviving an original, essential Christianity. The Light of Christ was eternal, not historical, universally given to all people at all times. George Fox and his followers would be imprisoned many times for this belief, and some would die in England's damp and terrible cells. Still, they persevered, and for the next three hundred years, Quakers met and grew in number and spread across the world. Their ideas often conflicted with social norms. They were early feminists and early pacifists. They worked to reform prisons and mental hospitals. They ferried slaves on the Underground Railroad. God was in each of us. It all followed from that.

The early Quakers believed that God was in nature, too, and their form of worship—silently waiting for the Light—encouraged a mysticism that led to a sense of oneness and Unity. They felt the immanence of God. They felt the Light everywhere and in everything. They were not pantheists. But their mystical tendencies and respect for the personal experience created a tradition in which Quakers today can welcome pantheists into their circle.

After that first discussion, Spinoza was invited to a Quaker Meeting for worship. Unfortunately his Quaker hosts were imprisoned before he could attend. He was also given a pamphlet on Quaker thought written by Margaret Fell, another Quaker leader and wife to George Fox. It is likely that the philosopher translated this work into Hebrew. Certainly he became well acquainted with Quaker ideas and would include Quakers as students and friends. In Spinoza's own work, he often used Quakerly language, referring to God as spirit or light or inward knowledge.

In turn, his writings would influence Quakerism. The pamphlet *The Light on the Candlestick* was written by one of Spinoza's close companions, echoed Spinoza's philosophy, and tried to articulate a rational basis for spiritual vision. This tract was widely circulated among Quakers as one of their own. At times, Spinoza seemed to be a Quaker voice more blunt and plain-spoken than any Quaker dared to be. Concerning the Bible, for example, he concurred that knowledge of God from reading this ancient text—written by humans and then rewritten by humans—was limited knowledge. Implacably, he concluded that "the Word of God is faulty, maimed, adulterated, and contradictory to itself."

Spinoza did not, of course, become a Quaker. The Quakers had come to Amsterdam to convert the Jews to Christianity, an idea that would not have appealed to the philosopher. Quakers were still theists who spoke easily of a personal relationship with a loving Father. Their ideas about religion were different enough to get them thrown into jail (and hanged in New England by the Puritans) but not nearly so different as what the excommunicated Jew had in mind.

He chose a more radical path.

Within a few years after his expulsion, a still tender Spinoza wrote a treatise in which he described the ordinary goals and ambitions of life as vain and futile. His experience of disinheritance, poverty, and exile had shown him that good fortune was not to be trusted. Yet surprisingly, his reversal of fortune had not harmed him. More accurately, he had not allowed himself to be harmed and so realized that events in themselves were not necessarily good or bad "except insofar as the mind is affected by them." He resolved to spend the rest of his life searching for "the true good, that which would affect the mind singularly, to the exclusion of all else . . . something which once found and acquired, would give me continuous, supreme, and everlasting happiness."

This treatise included three rules that allowed for such a pursuit: (1) Avoid trouble by behaving politely and following the accepted rules of society. (2) Seek out only enough wealth so as to live a simple and comfortable life of the mind. (3) Enjoy the pleasures of the body solely as a way to sustain good health.

With these rules as a guide, Spinoza began. To earn his living, he became a professional lens maker, shaping and polishing slabs of glass to be used in telescopes and microscopes. He never had a family but lived in villages outside Amsterdam in rented rooms in other people's homes, where he would sit alone at night reading and writing. He published under his own name an essay criticizing the philosophy of Descartes and finished a political treatise that he published anonymously. Mostly, though, he worked on the masterpiece he titled *Ethics*—which he presented as a logical argument that proved the idea we now call pantheism, beginning with definitions, then axioms, propositions, demonstrations of these propositions, and a corollary or two.

It was all so obvious and irrefutable. God was defined. Substance was defined. The ideas of finite and infinite were defined. By definition, God was shown to be an infinite being who consisted of only one substance and who contained everything in the world—everything created from the divine substance. We were all modes in the Body of Being. God was existence itself, the universe, nature, what is. This existence, this nature, this God was self-created, self-creating, and ineluctable. Existence was the divine nature, and existence flowed casually out of the divine nature.

Like the earlier Stoics, Spinoza imagined a predetermined universe. Proposition Twenty-nine: "In nature there is nothing contingent, but all things are determined from the necessity of the divine nature to exist and act in a certain manner." And Proposition Thirty-two: "Things could have been produced by God in no other way and in no other order than that in which they have been produced."

Also like the Stoics, Spinoza could not imagine an irrational universe. We lived in the Mind and Body of God, and at the very least this Mind and Body were sane. In fact, by definition— being God—the universe was perfect. What we perceived as imperfect, as pain and suffering, was a problem of our perception and limited human understanding.

For Spinoza, Nature or God had no goal or end result: "All final causes are human fictions." Nor did Nature or God have a special interest in humanity: "He who loves God cannot strive that God should love him in return."

Although God was a single substance, that substance had two attributes: extension and thought, roughly equivalent to matter and mind. The human body was one mode of God's attribute of matter. The human mind was one mode of God's attribute of thought. Spinoza described the body in medical terms as a complex whole made up of individual parts that were themselves complex. Some parts were fluid, some soft, some hard. He described the human mind as "the idea itself or the knowledge of the human body." The mind could not perceive except through the body.

Today, the neuroscientist Antonio Damasio argues that Spinoza intuited some three hundred years ago one of our most modern scientific beliefs: the biological source of human emotion and consciousness, which is the complex interaction of neurons and hormones. "What is Spinoza's insight then?" Damasio asks and answers, "That mind and body are parallel and mutually correlated processes, mimicking each other at every crossroad, as two faces of the same thing." The leader in this dance is the body, which shapes the mind rather more than the reverse.

Spinoza believed that most of what goes on in the human mind was untrustworthy, impressions from the senses and products of the imagination. Still, humans were capable of forming "adequate ideas" based on reason. Through such adequate ideas—through logic and rigor—we could know and experience God's attribute of thought. It was in the name of logic that Spinoza followed the form of the geometric proof. Similarly, he wrote in a learned and obscure Latin, hoping that by using a language that had lost its cultural associations, he could rid his work of figurative or emotional images. (He may have also hoped never to be compared to or in the same book as Giordano Bruno, a fellow pantheist who revealed God's immanence quite differently— through imaginative leaps, symbol, and metaphor.)

Spinoza did not stop at a proof of the divine universe. He was equally concerned about how we should live in this universe. Part One of the *Ethics* deals with God. Parts Two through Five, the rest of the book, are about being human, the quest for happiness, and the ethical life.

First, we had to accept that human psychology followed the same laws as everything else. We were the product of childhood, culture, neurons, and liver function—the flow of cause and effect that came out of the necessity of the divine nature: "In the Mind there is no absolute or free will but the Mind is determined to will this or that by a cause that is also determined by another, and this again by another, and so to infinity."

Our emotions, especially, were tied to cause and effect. In an effort to understand the emotions better, Spinoza cataloged them. Love was "Joy with the accompanying idea of an external cause." Hatred was "Sadness with the accompanying idea of an external cause." Hope was "an inconstant Joy which has arisen from the image of a future or past thing whose outcome we doubt." Since emotions were always connected to something external, and since external things were beyond our control, the man controlled by emotion was not his own master but "mastered by fortune."

Fortunately—and again Stoically—we could moderate our emotions by examining our value judgments. Spinoza had learned this after being cursed by the Jewish community when he discovered that his experiences did not contain in themselves anything good or bad "except insofar as the mind is affected by them." He had learned to accept his fate with cheerful affection.

He could do this because he had, in fact, found a source of continuous, supreme, and everlasting happiness. Spinoza believed that all beings act out of self-interest or "to persevere" in their beingness. Humans were no different. Unknown to most of us, however, our greatest state of being was a life of reason and knowledge of the world—the intellectual love of God. This was our virtue and our freedom. This was our happiness and "blessedness." This was our self-interest.

In this state, we tried to live moderately and healthily. We did not fear death. We knew that our personality would not live on except in its relationship to those adequate ideas that were part of God's attribute of thought. We also knew that we would never be completely destroyed, for something "remains which is eternal." We knew our place in Nature, another word for God, and we found peace in this knowledge.

Moreover, we worked for a just and tolerant society that permitted the intellectual love of God because that society, too, was in our self-interest. Spinoza may have been driven by political concerns as much as philosophical ones. Repeatedly, if anonymously, he advocated a democracy in which every man could "think what he wants and say what he wants." In his quiet way, writing his evil opinions in a rented room, he undermined the foundations of a Europe that still harshly demanded obedience to church and state, a place of cruel oppression and narrow prejudice. (Spinoza also reflected certain prejudices of his time. For example, he concluded that women naturally had fewer adequate ideas than men and should be under their authority.)

On paper—reading the *Ethics* and treatises—Spinoza is unattractive. A bit too superior. A bit too preachy. You wouldn't want *him* to be your father or uncle or friend of the family. What would you say to such a dry stick, full of propositions and axioms? To a man who intones, "After the enjoyment of sensual pleasure, the greatest sadness follows"?

In his actual life, the philosopher was more amiable. An eccentric recluse, he was also loved and respected by many friends, who wrote and visited him often. For his last seven years, he lived companionably as a boarder with the painter Henryk Van der Spyck, the painter's wife, and the painter's seven children. At times he sat in the parlor to chat with them about current affairs. According to one reliable account, when asked by the mistress of the household what he thought of her Lutheran religion, the scholar replied gently that it served her well and that she would indeed be "saved" if she lived a pious and quiet life.

In short, Spinoza followed Rule 1 of the three rules he had decided upon in his first treatise written when he was still a young man. He got along with people. He avoided trouble by behaving politely and agreeably and following the accepted rules of society. For the most part, he kept his feelings well under control and was described variously as modest, friendly, pleasing, even-tempered, and affable—and this from biographers who did not like him. (Only rarely do we glimpse another, more passionate side—as when his landlord Van der Spyck was forced to lock the door and prevent a distraught Spinoza from leaving the house to protest the death of a progressive Dutch leader. The politician had just been killed by a mob who were quartering his remains and selling them as souvenirs. A weeping Spinoza had prepared a sign to post at the bloody scene: "You are the Greatest of Barbarians." Such intemperance, fortunately, was the exception.)

Spinoza also heeded Rule 2 by seeking out only enough wealth as to live a simple and comfortable life of the mind. One of Spinoza's friends was the rich merchant and Quaker Simon de Vries, who studied the philosopher's writings with a group of like-minded students. De Vries died young and made Spinoza his heir. The lens maker insisted on accepting only a small annuity, however, which he later reduced even further. Later still, he refused the offer of a professorship at the University of Heidelberg. On occasion, he told the story of the Greek philosopher Thales, who used his understanding of weather to profit by buying olive presses and then donated all the money to charity. Spinoza's moral: "It is not out of necessity but out of choice that the wise possess no riches."

As for Rule 3—enjoy the pleasures of the body solely as a way to sustain good health—in general Spinoza lived a balanced life guided by a sense of moderation. Often he ate only gruel for the day, but with raisins and butter, washed down by beer. His main indulgence was his daily tobacco. He dressed simply yet liked his good leather shoes. He painted as a hobby, enjoying aesthetics even as he gave his allegiance to logic. He mixed prudence with courage and published his most controversial work anonymously or posthumously. He had no wish to be martyred.

He suffered always from a weak chest and spent his last years coughing. The condition worsened suddenly, and Spinoza died at the age of forty-four, possibly from tuberculosis or possibly from inhaling the dust from the glass lenses he had diligently ground for so many years—the telescope lenses and microscope lenses that served the growing effort to see the world more clearly. When death came, I do not think he feared it. He had had his share of continuous, supreme, and everlasting happiness. There was that in him which remained eternal, and his many adequate ideas flew up into the heavens to join the attribute of God's thought.

Peter and I miss the first day of bird banding this May because we are in Albuquerque watching our daughter, Maria, graduate from college. Peter's eighty-six-year-old father joins us. Five of us sit in the audience: mother, father, brother, grandfather, and a friend. Afterward, we pack up Maria's computer, furniture, and knickknacks from her apartment. Our son, David, is also going to the University of New Mexico in Albuquerque, and we pack up his junk, books, and mattress, too, driving it all back to Silver City in the eternal American transport of things. David starts a job with the U.S. Forest Service to earn money for a study-abroad program in the fall. Maria will stay with us this summer before joining AmeriCorps to work in a public school in rural Washington state. I feel centered again, both children at home, their lives nicely planned.

Families are more complex than that, of course. Spinoza wrote, "Devotion is love toward an object which astonishes us" and "Marriage is in harmony with reason." Such statements do not take in the whole of domestic life, but they hint nicely at certain complications. My nineteen-year-old son certainly astonishes me. Marriage and reason often seem compatible, although that is hardly the guarantee of a fun evening. If I do not write more on this subject, it is not because I do not long to but because the husbands and children of writers do not really want to be written about. They think of their lives as belonging to them, not another narrator. I could negotiate this—give up a confidence, paint a few scenes—and probably end up with a better paragraph, even a better chapter. But the price seems high.

May 14, the first day of bird banding, is busy. Without my help, the banders catch seven Lucy's warblers, eight Wilson's warblers, an Audubon warbler, a common yellowthroat, a red-winged blackbird, four Bullock orioles, a spotted towhee, a summer tanager, three green-tailed towhees, two white-crowned sparrows, a yellow-breasted chat, an ash-throated flycatcher, five MacGillivary's warblers, a Cassin's vireo, and a northern cardinal. They recapture a common yellowthroat, two Bewick's wrens, two yellow-breasted chats, and an ash-throated flycatcher. Most songbird species live only two or three years. These recaptured birds are adults that were banded last season. Their survival for one more year is always cause for celebration. "Hey," we say, "a recapture!"

On the second day of bird banding, May 21, we band three Wilson's warblers, a dusky flycatcher, two yellow warblers, three common yellowthroats, a warbling vireo, a Bewick's wren, two spotted towhees, three yellow-breasted chats, and three red-shafted flickers. We recapture a yellow warbler, a MacGillivary wren, two yellow-breasted chats, and a Lucy's warbler.

My job is to check the nets and untangle birds. This is not easy. For me, it requires a mental effort somewhat like that of a dyslexic trying to read. There is a spatial understanding I am supposed to have—from which direction the warbler flew into the net, how it half bounced out, how it thrashed and fought and turned itself around, which wing got caught, and which shoulder—and from this I am supposed to intuit whether to free the head first or the feet. There is a physical confidence I am supposed to have, pulling firmly at impossibly thin legs and trusting they will not snap off, feeling the rapidly beating heart and trusting it will not stop. As my fingers search for invisible strands of nylon tangled in tail feathers or balled around toes, I should know what will happen when I move these strands up or down. Meanwhile the bird has its own opinion. Untangling a bird from a net requires an unfamiliar meshing of my mind and body, those two seemingly separate modes. It makes me feel anxious and then weirdly centered—as though the coordination of these two separate modes is really, after all, what I am supposed to be doing.

I concentrate. I pull a few strands. And the yellow warbler is free, held firmly in my bander's grip. I pause a moment now to gape and admire. This bird is very yellow. Its color rings like a carillon. Its color could power a nuclear reactor, containing all the energy we would ever need in the world. I feel as if I have just raided a treasure chest. I am king. I am triumphant. I have the rare and singular golden prize.

In fact, yellow warblers are widely distributed across North America, from the Mexican border up to the Arctic Circle. Males defend their nesting territory from other males by singing beautifully and sweetly, with fluttering flight displays. Their cuplike nests, placed in the branches of trees and shrubs, are easy to find, especially by cowbirds. The warblers often respond by covering up the cowbird eggs, the female warbler laying a new clutch on top. Sometimes the cowbird returns. The yellow warblers might then add another floor to the nest and another clutch of eggs. In one recorded case, a cowbird returned five times and the yellow warblers built six layers of a nest floor.

With my bird in a cloth bag, I return to the banding table. The scene before me has a tribal feel, a mix of people of all ages. Eleanor's daughter and grandsons from Tucson are visiting, and Carol is showing them how to look at molt feathers on a Bewick's wren. Peter's father is here from his home in Washington, D.C., and has stopped by to watch the bird banding, too. Carol and Mike's son, Dominic, is pretending to be a fox in a hollowed log. His babysitter, Nena, watches and encourages. "I can see your little nose," she says. Dominic has also brought his collection of toy cars and is building a parking garage in the sand. Adults walk around purposefully, carrying net bags or radios, which we use for communication in the long run from Net One to Net Ten. Voices are generally low, although there is the occasional laughter. We could be back in the Paleolithic, a small group of hunters and gatherers intent on work and play, except that instead of skinning an animal or pounding seed, we are putting tiny bands of metal around the tiny legs of birds and swabbing their genitalia and parsing out the sex of an ash-throated flycatcher, which is surprisingly hard to do.

At Spinoza's death in 1677, his friends shipped his desk with the manuscript *Ethics* hidden in a drawer to Amsterdam, where the work could be published. Within a year, the book was banned throughout Europe and condemned by the Vatican, the Jews, and the Calvinists. The Quakers were probably also shocked by the idea of a divine substance so completely impersonal and uninterested in human affairs. Publishing or selling *Ethics* became a criminal offense.

For the next century, Spinoza would be treated carefully by the scholars of the day. Religious authorities maintained a harsh view of heretics, and in 1697, a medical student in Edinburgh was burned to death for his views on the Holy Trinity. Even when the burnings, tortures, and imprisonments began to taper off, disagreeing with the church could still ruin a man's career. The general practice was to refer to Spinoza's work with automatic pejoratives such as pestilent, shameless, or hideous. No one wanted to be associated with such unorthodox ideas—of an intelligible and impersonal universe, a self-created, self-creating Nature independent of an anthropomorphic God. And yet these ideas were so intriguing. The word pantheism entered the lexicon: pan = "all" and theism = "God." The pestilent, shameless, and hideous hypothesis was read and reviled, read and dismissed—and then read again. In the mid-eighteenth century, more than one published dictionary or encyclopedia included large entries that described Spinoza's theories, even as the authors criticized them.

By now, the cultural movement we call the Enlightenment had begun in Europe and the American colonies. Its foundation was a belief in the virtue of reason. Spinoza had been a significant influence on the Enlightenment, although he was not often publicly recognized. Promoters of this new worldview also pointed to scientific discoveries such as Isaac Newton's law of gravity. Through the observation of nature—through experience and experiment, curiosity and education—we could unlock the secrets of the universe. These answers would come not from the past or church authority but from the determined labor of the enlightened mind.

(Later still, the scientist Albert Einstein would say, "I believe in Spinoza's God," meaning that he accepted "the orderly harmony" of the universe while rejecting conventional theism.)

In the pursuit of such a goal, liberty and democracy were now seen as key values in a healthy society. Every citizen had certain basic rights. Tolerance and freedom of speech were compatible with social order. Although early leaders of the Enlightenment were sometimes jailed for these beliefs, by the 1770s, most thinkers and writers could pursue their ideas without fear of reprisal.

The romantic poets were reading Spinoza, too. This varied group of literary artists countered the Enlightenment's emphasis on science and reason by heralding the equal importance of intuition, imagination, and strong feeling. Spinoza would seem an odd mentor. Yet the most celebrated romantic poet of his time, Johann Wolfgang von Goethe, wrote that *Ethics* had affected his entire way of thinking: "I found in it a sedative for my passions, and it seemed to unveil a clear broad view over the material and moral world." In particular, "what riveted me to him was the boundless disinterestedness which shone forth in every sentence. That wonderful sentiment, 'He who loves God must not expect God to love him in return.'" In his poetry, Goethe would write of a God who "harbors the world in Himself, Himself in the world," a divinity woven into the fabric of being.

Following Goethe's lead, the romantic poets in England also admired Spinoza, especially Samuel Taylor Coleridge, although he would soon abandon pantheism for Christianity. Even so, his poetry echoed ideas from the Dutch philosopher: "One intellectual breeze, at once the Soul of each and God of all" and "Himself in all, and all things in himself."

Coleridge collaborated with William Wordsworth in the publication *Lyrical Ballads,* a collection that established some of the principles of romantic poetry: the celebration of nature and the use of informal rather than formal language. Throughout his career, Wordsworth would be accused of pantheism by his Christian friends, especially in the earlier poems. Sometimes he denied the charge. Sometimes he sounded rather vague, as though not certain himself what he thought. His poetry expressed his pantheism more strongly:

> *And I have felt*
> *A presence that disturbs me with the joy*
> *Of elevated thoughts: a sense sublime*
> *Of something far more deeply interfused,*
> *Whose dwelling is the light of setting suns*
> *And the round ocean and the living air,*
> *And the blue sky, and in the mind of man:*
> *A motion and a spirit, that impels*
> *All thinking things, all objects of all thought*
> *And rolls through all things. Therefore, am I still*
> *A lover of the meadows and the woods*
> *And mountains; and of all that we behold*
> *From this green earth . . .*

Meanwhile, the English poet William Blake was seeing eternity in a grain of sand and infinity in a wildflower, writing, "God only acts and is through existing beings and men." And now there were philosophers, too, like Hegel ("What God creates, he himself is") and Schelling ("Nature is visible Spirit; Spirit is invisible Nature").

And suddenly there were pantheists—or people dabbling in pantheism—everywhere, like birds in the trees. Most of these pantheists were not singing about an intellectual love of God or a predetermined universe or the need to control your emotions. They were singing about beauty and joy and passion. They loved the meadows and the green woods. They were bursting with good news.

On June 4, we band a common yellowthroat, a western wood pewee, two red-winged blackbirds, two brown-crested flycatchers, a summer tanager, a ladder-backed woodpecker, four yellow-breasted chats, two blue grosbeaks, and a red-shafted flicker. We recapture two yellow-breasted chats, a common yellowthroat, two summer tanagers, and a Bewick's wren. Carol refers to the latter as avian mice because they are so agile and determined to escape the net.

In Net Eight, we find a female broad-tailed hummingbird fiercely entangled. After Mike unwraps the tiny bird, she is perfectly still, and Mike asks me to take her back to the banding table, where Carol can feed her sugar water. I walk the quarter mile like a funeral procession, the body of the dead in the palm of my hand. Suddenly the dead body whirrs with the noise of a plane about to take off, and the hummingbird flies away.

Later I take a turn recording information, and Carol points out that the spelling is *Bewick's,* not *Buick's,* wren, so that I have to reimagine the story of this animal, which I had happily associated with a sturdy American engine. The Bewick's wren is in decline all over the United States and has disappeared east of the Mississippi River. The Gila Valley is one of its strongholds. After recapturing one bird, we check back through banding records to discover that this particular wren is five years old! This is a very old, very lucky, very wise Bewick's wren, and we look at it differently now, with more respect. Carol marvels at its unusual plumage, the bird version of gray hair.

Mike and Carol are also excited by the appearance of a grasshopper sparrow on the Gila River Farm. A few weeks ago, Carol had been taking Dominic on a bicycle ride when she heard a familiar vocalization, a few high chip-chip notes followed by a grasshopper-like buzz. She knew the sound well from working with grasshopper sparrows in the tall grass prairies of Oklahoma. But what was that chip-chip-buzz doing here?

Soon after, the ornithologist Dale Zimmerman visited the Gila River Farm. Dale is a trim man in his seventies, an acclaimed illustrator, former professor at Western New Mexico University, and author of the definitive *Birds of New Guinea* and *Birds of Kenya and Tanzania*. Carol asked him, "Could I have heard what I thought I heard?" Dale also got excited because, indeed, she could have heard what she thought she heard if she had heard the Arizona grasshopper sparrow, a declining subspecies. These birds are still seen in the desert grasslands of Arizona, but not in southern New Mexico. In southern New Mexico, they do not exist.

Mike went to the Internet, where he found and recorded a male Arizona grasshopper sparrow's song. These sparrows are so territorial that any other male will respond almost instantly to such a noise, ready to defend his property and sing away all rivals. Mike and Dale set up a tape recorder in an alfalfa field on the farm, played the song, and waited. Within minutes, a male Arizona grasshopper sparrow was perched on a tall weed vigorously shouting at the offending tape recorder, his tune high-pitched and unmelodious. Next, Mike and Dale set up a net and caught the sparrow. Mike explains, "The Arizona subspecies has a particularly large bill—a big nose." This bird had a big nose.

Telling his story at the bird-banding table, Mike reports that at this point Dale Zimmerman was "almost giddy" with delight. Dale is a man who has traveled throughout the world: Africa, Asia, South America. He has seen and illustrated the most glamorous of bird species: white-crested turacos and crowned hornbills and spotted eagle owls. Now the Arizona grasshopper sparrow was expanding its range into New Mexico, and Dale Zimmerman was ecstatic. Overjoyed by a sparrow. Listening to Mike, we all nod and think: This is exactly the kind of person I want to be.

The grasshopper sparrows were passing through to lay eggs and rear their young. On the Gila River Farm, flood-irrigated fields of hay had created an artificial oasis, something like the grasslands in Arizona. Immediately, Mike began to scheme. Could the Nature Conservancy manage the farm for breeding Arizona grasshopper sparrows?

Dale Zimmerman has a relationship with the Arizona grasshopper sparrow and with hundreds of other bird species, with every species he meets, bird or butterfly or moth—as do

Mike and Carol. When Spinoza set aside the personal God, when he set aside his relationship with an all-loving God, he replaced that with a relationship to everything in the world. We are connected to everything. We are related to everything. In the pantheism that evolved beyond Spinoza, we do not need to control our emotions in response to external things so much as we need to broaden our relationship to external things. In this way, we will not have four or eight or ten things that make us happy and that "master" us the more we depend on them. Instead, we will have twelve hundred or twelve thousand or eight million relationships with the world. We will be mastered by none and giddy with happiness every day.

As the novelist and pantheist D. H. Lawrence wrote, "This is how I 'save my soul,' by accomplishing a pure relationship between me and another person, between me and other people . . . me and the animals, me and the trees or flowers, me and the earth, me and the skies and sun and stars, me and the moon. . . . This, if we knew it, is our life and our eternity: the subtle perfected relation between me and my whole circumbient universe."

On June 11, Sunday morning, we catch a Lucy's warbler, a Bewick's wren, two red-winged blackbirds, a yellow-breasted chat, and a blue grosbeak. The Bewick's wren escapes before we can weigh her. We recapture three yellow-breasted chats, a Bewick's wren, a yellow warbler, and a white-breasted nuthatch. The white-breasted nuthatch is sparrow-sized, white-faced, and quiet.

The blue grosbeak, on the other hand, screams in the net, "Murderers, torturers, thieves!" He is loud and excitable, a large bird with a thick bill. No one wants to get a finger near that

beak. At the banding table, the grosbeak never lets up, squawking and squawking and squawking. This is his nature. Carol simply laughs at him. I have often seen blue grosbeaks in front of
my house, perched on weed stalks, flicking their tails nervously
and looking like fallen chunks of sky. They squawk even then,
always something to complain about.

It sounds good on paper. Me and the earth. Me and the animals. Me and the sun and moon and stars. But when I am in a
bad mood, pantheism feels more like unrequited love, the dreary
task of whipping up both sides of a relationship. The truth is
that I often feel lonely. I am talking to myself and no one answers. Yada-yada-yada. Blah-blah-blah. The same stuff I have
heard all my life. I am so tired of this voice. I am so bored. It
may sound strange, but I don't want to be alone in my body and
mind. I want someone with me.

This is an ontological loneliness that my husband can not re-
dress, although I love him and he loves me. My children distracted me from this feeling for a long time, twenty-two years,
and then they grew up and went away. (Which was, of course,
the right thing to do. Still, you can't help but feel—ungrateful
wretches.) Now I am no longer distracted. I have more time to
talk to myself. Yada-yada-yada. Blah-blah-blah. Now this loneliness seems unending and almost unbearable.

I have a few theories as to its origin. (1) It is my mother's
fault. That's a given. (2) It is a flaw in my character, and I would
have more friends and never feel lonely if I were a better, more
extroverted, more gregarious person. Also quite obvious. (3) I

started out in the womb with a twin sister, but then she died and was absorbed into my body, and I've carried that grief ever since. (4) We are all hardwired for that Paleolithic tribe of thirty to forty people with whom we feel intimately linked, but instead I grew up in the suburbs of Phoenix. (5) It is chemical. It is menopausal. It is neurotic. It is imaginary. It is the empty nest. (6) It is the loss of the personal God.

It is the loss of the personal God. In some ways, I think I would have done better in another religion. Without doubt, I would believe in God or gods or goddesses if I could. I would like Someone to pray to, Someone to note my fall and care about my scraped knee. I would like that Shoulder, that Chest, that Arm. It is less a matter of won't than can't. Did I believe in these things once? Maybe, as a child. But even that belief felt more pretend than real.

Sometimes I feel envious of other faiths. Then I remember the story of Abraham and Isaac. My first response is that I want God to speak to me. My second is that it depends on what he has to say.

I have been thinking a lot about going back to Quaker Meeting. I would have to think hard to count up how long it has been since I last attended, three years perhaps, or maybe four. From my perspective, my absence from Meeting does not really mean I am not there or that I am not a Quaker. I have never withdrawn my letter for membership. I pay my yearly dues and receive my monthly newsletter. I still have good friends among Gila Friends. I still feel I belong. I know I would be welcomed into the circle, and it would be as though I had never left.

I am ready again to sit in silence and wait for the Light. I understand one meaning of church to be a social network, a kind of tribe, and I know that Quakerism is a natural church for the churchless pantheist (as is Unitarianism and a few other groups). I know Quaker Meeting will make me feel less lonely.

Unfortunately, Quaker Meeting is every Sunday morning, the same time we bird-band. Unfortunately, the weekends are the only days Peter and I can come out to the Gila Valley and our little yellow house.

At first glance, in his catalog of emotions, Spinoza seemed to be quite thorough. One by one in *Ethics,* he parsed the meaning of desire, joy, sorrow, astonishment, contempt, love, hatred, inclination, aversion, devotion, derision, hope, fear, confidence, despair, gladness, remorse, commiseration, favor, indignation, overestimation, contempt, envy, compassion, self-satisfaction, humility, repentance, pride, despondency, self-exaltation, shame, regret, emulation, thankfulness or gratitude, benevolence, anger, vengeance, cruelty or ferocity, audacity, pusillanimity, consternation, courtesy or moderation, ambition, luxuriousness, drunkenness, avarice, and lust.

He did not, however, define loneliness. The absence seems odd in such a complete list. Apparently Spinoza did not see loneliness as an emotion. Perhaps he simply never felt lonely.

CHAPTER 7

The Peaceable Kingdom

INSTEAD OF ACTUALLY going to Quaker Meeting, I have lunch with Polly, the current clerk of the Gila Religious Society of Friends, and with Elisabeth, one of the weighty Quakers who came from Pennsylvania and helped start this Meeting. Lunch with these two older women is nothing new. Both were among my first friends when I came to southern New Mexico in 1981. Polly is now seventy-five and Elisabeth is eighty-five. It was Elisabeth who taught me about Quaker tradition, along with Josephine, who died six years ago at the age of ninety.

Equality—Josephine once explained—is a defining tradition for those who follow the early Quakers. There is that of God in everyone. In the seventeenth century, the word you was reserved for social superiors. Quakers rejected that distinction and used the informal thee and thou, an impertinence for which they could be jailed. Equality leads to the idea of consensus, a process in which all opinions are valued in the pursuit of a unity of agreement, not a majority. The business of a Quaker Meeting is done by consensus, and by volunteers, without a paid preacher or priest. There can be no hierarchy among Friends. Business meetings are also called meetings for worship, for as Josephine said, "We listen to each other's concerns with our hearts and minds open. Out of that will come a richness no one person could have dreamed of."

In my memory, Elisabeth sighed and looked skeptical at this remark. She noted that business meetings could be quite long. Josephine acknowledged that every Meeting she had ever attended included some "neurotic or contrary soul," sometimes two or three. Quakers had to know when something was obstructive and "enclose this with tenderness." Quakers had to learn to disagree with Meeting and then choose to stand aside, to not stand in the way.

Silence is another defining tradition. We know the divine best through personal, immediate experience, and that divinity, that Light, is here right now, all around us. Silence is how we listen for the Light. In a moment of listening, we will hear a small inner voice, the voice of God within. We will know what we have always suspected: Eternal life is under the words.

For this reason, Quakers in my Meeting start sitting at ten o'clock every Sunday morning and remain sitting quietly for an hour. Sometimes one of us is prompted to speak, words meant to come from the inner Light. Most often, an entire hour passes and no one says anything. We try to be still. The world slows down. We try to listen.

After silence, we have announcements and perhaps a business meeting. We are bound here by tradition, too, and Quaker language. A threshing is a discussion, the winnowing of answers. Eldering is a form of counsel and advice, done privately "in a Friendly way" by an older member of the Meeting. Clear is a favorite word. Seeking consensus or "the sense of the Meeting," the clerk might ask, "Are we clear about this?" Members who wish to be married under the care of the Meeting will ask for a Clearness Committee to confirm their readiness. A Clearness Committee also forms to assess a letter asking for membership or to help a member with a personal problem. The very names of our committees "speak to us": the Committee on Sufferings, the Committee on Ministry and Oversight, the Committee on Unity with Nature, the Committee for Peace and Social Action.

In a religion famous for committees, this last committee is an important one. At every Gila Friends Meeting, we will be urged to do something political: write our senator about AIDS in Africa, bring food for illegal immigrants crossing the Mexican-American border, or protest the war in Iraq. Our empathy takes us around the world. Just as some people hand out recipes, Quakers clip out newspaper articles and give them to each other, horrible stories about injustice and death. Perversely, we seek out pain.

As Americans, we are particularly haunted by our country's violence, past and present. Often we feel paralyzed with guilt. In 1660, George Fox, the founder and principle leader of Quakerism, presented to Charles II, king of England, *A Declaration from the Harmles & Innocent People of God Called Quakers*: "We utterly deny all outward wars and strife and fighting with out-ward weapons, for any end, or under any pretense whatsoever; this is our testimony to the whole world." In part, this statement was meant to assure the king that the Quakers would not at-tempt to overthrow the monarchy as other groups were doing. Mostly, however, the peace testimony followed from the Quaker belief that there is that of God in everyone. How could you try to kill that of God?

Pacifism is what people know best about Quakers and agree with least. When I first joined the Meeting, a friend asked with real interest and all in one breath, "So what would you do if you and Maria were walking down the street and a man jumped out and attacked your daughter and tried to rape her?" I answered, "I would try to stop him." She insisted, "And if you had to kill him to stop him?" I answered, "Then I would kill him."

I may not be a stellar Quaker, but I am not so unusual. Other Quakers will also fight in self-defense or in defense of someone else. In 1683, William Penn's city of Philadelphia, the City of Brotherly Love or Holy Experiment based on Quakerly principles and laws, began without militia and fortifications. By 1725, the Quaker Assembly had authorized a tax to arm them-selves against the French and Indians. Many "fighting Quakers" were part of the American Revolution, including patriots like Thomas Paine, Nathaniel Greene, and Betsy Ross. In the 1860s, the Civil War challenged Quakers as never before. Most Friends were opposed to slavery. They also felt a deep sense of patriotism and duty toward their country. Thousands of Quak-ers joined the Union Army, and some Meetings found it hard to deny them. After the war, Iowa Meeting declared only "fervent charity towards one another in relation to that which is past." Many more Quakers participated in World Wars I and II.

In my Meeting, most of us accept that our pacifism is not pure or absolute. In many ways, we worry out loud about our potential for violence. Often we feel an enormous anger against those politicians who have embroiled us in cruel and needless wars. We feel that anger rising up through the body, hot and self-righteous. We feel helpless in the grip of anger.

At the same time, we have been taught four precepts for dealing with conflict:

Facing an adversary, try to go into meeting with him.
Identify with your opponent; never use a man or woman as a means but as an end.
Speak truth to power.
Muster within thee all love, tenderness, and concern for the other.

Imagine doing this with someone you hate or fear. The first person who comes to mind is best.

Pacifism or nonviolence is something Gila Friends can sanely discuss. We can look at our relationships and try to understand our response. We can hope to muster all love and tenderness for the other.

Another Quaker testimony—simplicity—is in the realm of the absurd. When we sing the Quaker song "'Tis a gift to be simple, 'tis a gift to be free," we are surely being ironical. By and large, most Quaker Meetings in the United States represent a white middle class. Everyone drives a car. Everyone indulges in some luxury. We are embedded in a culture of buying and consuming.

If George Fox were to burst into the Gila Friends Meeting today, I think he would be dismayed at the scale of our struggle for peace and simplicity. But given his understanding of human nature, I do not think he would be surprised. What *would* shock him, I suspect, is that so many of us are no longer Christian. In 1646, the Light was another word for the eternal Christ. That small inner voice was the voice of Jesus. Over three hundred years later, Quaker Meetings like mine do not emphasize any one religion—not even theism. When Gila Friends break silence, speaking from the inner Light, we hardly ever say the word God. No one mentions Jesus. It is not exactly forbidden. It is just a little gauche.

In the nineteenth century, Quakers divided between those who continued the tradition of silence and those who wanted a more conventional Christian service with text, hymns, sermons, codes of conduct, and a stronger sense of organization. Richard Nixon was one of these "programmed" Quakers, as was my grandfather in Kansas before he joined his wife at the Methodist Church. Programmed Quakers now make up the majority of the over three hundred thousand Quakers worldwide. They no longer sit and wait for the Light but instead listen to a paid preacher. They praise the Holy Spirit and accept scriptural authority. George Fox would be shocked at them, too.

Unprogrammed Quakers, like those in my Meeting, further divide into Christ-centered Friends, who believe that Quakerism should still be defined in Christian terms, and Universalists, who do not believe this at all. Unprogrammed Meetings can differ enormously from one another, and this decentralization is another Quaker tradition. Among unprogrammed Quakers, the larger community is composed of Monthly Meetings that join together in Quarterly, Half-Yearly, and Yearly Meetings, that appoint delegates to national groups like the American Friends Service Committee or the General Friends Conference. These larger groups do not represent the top of the pyramid. There is no pyramid. Monthly Meetings are completely autonomous. While one Meeting still ponders its attitude toward gay couples, another Meeting is happily marrying them. While one hosts a Christmas bazaar, another celebrates the winter equinox.

My Monthly Meeting, the Gila Religious Society of Friends, are Universalists, an eclectic mix of agnostics, Buddhists, animists, pantheists, freethinkers, and a few Friends who talk to Christ. This has been true since the first time we gathered together as a worship group, a collection of people who sit and wait for the Light but have not yet formed an official Meeting with committees. We have always been far-flung in geography, sixty miles from one valley to the next. We also show that range in our religious beliefs, a spinning wheel kept from spinning off into outer space by the gravity of our traditions and Quakerly language. In truth, I never thought we would last this long.

I remember the beginning: 1984, crowded together in Josephine's house on a hill in the Gila Valley, a dozen people or more, mostly young in our twenties and thirties. I remember the land outside the living room window, the dark Mogollon Mountains broad-shouldered above the irrigated fields lime green and emerald green. Yellow grama grass rustled dryly. Pink arroyos zigzagged up canyons, and white bluffs crested in the summer air, sensual shapes breathed out by geology. So many of us were here because of this land. We had come as vagrants, wrapping our dreams around these colors: yellow, pink, and blue. We wanted to sink into the earth. We wanted our very houses to be made of mud.

In her bare-dirt yard, Josephine also had adobe bricks made of mud, lined up in rows and covered with black plastic against the rain. Josephine had come to the Gila Valley about ten years before from a lively Quaker Meeting in Chicago. When she moved to the Southwest, in her midsixties, she became a visiting Friend traveling north to Gallup and south to El Paso, slowly gathering around her a worship group in the Silver City area. Now, as we sat in a circle on well-worn couches and chairs, she spoke crisply, confidently, "As a worship group, we came together and held silence. But we didn't have the mass, the crucial weight to carry the responsibilities of a Meeting. We are here today to decide if we have that weight now."

She clucked and pressed us together, a dozen people against her breast. We stayed like that for hours. Elisabeth put down a bowl in the kitchen. Florence and Harry (one of those fighting Quakers, a Jew who had stormed the beach at Normandy) sat patiently and waited. These were our elders.

If we had that mass, if we felt weighty enough, we would write a letter asking for recognition from the larger Quaker community, starting with the Albuquerque Meeting. We began to thresh and winnow. Many of us had questions. What would our children do during silence? What about all those committees? Did we have to believe in Jesus? Did we have to be pacifists? What if we were walking down the street with our daughter and a man jumped out and. . .

Somehow the answer was implied in our questions. Somehow, unknowingly, we had gathered mass. In the end, a resolve formed. We had four Quakers willing to transfer membership from another Meeting: Josephine from Chicago, Elisabeth from Pennsylvania, Harry and Florence from Monterrey in California. We had three more people ready to write letters asking for membership. The rest of us would remain attenders, thinking-about-it Quakers who often make up the majority of a Meeting.

I remember the colors outside Josephine's window, the yellow grass and pink soil and bright blue sky. A few months later, my daughter, Maria, was born. In three years, we had David, our son. Soon after his birth, I dropped out of Quaker Meeting for the first but not the last time, the first of a succession of advances and retreats. You could ask me why. But I don't really know. I remember that we lived thirty miles from town. We had goats and a big garden and fruit trees and an outhouse and two adobe rooms. We did not have electricity or a reliable car. I started teaching full time at Western New Mexico University.

Every day, every evening, I breathed in the sweet smell of my children, which was all I wanted, all I needed.

"There is a Quaker belief," Josephine told me then, "that you can lay a thing down if that seems the right thing to do. There is no ought involved in coming to Meeting."

I laid down the Gila Religious Society of Friends just as the Meeting was strengthening and growing in profound ways. In the 1980s, many Quakers in the Southwest became involved in the Sanctuary Movement, a network of churches helping refugees from Guatemala and El Salvador. In these countries, the United States covertly supported repressive governments and political groups that were waging war against their own people. Teachers, lawyers, laborers, writers, hair dressers, even children were tortured and killed for wanting a more tolerant and just society. Military death squads terrorized the population. In Guatemala, which is 50 percent Mayan, Indians were killed just because they were Indian. Within a decade, 75,000 El Salvadorans would die and 150,000 Guatemalans. Millions of people fled the violence. When they reached the American border, they were deported as illegal aliens.

The Sanctuary Movement believed that the deportations themselves were illegal, violating a federal law meant to protect political refugees. Sanctuary united hundreds of Americans who risked jail and other penalties. Among them were Gila Friends. Elisabeth drove two men and two children north to Albuquerque, using the dirt roads through the Gila National Forest. Anxiously they bumped over deep ruts, past endless ponderosa pines and hidden canyons, through a long, yellow, grassy plain. The two men said little. The children never spoke. Florence, Harry, and Josephine also transported refugees north. They went up through the Zuni and Navajo reservations, taking lunch and dinner and stopping only for gas.

At Quaker potlucks, stories about Central America were passed around, clipped from the newspapers. In Guatemala City, a young girl was found sprawled in a dump, her tongue cut out. In San Salvador, a man's feet had been hacked off. A child died screaming. A mother went insane with grief.

In Quaker folklore, there is a chilling scene between George Fox and Margaret Fell, wife of Judge Thomas Fell, mistress of Swarthmore Manor and mother of seven. On hearing George Fox preach about the inner Light, Margaret Fell had her own revelation, and soon her home, Swarthmore Manor, became a center for Quaker meetings and efforts at social reform. Once while visiting a Quaker friend in prison, she was disgusted to see that children were also commonly jailed under terrible conditions. She began visiting more mistreated children in jail. She raged at the injustice. She despaired. She grew depressed. Finally, after watching a pitiable young boy hang from the gallows, she went to George Fox and demanded that he prove the existence of God's love.

But George Fox could not. Only she could prove God's love. How could God speak to the human heart? Through the trees? Through the animals? How could God help these children?

George Fox looked at Margaret Fell. "He has only thee."

Margaret Fell burst into tears.

I often feel the same way. In Quaker philosophy, God is not exactly in charge. He has no power to cast us into hell or lift us up to heaven. Heaven and hell are on this earth now. God's love is that Light in each of us, and we will be asked, each of us, to show that love ourselves.

In 1669, nine years after the death of Judge Fell, Margaret Fell and George Fox finally married. They did not spend much time together but were imprisoned themselves for months and years at a time. Margaret Fell lived to be an old, sharp-tongued widow, outlasting two husbands. Other Quakers, less lucky, died for their beliefs—raped, beaten, starved, and hung. There is no guarantee what will happen when you show God's love.

At their best, Quakers believe that the Peaceable Kingdom exists now, and they want to be among those who stand up— who stand in the Light—when that kingdom is threatened. I would never have finally written my letter asking for member- ship to become a Quaker if I had not known real Quakers who actually did this. These men and women were my inspiration, living examples of Quaker history.

Nena MacDonald is the woman who watches over Mike and Carol's son, Dominic, while we bird-band. In 1986, she worked as a nurse at a refugee center in Tucson, Arizona. Along with one of the leaders of the Sanctuary Movement, Jim Corbett, she was indicted for violating immigration law. The two faced years of trial and imprisonment as the Gila Friends Meeting took these Quakers on "as a concern" and "held them in the Light." Even- tually Nena and Jim were acquitted of all charges. Nena, her husband, Steve, and their two children packed up their things, left Tucson, and came to live in the Gila Valley, just down the road from Josephine.

A few years later, in 1990, the United States Congress stopped the deportation of El Salvadoran and Guatemalan refugees and made them eligible for temporary protected status. The Sanctuary Movement was over.

A different kind of conflict was still troubling the rural West, the bitter dispute between ranchers and environmentalists over how to manage huge tracts of public land. Cattle ranchers resented any regulation concerning their right to graze cows in the national forests. Environmentalists accused ranchers of overgrazing the uplands and destroying stream areas. Steve MacDonald is a biologist, and soon after coming to the Gila Valley, he became concerned about the degraded condition of the Gila River. Cows ranged freely throughout the river system, eating new seedlings and shoots of grass, trampling the eroded cut banks, and preventing the growth of vegetation.

I got to know Steve and Nena when I wrote a book about public lands grazing in the early 1990s. I also got to know their friend Jim Corbett, a thin, arthritic man in his sixties with a long, angular face. As a Quaker and former cowboy, Jim could help Central American refugees cross the Sonoran desert because he had grown up in the area and knew it so well. A mix of shepherd and scholar, he was author of the extraordinary book *Goatwalking*, in which he described living for weeks in wild-land areas as a nomadic member of a herd of goats, drinking goat's milk and wandering wherever the herd wandered. Now he was part owner of a small ranch in eastern Arizona with forty cows he was trying to graze ecologically. He called this effort land redemption, "a choice between possessing the earth and trying to enter into a hallowing process." He was the first man I ever knew who quoted Spinoza and one of the most erudite men I will ever know.

By now, I had not been to a Quaker Meeting for a long time. But I enjoyed watching these three Quakers apply their ideas to a dispute that involved almost 70 percent of the American West—the percentage of land still grazed today. I felt privileged to see Quaker beliefs put into practice:

Facing an adversary, try to go into meeting with him. Identify with your opponent; never use a man or woman as a means but as an end. Speak truth to power. Muster within thee all love, tenderness, and concern for the other.

Steve and Nena formed a conservation group called Friends of the Gila River, a name with a double meaning. The group documented how cows were denuding parts of the national forest, places where the river had turned into long sweeps of gravel punctuated by a few old trees. They made phone calls, wrote letters, pole-planted willow, and pointed out where the fences were down. They pushed the Forest Service into enforcing its no-cow policy on a nearby bird refuge. They submitted a petition asking the government to make restoration of the Gila River a priority. Eventually they became part of a Forest Service management team that included ranchers and environmentalists, sportsmen and bureaucrats. They were forceful, but they were also Quakerly. They never demonized the ranchers. "We are all

rural people here," Steve would say. "What we share is important." They never forgot their priorities. "We need to listen,"
Nena would say, "to break down the barriers."

Their counterpart in this effort was Jim Corbett. As a
rancher, his beliefs went beyond just getting along with environmentalists. He insisted that ranching was an important part of
our relationship with the natural world—a world in which we
have become cocreators. Unlike farming, ranching did not rip
up the landscape but had the potential of adapting to its grasslands and forests. "Livelihoods like ranching," Jim would intone
earnestly, as though reading from a lecture, "are microcosms in
which to imitate humanity's ecological task, to discover how to
live at peace with the rest of life on earth."

Friends of the Gila River later evolved into the Upper Gila
Watershed Association, a locally based environmental organization that is still active and meets every month at the nearby
Lichty Ecological Research Center. On Jim's ranch in Arizona,
he formed the Saguaro-Juniper Association, which established
a covenant with the land and a bill of rights, addressing practical concerns such as soil erosion, pesticides, unleashed dogs,
native species, and hunting. Both groups were surprisingly successful in their long-term goals. The Gila River is a different
landscape from what it was fifteen years ago, with new bosques
of cottonwood, sycamore, willow, ash, and walnut up and down
the river, including on the Gila River Farm, where we set up the
bird-banding table and Nets One through Ten. The Saguaro-
Juniper Association remains a model of public lands grazing
and land restoration.

In the summer of 1992, I sat with Jim under the shade of a mesquite tree, talking about cows and much more. Jim and his wife lived nearby in a dingy trailer, surrounded by goat pens, a large garden, and the sound of chickens. That day, Jim quoted Moses Cordovero, a sixteenth-century Jewish kabbalist: "All existence is God, and a stone is a thing pervaded by divinity." (My heart seemed to pause and then went on beating. I had never heard of Moses Cordovero. So why did these words sound so familiar?) He traced Quaker roots to the twelfth century and Spain's cross-fertilization of Moslem-Christian-Jewish mysticism. He spoke of the power of a Quaker community, which gathers in silence to listen for the Light and Love that passeth human understanding. He smiled and nailed me to my chair with Spinoza: "We are all modes in the body of Being. Nothing is outside the Body of Being."

He smiled and recited a passage from his favorite book, *Don Quixote,* and his favorite author, Miguel de Cervantes. Jim happened to look a lot like Cervantes's description of Don Quixote, only with glasses. "Errantry is a sallying out beyond society's established ways," Jim said. By now we had moved inside the trailer after his wife had revved up the swamp cooler. Jim's grip around the coffee cup looked painful, his fingers twisted with arthritis, his toes wrapped around each other. "Unlike formal religion, errantry is wanderings and openings, uncertainties, and beginnings. From the time I turned Quaker, I've never reached a destination."

In 1996, Peter and I and Maria and David sold our small homestead and bought a duplex in Silver City. Maria was

twelve years old. She would forever see this as leaving Eden, a
division in her childhood from the mythical innocence of country to the complexity of town and puberty. Of course, we moved
largely for her, so she could go to a better school. Of course, we
changed her life.

Soon after, I sat on my porch step wondering if I should become a member of my Quaker Meeting. Was I finally ready to
be labeled, boxed in the very box you are thinking of—the one
with the picture of Ben Franklin selling oatmeal? Did I believe
in something called the Light, or was I simply attracted to
Quaker tradition and the far-flung community of Elisabeth and
Josephine, Nena and Steve and Jim Corbett?

In front of me on my porch step was a strip of grass, a sidewalk, a strip of asphalt, more sidewalk, a stone wall, pine trees
and, higher above, electrical wires. Cars drove by. A raven gurgled. White clouds floated in the blue sky. I had my epiphany.
"The Light is all this," I said to myself. The Light was the steps,
the street, the raven, the sky. The Light was everything, the
universe-conceived-of-as-a-whole, mysterious and material and
right here.

At that moment, my understanding of the Light had nothing
to do with El Salvador or human suffering or land redemption.
It was a little inhuman and a lot untested, a tiny experience on
concrete steps in a nice American town where I was safe,
healthy, and happy. No fleas on me.

At the same time, looked at another way, my understanding of
the Light had everything to do with El Salvador and human suffering and land redemption. It had everything to do with my

connection to the world. "I don't like the word religion," Harry, the fighting Jewish Quaker, once said in Meeting. "I don't know what spiritual means. What's spiritual? But I need to take a stand on certain issues, and these are the people I want to stand with."

I wanted to stand in the Light, and I wanted to stand with these people. I wrote my letter asking for membership, met with a Clearness Committee, and went back to attending Quaker Meeting.

Because our Meeting is small, and because there are so many committees, soon after joining the Gila Religious Society of Friends, I became involved in the business of one thing after another. Eventually, I was clerk. "What do I do?" I asked my Quaker friend Ruth, who was a funny woman, and a short one, about five feet tall. ("I come in sample size," she once explained.) Now she replied, "You are the Great Pooh-bah. You don't have to do anything."

She was kidding. As acting clerk of the Gila Religious Society of Friends, my job was an important one: to watch the clock, opening and closing the hour of silence. I also ran the business meeting held once a month and according to my *Quaker Faith and Practice,* a six-hundred-page guide to being a Quaker, was supposed "to enclose obstruction with tenderness" and demonstrate "a spiritual capacity for discernment and sensitivity to Meeting." Such expectations aged me twenty years, which was just about the age I needed to be.

I learned some Quaker jokes:

I am a Quaker. In case of emergency, please be silent.

Why do liberal Quakers sing hymns so badly? Because we are always reading ahead to see if we agree with the words.

So one day Herbert Hoover, a birthright Quaker, was traveling on a train with another man. They passed a flock of grazing sheep. The man remarked, "Look, those sheep have just been sheared." "Yes," Herbert Hoover agreed, a fine example of Quaker caution, "On this side, at any rate."

The jokes weren't so very funny, but they would make any Quaker smile—as we smile at relatives who snore at the Thanksgiving table, call us by someone else's name, and remind us that imperfection is part of being in a family.

Five years passed. It was the start of a new century. I dropped out of Meeting once again. This time, I didn't discuss my decision with anyone. I didn't really make a decision. I just drifted away. Now I am thinking of going back. It seems so irresolute! Not at all the pattern of someone who has stayed in the same marriage for over twenty-five years and in the same job for over twenty, and who has been writing since she was eight years old.

This time, I have some theories about why I left: (1) Quakers can be so earnest, so loopy. They can drive you crazy with their attention to minutiae and process. They can be hypocritical. They talk about being good, but they are not always good. They can be hypercritical. They nitpick. (2) I ran for the local school board, which at that time was leaning heavily to the religious right. Now school board meetings, coupled with university meetings, began to exceed my internal limit for meetings. (3) My back hurt. I had a prolapsed disk. It was painful to sit for as long as an hour. (4) Polly and I went to Guatemala.

Polly and I went to Guatemala in 1998, a few years after the Peace Accords in which the guerrillas and the Guatemalan government agreed to end their thirty-five-year-old civil war. Polly had not yet joined the Meeting then, and she went to Guatemala to see Mayan ruins and be a tourist. I also wanted to see Mayan ruins, as well as talk to Quakers working with the poor. I wanted to see how Guatemalans had survived during those terrible years only a decade ago. I wanted to understand more about violence and social justice.

Before the trip, as is sometimes the case, I read too much. I read about Hector Gomez Calito, a leader in an organization of grieving mothers and wives, relatives of the disappeared. In March 1985, Hector Gomez was burned by a blow torch and his tongue cut out. At his funeral, Rosaria de Cuevas took the microphone to promise that his death would not be in vain. Three days later, Rosaria was found dead, raped and mutilated in a ditch, along with her brother and two-year-old son. At this second funeral, mourners stared at the hands of the baby. His fingernails were missing.

I read about the massacres of the 1980s, the men and women set on fire, leaping into the air. I read about the School of Americas and the manual on torture produced by the American military. I read about the *capucha,* the hood made of rubber that is tightened around a victim's neck until he suffocates. I read about the Mayans a thousand years ago and how they tortured their captives, too, more fingernails pulled out, more skin sliced slowly with knives. Later, when the Spanish conquered the Mayans, they also took prisoners, Mayan lords whom they also mutilated and burned alive. I read and read and filled up with fear.

In the month that Polly and I visited Guatemala, a Mayan leader and his son were dragged from their home and shot; two community leaders were stabbed; a Mayan woman lobbying for land rights was killed; two more activists were tortured and killed; five men were found executed; five more bound and shot at close range; two more dumped in a football field. Dozens of people working for human rights received death threats. Terror and heroism were still part of Guatemala as they had been part of Guatemala for so long, for as long as people wanted something more, something better.

At the Mayan ruins in Tikal, surrounded by temples from the Classic Period, Polly and I talked to our hotel owner, whose father had been executed by a military death squad, and to a guest at the hotel, whose brother and sister-in-law had been killed by guerrillas. In Antigua, we visited a Quaker woman setting up a Montessori day care; for seventy-five dollars, she told us, we could send a child to public school for a year. In Guatemala City, with a Catholic nun as our guide, I dragged Polly through a garbage dump, where diesel fumes and rotting food mixed with the odor of human waste. A man squatted in a corner defecating. He saw us and glared. A truck brought in a new load of garbage as men and women stood and waited to go through it. More angry young men sat on the tires that seemed to be everywhere. The nun led us into a shack, where we met a mother whose fourth child, a girl with polio, was going to college to learn accounting. This woman had gotten up before dawn to wash her clothes for a fee at a public laundry two miles away. She had no water or electricity or toilet. But she had a child in college. She seemed to tremble with hope.

In Guatemala, I learned how much I was willing to help, and it wasn't much. A little money, not much. I learned that I could turn away from children in need. In that turning away, I did not feel separate from anyone, not even those men who torture two-year-olds. For a while I thought I had come to Guatemala to die—not because I was ever endangered but because I felt so much death all around me. How I loved my life when I thought I was going to die in Guatemala! How I missed everything I had so foolishly left behind!

In Guatemala I saw that my children, my husband, my home were all I had. Sleepless in the hotel room, staring up at the ceiling, I swore to myself that I would go back and live my intimate life with integrity and awareness. I would be as luminous as the flame in a candle. But I would also be as small and as extinguishable. I would not be living in the Light. This fear had nothing to do with the Light.

In Guatemala, I learned about selfishness. This self was all I had. My connections were fragile and finite. Without them, I was unanchored. I had no place. I could do nothing for the rest of the world, which was unanchored like me, crashing about. I could not stop the burning of people or the anguish of those young men sitting on tires and waiting for garbage. I could only hunker down. It was not simply that I was not good enough. I did not want to be that good. In Guatemala, I wanted only to rush home, gather my family, and put us all on the bed. Bring up the covers. Hold onto each other.

Instead, I went back to Quaker Meeting and became clerk. I served on the Ministry and Oversight Committee. I took my turn on the Nominating Committee and the Hospitality Committee. I went to a Half-Yearly and Yearly Meeting. I sat in Internet chat rooms with the Committee on Unity with Nature.

But nothing was ever quite the same.

Today at lunch—and let me stop here and marvel at how the years have flown by. I know it is a cliché. But flight seems to be the only metaphor, a sense of speed and blurred scenery. It is 2006, and Josephine and Harry are dead. Jim Corbett is dead. Ruth is dead. Florence is in a nursing home. Nena and Steve and I are on the far side of middle age. Elisabeth is eighty-five, and Polly is seventy-five and will be moving soon to Oregon to be near her daughter. The Meeting is still almost vigorous, with new people writing letters asking for membership. The years have flown by, but Quaker tradition has remained, the very notion of clerks and silence and consensus.

Today at lunch, Elisabeth says my account of how our Meeting started twenty-two years ago is not true. She insists that our resolve did not form that day at Josephine's house but took much longer. "What we said then," she remembers, eating her salad and trying to get the waitress's attention, "is that 'Way will open.' And it did."

I do not contradict her. She could be right. We ask for more coffee. We ask Polly about her cataract operation. Elisabeth and Polly ask me about Maria and David and my current writing project. ("Ah, well," I say, "I'm writing about you. About this lunch.") Elisabeth has some newspaper clippings to share. Of course, she does. Elisabeth has always been the worst of a bad lot, deeply engaged in politics, worried now about the fence the government wants to build on the Mexican-American border, about Fox News and their shamelessly biased reporting, about hunger in the Sudan, about hunger in America. She writes a check now for my local school-based food pantry program. She is constantly writing checks to one charitable organization after another. She has a heart like the Great Plains.

At Quaker Meeting, we chirp about the Light. We want to stand in the Light. We hold people in the Light. I have never heard anyone use its antonym: the dark. I have never seen it capitalized. At the same time, Quakers can seem obsessed with the darkness of what people do to each other. They are acutely aware that something is wrong in the Peaceable Kingdom.

It has been eight years since I went to Guatemala. Today after lunch, walking home, I understand my response a little better—for that small inner voice does not occur just in silence. The universe is either a very bad parent, favoring some children (you get enough to eat, you get love, you get to live in Sweden) and denying others (you get to be raped before you are three, you get to live in a garbage dump), or the universe really does not care about these things. In Guatemala, the indifference of the universe had been too much for me.

Unlike the universe, Quakerism is not indifferent and cares about human suffering. But the Quaker answer to human suffering is not much of a comfort. He has only thee. What human love exists in this world will come from humans. What human understanding exists in this world will come from humans.

The indifference of the universe is not necessarily absolute. Although the universe may not care about us in the particular, it might in a more general way. The Stoics and Spinoza believed that the Logos in us reflected a larger Logos. Mystics believe that the human love in us reflects a larger love. Jim Corbett was something of a mystic, and in his darkest hours as a young man, he felt such a love, a love "or something like love that doesn't split, the way love does, into loving, and being loved."

I walk home through the neighborhoods of Silver City, each house and yard unique, mostly small and mostly beloved, with fillips of paint and landscaping. I realize how much I persist in thinking of the Light as something good and nice. Like Christmas tree lights. Like these little neighborhoods. This may be an idea I have to rethink. Light is also a name for vision, for insight, the act of bringing the unseen into seeing. And what I have to see or rather hold in my mind and body is the enormity of it all: Guatemala and lunch with Elisabeth, the angry man defecating and my son David, joy that is not canceled out by pain and pain that is not canceled out by joy. I have to hold these contradictions the way you hold a trembling bird in the hand. I have to live in a world that doesn't split, the way the world does, into one thing and then another.

There is a Quaker belief that you can lay a thing down if that seems the right thing to do. Today at lunch, neither Elisabeth nor Polly urges me to come back to Meeting. There is no pressure. Way will open.

On June 25, an American kestrel flies into Net Nine. In the same net, Mike finds a dead vermilion flycatcher. This bird species is one of the prettiest on the Gila River Farm, the male the color of a matador's cape: fire truck red, Chinese red for luck. Mike untangles the living kestrel and dead flycatcher and brings them back to the banding table. We theorize that either both birds were caught in the net and the proximity of the kestrel scared the flycatcher to death or that the kestrel had already killed the flycatcher and dropped it in the net when he himself was caught.

With some trepidation, Carol takes North America's smallest falcon out of its cloth bag. Happily the kestrel is not injured, and neither is Carol, and we stare at this predator, which stares back, only inches away.

In raptors, bony shields above each eye angle down to give the bird a fierce and perpetually angry expression. These shields protect the eye from glare, tree limbs, struggling prey, and aggressive nestlings. The kestrel's eyes are large, round, black, and glowing. The hooked beak is short and sharp, ready to stab apart a mouse or vermilion flycatcher. The face is striped white and black, a pattern that also reduces the sun's glare. The shoulders are slate gray, the breast rusty brown with delicate and beautiful black spots. We are not licensed to band this species, and Carol's bander's grip is not going to hold the bird for long. For seconds, then, we feast with our own eyes, taking in the glow, the essence, before she must open her hand.

The kestrel swoops quickly to a nearby cottonwood. Carol examines the dead vermilion flycatcher, takes its measurements, and puts the corpse on the ground near the tree. But the kestrel never reclaims its prey. (This particular dead vermilion flycatcher is a female, not male, drab, not red. I do not think it is my imagination that we mourn a little less.)

Later we will see the falcon and his mate hunt food for their nestlings and hear the shrill *kleee, kleee, kleee* of an unsuccessful pursuit. Young kestrels grow quickly. In two weeks, they are almost as big as adults. Once out of the nest, the fledglings sit and walk about on nearby tree branches while their parents keep feeding them for another week or two. About a month after hatching, the birds take their first flight. We will see some of this, too, the whole family drama of feeding and *kleeing* and waiting and flying, since the kestrel nest is near Net One.

That same day in June, Patricia and I visit Net Three and disturb an unusually large black-tailed rattlesnake that coils under the mesh and shakes its tail, ready to strike. The snake is scared away, but from then on, Net Three remains a source of pride, a cultivated fantasy that our lives, as bird banders, are dangerous and full of adventure.

We also catch and bird-band three Lucy's warblers, two common yellowthroats, four Bewick's wrens, a bridled titmouse, four red-winged blackbirds, a western kingbird, two white-breasted nuthatches, two blue grosbeaks, a brown-headed cowbird, and a yellow-billed cuckoo. We recapture a Bewick's wren, a yellow-breasted chat, a common yellowthroat, a Lucy's warbler, and a blue grosbeak.

CHAPTER 8

Walt Whitman

WHO WOULD NOT want to be a transcendentalist? The very name seems like a promise. In nineteenth-century New England, the American transcendentalists were a group of writers and scholars that included Henry David Thoreau and Ralph Waldo Emerson. They believed human beings had inherent ideas or intuitions that came not from reason but from spirit—from God or God's immanent presence. There was something in us that transcended matter. From most religious viewpoints, this may seem obvious. But the transcendentalists were rebelling against the religion of their day by not endorsing a conventional Christianity. At the same time, they disagreed with the new science or rationalism that based all knowledge on sensory experience. They believed that each of us (women as well as men, black as well as white) had an inner spiritual "body," sometimes called the oversoul, or inner light, or conscience, that corresponded to the body of the external world. Together, the spiritual and physical made a whole.

The transcendentalists were influenced by the romantic poets—particularly Goethe, Coleridge, and Wordsworth—in their celebration of the divine in nature. Forest, pond, mountain, and sky were a beautiful mystery full of symbols and signs that reflected our inner self. As human beings, we embraced this mystery and studied ourselves through studying nature. Most transcendentalists emphasized the present moment rather than a belief in heaven or a supernatural afterlife. God was right here, all around us, in every glen and wood, every wildflower and grain of sand. As Thoreau wrote, "Give me one world at a time."

Thoreau also declared, "I was born to be a pantheist—if that be the name of me." The word pantheism was still a pejorative, and one reviewer complained of Thoreau's first book, "His philosophy, which is the pantheistic egotism vaguely characterized as Transcendental, does not delight us."

At times, the transcendentalists could sound quite Quakerly. They believed in the importance of inner conviction and of listening to that voice within: the voice of intuition, personal communion with the divine spirit, and direct experience. They identified themselves with progressive political movements such as abolition and feminism, which seemed to follow from the belief of "that of God in everyone." In 1838, an early transcendentalist set the tone: "It is only on the reality of this inner light, and on the fact that it is universal, in all men and in every man, that you can found a democracy."

Although universal, the inner light for a transcendentalist was also highly individualistic and could manifest itself in different ways. Members of this elite club prized their independence and did not feel the need to agree with each other. As one of them noted, "We are called like-minded because no two of us think alike."

In his understanding of the larger whole, for example, Emerson privileged spirit over matter. He acknowledged the importance of the material world but went on to affirm something more, a "higher nature." As a pantheist, he would be among the idealists, the Hindus and Buddhists and Neoplatonists, whose traditions he knew well. Everything is God, and God is consciousness.

Thoreau, of course, composed paeans to matter, like the long quote memorized by Mike and once recited to me as we walked to Net Nine: "Matter in its home! I stand in awe of my body, this matter to which I am bound. . . . Talk of mysteries! Think of our life in nature—daily to be shown matter, to come in contact with it—rocks, trees, wind on our cheeks!"

A transcendentalist was as willing to contradict himself as anyone else. At one moment, Thoreau might declare, "My happiness is a good deal like that of the woodchucks," and then in the next, "We soon get through with Nature. She excites an expectation which she cannot satisfy." Perhaps Emerson rationalized this trait best. "A foolish consistency," he wrote, "is the hobgoblin of little minds."

Critics of inconsistency were less impressed. The transcendental movement was short-lived, lasting roughly from 1836 to 1860. Part of the problem seemed to be its lack of coherence and support from other intellectuals. Edgar Allan Poe suggested that the best way to discuss transcendentalism was to use small words but turn them upside down. On his visit to America, Charles Dickens was advised that "whatever was unintelligible would certainly be transcendental." And a 1913 Webster's Dictionary listed transcendentalism as a synonym for "that which is vague and illusive in philosophy."

Maybe. But the legacy of these men and women has proven to be surprisingly strong. Bronson Alcott was a transcendentalist whose ideas on education are still progressive. The feminist Margaret Fuller could be quoted today. Emerson's discussion of language influenced poets like Walt Whitman and Emily Dickinson, and then onward into the twenty-first century. Thoreau's essay on civil disobedience helped inspire Mahatma Gandhi and Martin Luther King, Jr. Moreover, Thoreau's account of two years in a cabin on Walden Pond, a time in which the twenty-eight-year-old tried to live out the themes of transcendentalism, is considered by many the beginning of the environmental movement. For Americans, transcendental ideals of the solitary retreat into nature, the unique spirituality of each individual, and the importance of self-examination and self-expression both reflected and influenced a national ideal.

Of all the transcendentalists, Walt Whitman stated his pantheism most clearly and is the one I blame the most for who I am. Whitman proposed to write an "indigenous" or uniquely American poetry that reflected the country's abundance of resources, energy, ambition, and political idealism. He brought together mysticism and matter and fused them in a fiery circle. He would allow for no separation, certainly not the separation of humanity from the natural world. He infected me when I was young and impressionable with his dreams of democracy and his cries of celebration. His "barbaric yawp" proclaimed that this was our job: to celebrate and be joyous.

I read his long and perhaps best-loved poem, "Song of Myself," like the Book of Psalms. We were all meant to be Walt Whitman, children of the cosmos, male and female, young and old, plantation owner and slave. Like his, our bodies are made of earth and sidewalk. We spread sideways into nature. We burrow into people. Animals adorn us. Plants grow in our ears. We have lived a trillion summers and will live a trillion more. Unlock the doors, unscrew the door jambs, take down the walls! We go naked and undisguised to the riverbank, mad to be in contact with the air that is for our mouth forever. Logic will never convince. Sermons do not convince. The damp of the night drives deeper.

Walt Whitman urged me to connect with the world, and in 1975, a college student at the University of California at Berkeley, I thought I could do it standing on a street corner—behind me a shop that sold falafels in hot pita bread, the taste peppery and exotic, before me a traffic light blinking green and red. Just past the light, I could see the papery trunks of the eucalyptus trees on campus. I knew their sharp medicinal smell. People jostled by. The life of the senses, the life of the mind. I could make contact, naked and undisguised, and I didn't have to go to parties and talk awkwardly with other college students or go on dates and find a boyfriend. I could do it much more easily through the cadence of Whitman's poem. I am the old artillerist.

I am the mashed fireman. I am the captain on deck. I am the mother of captains. The language was a little archaic, but still, it seemed that I *was* all those things. And that the bigger questions about life were answered here or would be answered.

> *And I call to mankind, Be not curious about God,*
> *For I, who am curious about each, am not curious about God;*
> *(No array of terms can say how much I am at peace about God,*
> *and about death.)*
>
> *I hear and behold God in every object, yet understand God not*
> *in the least,*
> *Nor do I understand who there can be more wonderful than*
> *myself.*
>
> *Why should I wish to see God better than this day?*
> *I see something of God each hour of the twenty-four, and each*
> *moment then;*
> *In the faces of men and women I see God, and in my own face*
> *in the glass;*
>
> *I find letters from God dropt in the street—and every one is*
> *sign'd by God's name,*
> *And I leave them where they are, for I know that*
> *Others will punctually come for ever and ever.*

Today, rereading "Song of Myself" (which was originally titled "Walt Whitman" in 1855 and which turns out to be the only poem

I really read in Whitman's collection of poems *Leaves of Grass*), I am still struck by how well he held the enormity of it in his mind and body, in his hand, in his words. He saw God every day. He understood God not at all. Does he contradict himself? Very well, he contradicts himself. We are large and contain multitudes. Joy and pain are braided. With broken breastbone, the mashed fireman lies on the cold earth. The voices of his comrades hush. Elsewhere, the judge also proclaims the death sentence in a hushed voice. Elsewhere, stevedores shout, "Heavy-e-yo," and strong men laugh and homely girls croon to babies. Agonies. Good times. The procreant urge.

Elsewhere, everywhere, birds, wheat, whales, cows, and blackberries. A leaf of grass, the egg of a wren. We could live with these cows all day long. We are staggered and triumphant. We are braided into nature. We are reflected there. Celebrate every part, mollusk and hat.

> *Dazzling and tremendous, how quick the sunrise would kill*
> *me,*
> *If I could not now and always send sun-rise out of me.*
>
> *We also ascend, dazzling and tremendous as the sun;*
> *We found our own, my Soul, in the calm and cool of the*
> *daybreak.*

In southwestern New Mexico, we wait for the monsoon season, the rains that fall in the months of July, August, and September. The monsoons provide us with half our annual precipitation, which still adds up to only fifteen inches a year in Silver City and twelve inches a year in the Gila Valley. Commonly, the thunderclouds build up in the afternoon, growing darker and heavier until they drop their burden like a woman throwing water from a saucepan, hard and focused on a few choice spots, with flashes of lightning to make the humans run to shut down their computers. We hope to have rain now in the Gila Valley every day for some sixty days. We hope for the majority of our annual, meager twelve inches of rain, and we are always anxious that we might get less, that the rains will not be good this year or may not come at all.

The skies are tremendous, the clouds huge and masted flat-bottomed ships. Fleet after fleet set out for conquest. Majesty embodied. This is true democracy, beauty for everyone. You don't have to be rich or successful or good. You don't have to live by the ocean or in the middle of wilderness. This is drop-dead gorgeous scenery, the ephemeral version of prime real estate. This could be your ticket to a mystical experience, and the show runs through the rest of summer, almost every day. This is a grandeur that most of us, most of the time, barely notice, looking up and then away, intent on some errand.

Cumulus clouds form when the sun heats the earth. Packets of warm air rise from the ground, cool, and condense. The cloud's flat base is the level where condensation begins, as the rest of the air continues to rise into stacks of puffy white balls. Fair-weather cumulus often line up in cloud streets, clouds on a string stretching hundreds of miles, clouds following each other like ducklings. They live for five, ten, thirty minutes. They are low, perhaps a mile high, and small, perhaps a city block.

In the monsoon season, however, in less stable conditions, these packets of warm air rise through rapidly dropping temperatures, and the cloud develops higher and more vertically, with peaks and towering cliff walls. Inside the cloud, there is further rising and falling, condensation, coalescence, until water droplets become heavy enough to fall. In cloud language, the word nimbus means rain, and a cumulus cloud has just become a cumulonimbus, perhaps seven miles in height and several miles wide. High-altitude winds shear its top, the anvil from which trails of ice crystals or cirrus clouds spin out in thin, fibrous wisps, also called mare's tails. Electrical energy builds up as water and ice particles are repeatedly split and separated. Suddenly there is a flash, brightness, cracks, and rumbles. The force of ten Hiroshima-sized bombs can be released in a single thunderstorm. The Greeks were not wrong to imagine gods.

I walk Sacaton Mesa surrounded by cloud streets, cloud turrets, a small cloud East Asian art museum, cloud doorways arched and dissolving. It is architecture on the move. A storm builds in the east. The cloud cliffs grow taller. The prow of a ship crashes into another. Already there is rain over the Mogollon Mountains, the line clear between where water is falling and where it is not. Already I should turn back and hurry home if I do not want to get soaking wet.

I feel what the transcendentalists might have called a correspondence. This beauty is not a doorway into something better. This beauty is my other half. This sky, this majesty, is my other self. I feel the yearning to reunite, join with the sky. In some way, we reflect each other. I am transparent, and the clouds pass through me. I have felt this before on Sacaton Mesa, and I am careful now not to get too excited or try to hold onto the moment with words. The Quaker tradition of silence works best. There is something under the words. There is something calm and whole under the words.

At the banding station on Sunday morning, July 10, we hardly catch anything. A Lucy's warbler, two red-winged blackbirds, a brown-crested flycatcher, and two brown-headed cowbirds. We recapture a Lucy's warbler and a blue grosbeak. We complain about the mosquitoes at Net Nine and count our bites. In birder language, fondle list refers to the birds that someone has personally handled as a bander. We talk about our fondle list. We don't have much else to do but talk, and then Sarah does an imitation. She hops and stops and hops and stops, and we must guess. Finally, someone says robin. Next, Carol does a credible wren. Peter follows with a pigeon. He has all the moves, the back-and-forth neck, the puffing breast. Carol counters with a towhee, jerky, robotic, a little scary. Most of us are laughing quite hard by now at the comedy of someone so large trying to act like fifteen ounces. The human body just looks silly hunting for worms.

On July 16, we have a little more luck, banding three lesser goldfinches, a Bewick's wren, two bridled titmice, a black-headed grosbeak, two hairy woodpeckers, a blue grosbeak, two ash-throated flycatchers, a house finch, and a lazuli bunting. We recapture a blue grosbeak.

My personal prize is the male hairy woodpecker, which I disentangle from Net Three while holding my breath and thinking good thoughts. Woodpeckers, of course, are always personable with their erect stance, thoughtful probing, and energetic tapping like a very good carpenter going about the business of fixing up your house—fixing up the world. Tap, tap, tap. The hairy woodpecker has a white breast, a masked face, black-and-white patterned wings, and a red cap. The males incubate the eggs at night, the females in the day. My hairy woodpecker tries to peck me with his long bill and looks annoyed at this interruption of his day. He has work to do.

In Net Four is our first lazuli bunting of the season. This migratory songbird is small, under six inches. Each male two years and older has a unique song, only one, which he developed by listening to other males, combining certain fragments and synthesizing his personal arrangement. The head of the male is brilliant turquoise, with other shades of blue on his wings, tail, and lower breast—the upper breast a rusty orange red. The female is commonly described as dull brown. I have never been much interested in jewelry, but the male lazuli bunting is the wire to that electric socket, plugging me into an obsession long part of human culture. I want to wear this blueness, too. I want to keep this blueness close to me, around my neck or in my hair. I feel the correspondence, my other half, but this time with a sense of possession. I covet a blue feather. Who will ever know?

As a child, Walt Whitman absorbed a Quaker sensibility through his grandmother, described by the nature writer John

Burroughs (a companion to Whitman in his later years) as a Quakeress with a sweet character, deeply intuitive and spiritual, as well as being a good housewife. Neither Whitman's mother nor father ever joined the Religious Society of Friends, but they were freethinkers who participated in Quaker culture.

Whitman's parents particularly admired Elias Hicks, the charismatic Quaker preacher at the center of the nineteenth-century break between those Quakers who believed in the tradition of silent worship and direct personal experience and those who wanted more words, more structure, and more external authority in their church. Elias Hicks was a gentle man who understood suffering, having watched each of his four sons die of the same mysterious disease. He promoted the eternal Inward Christ and rejected any material or historical version: His Jesus was an inner law, nothing less. In 1827, at a Meeting in Philadelphia, the preacher said almost thoughtlessly, "The blood of Christ—the blood of Christ—why, my friends, the actual blood of Christ in itself is no more effectual than the blood of bulls and goats—not a bit more—not a bit." The audience sat stunned, and then hundreds stood to mutter, shout, and thump their canes. Some Quakers left. Some stayed to argue or listen more carefully.

The moment marked an important Quaker schism. The Hicksites, or unprogrammed Quakers, emphasized the original ideas promoted by George Fox. There is that of God in everyone, a reflection or correspondence to the Universal Spirit that reveals its truth to each of us, even difficult or seemingly blasphemous truths. The Orthodox, or programmed, Quakers preferred a reliance on outside sources, specifically the Bible, as well as the authority of church elders who had the power to dictate behavior and belief.

In 1829, a ten-year-old Walt Whitman listened to Elias Hicks's last public performance in a handsome building in the city of New York. Sixty years later, the poet still remembered that night, how his father had come into the kitchen and thrown down a pile of kindling blocks so that they bounced on the floor. "Come, Mother! Elias preaches tonight." At this, Mother hurried the supper, found a babysitter for the younger children, and—because Walt had been behaving especially well—agreed the boy could accompany them. Whitman entered "a cheerful gay-color'd room with glass chandeliers bearing myriads of sparkling pendants," where the Quaker preacher stood tall and straight with an expansive forehead, large black eyes, and long white hair. Behind him, facing the audience, sat a dozen or more Friends, most of them old, grim-looking, and still wearing their broad-brimmed hats. A few women also sat on the stage in Quaker dress and bonnet.

Elias Hicks began slowly and emphatically with the question "What is the chief end of Man?" After that, Walt could hardly follow the preacher's speech, which became fervid and pleading, tender and agonizing, "a magnetic stream of natural eloquence, before which all minds and natures, all emotions, high or low, gentle or simple, yielded entirely."

Walt Whitman yielded more than most, and the preacher's natural eloquence would eventually play a role in the poet's own work. Elias Hicks believed that nature reflected the Light, which filled the entire world. So he could proclaim that "the fullness of the godhead dwelt in every blade of grass." In Whitman's "Song of Myself," the poet would "lean and loafe at my ease observing a spear of summer grass," which then became the flag of his disposition, the handkerchief of the Lord, a child, a hieroglyphic, and the uncut hair of graves. Hicks believed that heaven and hell were what we experienced right now. In "Song of Myself," Whitman would write that there is never "any more heaven or hell than there is now." For both men, revelation was ongoing, continually available to every human being, even the lowliest. The entire manuscript *Leaves of Grass* would testify to that power, the power of this moment, this time, this world.

In his preface to *Leaves of Grass,* Whitman prescribed what might have been an idealized biography of Hicks's life, as well as his own:

> This is what you shall do. Love the earth and sun and the animals, despise riches, give alms to everyone who asks, stand up for the stupid and crazy, devote your income and labor to others, hate tyrants, argue not concerning God, have patience and indulgence toward the people, take off your hat to nothing known or unknown, or to any man or number of men—go freely with powerful uneducated persons, and with the young, and with the mothers of families—re-examine all you have been told in school or church or in any book, and dismiss whatever insults your own soul; and your very flesh shall be a great poem, and have the richest fluency, not only in its words, but in the silent lines of its lips and face, and

between the lashes of your eyes, and in every motion and joint of your body.

It is essential Whitman that we move in a long sentence from the earth and sun to the skin between eyelashes. The poet greatly admired the human body, and although the release of *Leaves of Grass* in 1855 was first met with praise, critics were soon pointing with disgust to those passages that celebrated sexuality. The poems were "a mass of stupid filth," "bombast, egotism, vulgarity, and nonsense," and the writer was "some escaped lunatic, raving in pitiable delirium." Even Thoreau, who also praised the work, complained, "It is as if the beasts spoke."

But Whitman never wavered. In the coming decades, he continued to revise, expand, and republish his poorly selling manuscript. He sometimes lived in poverty. He was sometimes depressed, lost in his soul and in his relationships. Sometimes he wrote bad poetry—didactic and stiff, glorifying an increasingly mechanized and can-do America. But he never denied what the Light whispered to him about the beauty of physical love, the beauty of flesh, the sensuous details of being human.

He did, of course, deny his yearning for other men. In his poetry and prose, Whitman seemed to write frankly about male-male love, only to say later that sexuality was not what he was talking about, or that maybe it was, but he wasn't sure, "perhaps I do not know what it all means—perhaps never did know." Throughout his long life, he fell in love with younger men but never gave a hint as to what progressed from those first chaste kisses. Some scholars believe that in 1841 the twenty-two-year-old Whitman, then a schoolteacher in Long Island, was actually charged with sodomizing his teenage pupils. According to local history, a small-town mob dragged the teacher from his hiding place, tarred and feathered him, and rode him on a rail. Seriously injured, Whitman left the area, soon left teaching, and stopped writing for half a year. The evidence for this event is hardly conclusive. But the story works symbolically. The poet beat the drum for the common man, he boasted of his universal acceptance, his vigor and his manliness—perhaps even, he protesteth too much—but he also wrote about exclusion and shame. He understood despair and betrayal. He understood self-betrayal. He lived a divided life.

Above all, he lived through a time of national division and darkness, the Civil War, when there was plenty of pain and suffering to go around. Moving to Washington, D.C., in 1862, Whitman became "an angel of mercy," visiting injured soldiers in hospitals, bringing them treats, wiping their foreheads, and holding their hands. The misery was unrelenting. The slow speed and heavy weight of Civil War bullets shattered bones and ripped out flesh. Following a hasty amputation—in which virtually nothing was sanitized—infection was the norm: pyemia, septicemia, tetanus, gangrene. Dysentery was said to have killed nearly one hundred thousand people, and Whitman would tell a friend that the war was "about nine hundred and ninety-nine parts diarrhea to one part glory." Doctors often made matters worse by bleeding, leeching, binding, chafing, and overprescribing a horrific array of drugs. Most awful was the liberal use of calomel, which caused mercury poisoning and the occasional mercurial gangrene, rotting the soft tissues of the mouth. (Bronson Alcott's daughter, the writer Louisa May Alcott, was also a nurse in a Washington, D.C., hospital. After being dosed with calomel for typhoid fever, she lost most of her hair and teeth and remained tormented the rest of her life by pains in her arm and back.)

In this particular hell on earth, heroism was matter-of-fact and everyday. Holding Whitman's hand, the young men died without complaint. They died with a tender kiss. They died needlessly but bravely. Eventually Whitman's volunteer work affected his health, and he began to suffer dizziness, weakness, and headaches. He may have gotten an infection from a gangrenous scalpel. He may have been dosed with calomel. Within ten years, now in his fifties, he had a debilitating stroke and declined into an early old age. Later he would say that the hospital work both ruined him physically and saved his life. For in these young men, in those waves of men, in sweet smile after sweet smile, in death after death, he saw his optimism justified. He experienced firsthand a breadth of spirit, generosity, stoicism, and true celebration. His earlier words from "Song of Myself" were now proved prophetic: "All goes onward and outward, nothing collapses. And to die is different from what any one supposed, and luckier."

The relationship between Whitman's poetry and his life was not always so pure or consistent. *Leaves of Grass* was what Walt Whitman wanted to be, written as a guide and game plan, before he had the opportunity to become that self. He knew his creation was artificial. He warned his readers that he was not always what he seemed. He hid his flaws when he could. He was occasionally confused. Perhaps he did not know himself what it all meant—perhaps never did know. I like his uncertainty as much as the rest.

For a pantheist, it comes down to this: As part of the larger whole, we are called upon to celebrate our existence in the universe, no matter what and who we are, blessed or not, whole or broken, deserving or undeserving. What is the alternative? We are braided into pain and joy, darkness and light. We are braided into nature, reflecting the sky. We transcend the material, the everyday, for we know these things themselves to be transcendent. We are called on to rejoice. Who calls us? We preach to ourselves. A child of the cosmos. Here we stand.

Soon after we moved from the country into town, when my daughter, Maria, was thirteen years old, we brought home two kittens: two brothers, yellow and black, Andy and Moon. Moon became a large, muscular, charming fellow who would lie next to my keyboard and bat my moving fingers, not helping me write but directly interfering. *Me,* he would say languidly, insistently. A black blissful Buddha. Celebrate *me.*

This year, before the mid-July bird banding, Moon begins to lose weight. At the veterinarian's office, they run tests. Perhaps he has an infection or leukemia. Perhaps he has been poisoned. We try this and that, Moon gets skinnier and skinner, and then we realize that he is dying. There is nothing to do but make his death more comfortable. Just before the euthanasia, Maria and I stroke the black cat, who by now cannot move his legs, who looks at me for the last time, panting as his systems fail. He is miserable and scared in a way I have never seen him scared before.

A pet dies, and you are not sure how to experience this sorrow. How much can you grieve? Whom are you grieving for?

The idea of poison lingers unpleasantly. The vet explains that this poison could have come from anywhere, that we are surrounded by poison, in our garages and homes, the cupboard, the bathroom. As a cat who spent time indoors and out, Moon was often exposed to cleaning products like bleach or cleanser. He could have eaten the stray pill—a single Tylenol is enough to kill a small animal. He could have drunk water carrying spilled insecticide. He could have brushed a plant drenched with weed killer and then licked his fur. He lived in a miasma of toxicity, just as we do.

On July 23, we catch a common yellowthroat, a western wood pewee, two Bewick's wrens, two bridled titmice, a brown-crested flycatcher, a yellow-breasted chat, a white-breasted nuthatch, a blue grosbeak, and a mourning dove. We recapture a blue grosbeak.

In Net Eight, we also untangle the federally endangered willow flycatcher, which we cannot band because Mike and Carol do not have a license to band endangered species. The southwestern willow flycatcher is disappearing from the world because rivers are disappearing or changing too much to support native wildlife. Despite its diversions of water for irrigation, the Gila River remains one of the last best places for these birds, of which there are only a thousand breeding pair left.

A few days later, Peter gets very sick. The Sunday before, after lunch and bird banding, we had watched a muskrat sit forever on a log on the Nature Conservancy pond. I had rubbed my fingers with the petals of a chocolate flower, a pretty daisy that actually smells like a Hershey bar. On our evening walk, we saw a great horned owl. Like so many others, this weekend was strung on a chain of small good moments—and then on Tuesday Peter is groaning. He has never experienced such pain in his arms and legs. There is fever and a strange rash. We go to a doctor. He does tests. Perhaps this is shingles, the reoccurrence of the chicken pox virus. Or hanta virus, a potentially fatal pulmonary disease caught by exposure to infected rodents. Or some other virus.

We wait for results on West Nile virus, which begins to seem the most likely candidate. West Nile virus is carried by certain species of mosquitoes that breed in open ponds and puddles, as well as by a common house mosquito found in city drains and sewers. The house mosquito is the more effective carrier, particularly during drought. In hot, dry spells, stagnant urban pools become rich with the rotting material required by the insects. The pools attract birds, on which the mosquitoes feed, and these birds carry the disease elsewhere. High temperatures speed up the development of the virus in the mosquito, increasing the chance that the virus will reach a mature stage while its host is still alive. In nonurban areas, a similar process occurs, the mosquitoes' natural predators—frogs, dragonflies, and lacewings—dying off as the drought continues. Serious outbreaks first began in Uganda in 1937, then Israel in the 1950s, and Romania in 1996—always following unusually hot weather. The first recorded case in the United States was in New York in 1999. Only six years later, the virus had spread to California and up into Canada.

This is a disease with subtext, symbol of a changing world in which we hear daily about the consequences of global warming. Increasingly dry summers mean ever more cases of West Nile virus, and that doesn't seem about to end soon. As the world gets hotter and as floods and droughts become more common, other diseases—malaria, cholera, dengue fever, and Lyme disease— are also traveling north to newly hospitable environments. Infectious diseases are resurging, reappearing, and emerging in places they were never seen before. Moreover, in the last thirty years, the World Health Organization has identified thirty new diseases, a veritable explosion that can be compared to the time of the Industrial Revolution and the sudden crowding of people into cities.

West Nile virus is not actually very dangerous. Eighty percent of its hosts feel no symptoms and fewer than one percent have serious complications such as encephalitis and meningitis. Some people do die: 177 in the United States in 2006. The response has been largely to get rid of mosquitoes by massive spraying with insecticide. Another idea is to drain areas where mosquitoes live. When the Nature Conservancy on the Gila River Farm wanted to create a second pond as additional wetland for the greater sandhill crane, one neighbor immediately protested, "But won't that bring in West Nile virus?" And, naturally, Peter and I think now, "Oh, those mosquitoes by Net Nine."

In the next week, Peter seems to be getting worse. We debate one night whether or not to go to the emergency room. We call two friends who are doctors for advice. One says Peter is dehydrated and should drink water. One says Peter is dehydrated and should get an IV at the local hospital. Peter refuses to go. I gauge the extent of his resistance. I can't quite see myself forcing him out the door, perhaps carrying him in the fireman's position. Neither of us wants to overreact or look foolish.

The very next day, the crisis is over, and Peter starts feeling better, although slowly. The tests come back negative. This was not West Nile virus. Our doctor doesn't really know what it was, except for something a little new and odd.

As Walt Whitman got older, his instinct to celebrate included even the industrial society of the post–Civil War with its growing mechanization of agriculture, overpopulated cities, and marvels like the Suez Canal and transcontinental railroad. Certainly, Whitman believed that America had a profound and glorious destiny. "A new worship I sing . . . you engineers, you architects, you machinists, yours." With these machinists and engineers, Americans would reach an even greater cultural and spiritual harmony. Sometimes the poet faltered in this belief. The wealth permitted by the new technology also brought new class divisions and political corruption. Urban poverty was replacing pastoralism. The skies were dirtier, much like the rivers and streams. Perhaps we were on the wrong track? Then Whitman rallied. We would do nature proud.

Other men of his generation disagreed. In 1864, the brilliant and self-taught scholar George Perkins Marsh published a book detailing the impact of a society rapidly cutting down its forests, destroying its topsoil, and polluting its water. "The ravages committed by man subvert the relations and destroy the balance which nature has established," Marsh thundered, "and she avenges herself upon the intruder by letting loose her destructive energies." The visionary predicted an impoverished earth with "shattered surface," "climatic excesses," and the extinction of many species, perhaps even our own.

Within a few decades, between 1870 and 1900, the population in America would double. At the turn of the century, some four thousand cars were on the road. In 1919, the Ford factories alone produced nearly one million. Life seemed to speed up. Progress had its own momentum.

Even as we changed the natural world, we mourned what was being lost. In the early twentieth century, nature writing became commercially popular and deeply sentimental—although the movement also included a revival of Thoreau and gifted new authors like John Muir, founder of the Sierra Club and one of the first activists in the new field of conservation. By now it was impossible for thinking men and women to enjoy a pantheistic celebration of nature without also thinking of "the ravages committed by man." Early in his career, Muir had written sadly, and softly, "Are not all plants beautiful? Or in some way useful? Would not the earth suffer from the banishment of a single weed? The curse must be within ourselves." By 1907, he was considerably more exercised: "These temple destroyers, devotees of ravaging commercialism, seem to have a perfect contempt for Nature, and, instead of lifting their eyes to the God of the mountains, lift them to the Almighty Dollar!"

Since then, the alarm bells have become a siren. We all know that sound. The sky is tilted if not yet fallen. "Give me one world at a time," Thoreau wrote. And that happened. We were given the world. We rejoice still. It's a lovely planet. But we feel the irony. A child of the cosmos. Here we stand.

CHAPTER 9

The Mind and Body of God

DESPITE OUR ANXIETY, the summer rains do come. It is what we call a good year, with lots of thunderstorms, mud in the driveway, and the river rising to swamp the beaver dam. Up and down the valley, the seed bank in the soil responds quickly. Shoots of grasses and forbs push up every day. The rolling hills dotted with juniper become carpeted with a numinous green. And there is the usual comment: "It looks just like Ireland." We try to say this as a joke, or perhaps with sophistication, as though recently back from a tour of the UK. But we can't pull it off. Because, to us, it does look like Ireland. It looks like a foreign country, amazingly and newly colored. A child has come along with her Crayola. Now we are emerald. Now we are transformed.

This August, I have a new mantra as I take my weekend walks on Sacaton Mesa or up the road into the national forest. I am walking through the Mind and Body of God. This is a rephrasing of Spinoza, who shocked his Jewish elders when he suggested that God was a kind of body—that the body of the world was God. It is easy to believe when you are surrounded by a 360-degree view, the Mogollon Mountains rearing north like friendly giants, the rumpled foothills of Black Mountain south in a catlike stretch, all those clouds, all that space, and the undulating rise and fall of land flowing out in mysterious movement, a mysterious lack of sound, and then more mountains—more shapes in the distance, more sky, and the shivery sense that this will never end.

I am walking through the Mind and Body of God. It is easy to believe down by the river, in the bosque of green cottonwoods and willow, a kind of intimate room—and there, in the center of the room, a gorgeous mound of jimsonweed, also called sacred datura, also called thorn apple and moonflower. The large blue-green leaves exude health, not often attacked by insects or other herbivores, and the large, trumpet-shaped, lavender white flowers exude a sweet, powerful scent, a favorite destination for the equally large and extravagant sphinx or hawkmoth. Here in the Southwest, I have grown up with sacred datura, and I know that every leaf and petal are poisonous, causing blindness, hallucinations, and death. I know the stories, how the Hopis, Zunis, and Navajos once used this plant for spiritual vision, how Anglo teenagers use it still for a cheap high. Most recently, three young people in southern New Mexico went out into the desert and made datura tea. Two died. The third stumbled home, delirious, forever changed. Especially at dusk, the flowers seem to glow. They radiate power.

I am walking through the Mind and Body of God. It is easy to believe when surrounded by mountains and moonflowers, by the Other which is my other half, which is also my source, where I came from, which is also my completion, what I will become.

I am walking through the Mind and Body of God. I like to think this walking through the streets of Silver City, too, all the different colors of paint and metal, straight lines, people, plants, trees, and cars mixed together. It seems so busy, not quiet like the hawk hunting the field. Someone waves. Someone speaks. I am walking through the Mind and Body of God. I like to think this as I pass a compound of three trailers and a shack in the small community of Gila, New Mexico. This is rural poverty, the yard full of junk and litter, a window broken, and the girl on the step looking sad. The girl breaks the spell. What happened? Why does she screw her face like that, as though holding back tears? I am walking through the Mind and Body of God. I would like to think this everywhere, in Lagos, in Baghdad and San Salvador, but it really works best on Sacaton Mesa or down by the river.

In college, I believed in the magic of the book. I was a disciple. This was real. I entered the language of a writer like Virginia Woolf; she entered my bloodstream—her syntax a shot of glucose; and then I knew what she knew. I absorbed, effortlessly, her powers and wisdom. Now her vision was mine: how consciousness moves with animal steps from person to person, how we are we all netted together in these dazzling connections, how everything is important, everyone is important and part of something profound.

I was drawn to the pantheists, although I didn't know that word, didn't know much about philosophy or history or religion. Really, I hardly knew anything at all.

I did not like the novelist D. H. Lawrence, whose pantheism was so fierce and angry and sexual. I have a memory of standing in the university bookstore, stuck in a passage of *Lady Chatterley's Lover*, thinking, "That can't be what a woman's orgasm is really like?" and then, "He can't be describing the only kind there is?" I didn't like his obsession with male power versus female power, his adoration of the phallus—"'So proud,'" one of his female characters murmured uneasily. "'And so lordly!'" I didn't like his rants or his arrogance. I knew he would not like me either. We would clash at any dinner table, and he would win. I would be annihilated.

Even so, I worked the voodoo. I gulped him down. And I saw what D. H. Lawrence saw, forever waking from an enormous egotism, waking and starting, noticing the world—and then embracing that world. He had his relationship with the fox. He had his relationship with the rooster. He was emotional and wordy. (Perhaps this reminded me of me.) In *Lady Chatterley's Lover*, the gentlewoman Connie—so tediously infatuated with the gamekeeper's penis—also falls hard for a domestic hen and her brood: "The slim little chick was grayish-brown with dark markings, and it was the most alive little spark of a creature in seven kingdoms. . . . Connie crouched to watch in a sort of ecstasy.

Life, life! Pure, sparky, fearless new life! New Life! So tiny and so utterly without fear!"

He wrote, I see now, with too many exclamation marks. He crouched under a pine tree and watched and wrote in a sort of ecstasy, aware of that pine tree as another living, intelligent, *experiencing* form: "And we live beneath it, without noticing. Yet sometimes, when one looks far up and sees those wild doves . . . one realizes that the tree is asserting itself as much as I am. It gives out life, as I give out life! Our two lives meet and cross one another, unknowingly: the tree's life penetrates my life, and my life the tree's."

He didn't stop with celebration. A young man at the beginning of the twentieth century, Lawrence saw the first appearance of the motor car, telephone, movie, airplane, and radio—and he had deep suspicions about this modern world. He asked the questions "Is it truer to life to insulate oneself entirely from the influence of the tree's life, and to walk about in an inanimate forest of standing lumber, marketable in St. Louis, Mo.? Or is it truer to life to know, with a pantheistic sensuality, that the tree has its own life, its own assertive existence?" He insisted, "Which is really truer? Which is truer, to live among the living, or to run on wheels?"

He lived with passion and surety, and he said so many clever and so many stupid things, and I would throw his books down, and pick them up again. We had a relationship.

I read Virginia Woolf quite differently. She was the river. I was the raft. Probably I should stop for a moment. Was Virginia

Woolf a pantheist? Perhaps no one else but me thinks so. You say tomato, I say tomato. I will argue that her novels supposed an interconnected Unity that she found numinous. I will argue on safer ground that she entered my bones, like Walt Whitman, and made me who I am.

In Woolf's novel *Mrs. Dalloway,* the point of view floats in less than ten pages from the wife of mad Septimus, a soldier who survived World War I, to Maisie Johnson, a girl on the street just up from Edinburgh, to Mrs. Dempster, "a little stout, a little slack, feeding squirrels in the park," to Mr. Bentley rolling up a strip of turf and thinking how aeroplanes are a symbol of man's soul, his determination "to get outside his body, beyond his house, by means of thought, Einstein, speculation, mathematics, the Mendelian theory—away the aeroplane shot." Next we are in the mind of the subtle and upper-class Mrs. Dalloway shopping for a party she is giving that night, an affair that would never include Septimus or Mrs. Dempster. A larger consciousness is implied, one in which we play our part. Just a few pages before, a motor car drives through London, and consciousness ripples in its wake, too. We see the car and think about the origins of the universe, the origin of London, the future of London when it is a grass-grown path. Past and future are in the present. The birds sing in Greek. Einstein. Mendel. Mrs. Dalloway's party. Nothing is trivial. Look up! The aeroplane is spelling something in the sky. "T . . . O . . . F . . . "

Similarly in Woolf's novel *The Waves,* a young girl becomes the field and barn and trees: "I cannot be divided or kept apart."

She is the hare who leaps aside at the last moment. She is the light that falls on the wooden gate.

Not insignificantly, in Virginia Woolf, I heard—and hear now—a woman's voice. As with most of history, to write about Western ideas of pantheism is to write about what men were thinking, what men were saying, what men were doing. Of course, women were somewhere, too, thinking and saying and doing something. But invisibly, for all the obvious reasons. Now we are in a bigger room. The other half of the human race has joined the party.

When I was in college at the University of California at Berkeley, the library stacks were hidden in secret rooms. You had to pass through a turnstile, show your ID, and creep up a series of narrow circular stairs to the floor you wanted. Floor after floor, aisle after aisle, row after row. Few other students seemed to visit this part of the literature section. There always seemed to be dust motes floating in a shaft of light. There always seemed to be another book to read. These writers never seemed to have died or to have stopped writing. I can still feel in my hand the heft of a small blue volume, perhaps Woolf's lyrical novel *To the Lighthouse,* or something red and heavier, Lawrence's *The Rainbow* or *The Plumed Serpent.* The air was darkened as in a confessional. But the intimacy here went both ways. The priests whispered their secrets to me.

Drawn to the pantheists, I read the poet Robinson Jeffers, who lived most of his life on the coastline of Big Sur some 150 miles south of my college apartment. Big Sur was and is outrageously beautiful, a national forest and wilderness area of pine and red-skinned madrone tumbling down to cliffs above a turquoise sea. Using this landscape as his setting, Jeffers wrote long narrative poems about incest and parricide and sexual abuse. Reading these poems, I was puzzled. I had assumed that natural beauty would bring out the best in humans. Jeffers seemed determined to show the opposite. He put his characters in the middle of unspoiled splendor and then let them behave very badly. I kept reading, shocked, resistant, and only later began to understand—how much history supports his case.

Jeffers took a dim view of human achievement. We were temporary. We were not as important as we thought. Even our greatest good and evil were only "excesses that balance each other like the paired wings of a flying bird." Our redemption could be found only outside ourselves, when we fell "in love outward" and entered emotionally and imaginatively into the natural world. The poet's understanding of this world was based on his understanding of science, and he often used scientific terms in his work, a device that irritated some critics.

In 1934, in a letter to a friend, Jeffers wrote a statement that could serve as a model for today's scientific pantheism:

> I believe that the universe is one being, all its parts are different expressions of the same energy, and they are all in communication with each other, therefore parts of one organic whole. (This is physics, I believe, as well as religion.) The parts change and pass or die, people and races and rocks and stars; none of them seems to me important in itself, but only the whole. The whole is in all its parts so beautiful, and

is felt by me so intensely in earnest, that I am compelled to love it and to think of it as divine. It seems to me that this whole alone is worthy of the deeper sort of love, and that there is peace, freedom, I might say a kind of salvation, in turning one's affections outward toward this one God, rather than inwards on one's self or on humanity or on human imagination and abstractions. . . . I think that it is our privilege and felicity to love God for his beauty, without claiming or expecting love from him. We are not important to him, but he is to us.

In the mid-1970s, this manifesto of pantheism would be discovered and quoted by the deep ecologist George Sessions. The term deep ecology had only recently been used to describe an ecological consciousness and spiritual approach to environmental concerns. The founders of deep ecology, Arne Naess and George Sessions, were influenced by Spinoza, whom they saw as an important figure in the tradition of what Aldous Huxley called the perennial philosophy: a belief in the seamless whole of God, nature, and humanity. Deep ecologists emphasized Spinoza's direct knowledge of God/Nature and took his intellectual love of God to mean a self-realization in which the self is not the personal ego but an identification with the larger organic Self—with all of life on earth. The corollary was that all living things had an equal right to fulfill their own potential. Human beings had no special right to disrupt the richness of the non-human world except to satisfy vital needs. (This reinterpretation of Spinoza left out his belief that all beings seek their own advantage. In fact, Spinoza saw nothing wrong with using or misusing other species.)

George Sessions described Spinoza as the closest the West had ever come to a rational and scientific statement of mysticism, and he saw the poet Robinson Jeffers as Spinoza's "twentieth-century evangelist." Jeffers had the advantage of knowing more science than Spinoza, from the nature of stars to subatomic particles, and he lived in a coastal Eden, not a rented room outside Amsterdam. He also saw the first use of nuclear weapons, and he wrote poems in protest of World War II and all wars. Shaped by a different time and place, his acute awareness of the destructive nature of humanity made him an advocate for the idea inherent in deep ecology: that our excessive consumption and interference with the natural world was a grave spiritual error.

In 1976, I graduated from Berkeley with a bachelor of science degree in conservation and natural resources. I could discourse on such topics as ecopsychology and ecotheology. I was reading Native American literature as well as the early pantheists of the twentieth century. I knew that I wanted to write. But what should I write about? Foxes, I thought. Hawks. I was a child of apartment buildings and swimming pools, the disconnected suburbs of Phoenix. Still I had taken a class in wildlife management from Starker Leopold, Aldo Leopold's son. I had written papers about the elephants in Africa's Tsavo Park and the minnow that stopped a dam in Tennessee. I had walked a summer on the Pacific Crest Trail in Oregon and camped in Canada's Rocky Mountains and bicycled alone from

Boston to Halifax. I felt connected to a tradition I could not yet name.

This summer, a book club I belong to in Silver City is reading *Mrs. Dalloway.* I haven't read this novel for thirty years, and I am surprised to learn that Mrs. Dalloway is so old, in her fifties. She is very upper-class and very English. Yet I felt close to her as a young adult, and I feel close to her again, today on August 13, the last day of bird banding. On a desultory net run, I stand by the Gila River, the play of sunlight and sparkle of water, and I realize that Mrs. Dalloway is who I have been missing in this recent time of children leaving home and perimenopause. I have missed her enthusiasm and passion for her party. I have missed the thrumming-humming intensity of a Virginia Woolf novel and the sense that my life, and everyone's life, is extraordinary.

We catch a yellow warbler, two Bewick's wrens, a summer tanager, and a yellow-breasted chat. Then, around eleven o'clock, twenty-one lazuli buntings come in a rush, five, seven, eight in a net. We *ooh* and *aah* and also begin rushing about, birds in hand, birds wiggling in cloth bags clothes-pinned to a line, birds banded, birds released.

The lazuli buntings are on their way back to Mexico. Carol explains that they have a unique pattern of molt and migration. The juveniles begin their first molt at breeding grounds in the north, then stop and come here—to what the Cornell Lab of Ornithology calls a "molting hot spot," one of a few such places in Arizona and New Mexico—where they finish the process of losing old feathers and growing new ones before flying south. As

I untangle these buntings and cup them in the bander's grip, they seem to eye me with more impatience than usual. They just want to molt and go home. It is sheer bad luck to be caught like this on the very last hour of the last day of bird banding, genitalia probed and a wing stretched out awkwardly.

By noon today, the end of banding season, we will have caught two hundred birds, mostly adults. The lack of young birds means that not many adults successfully raised nestlings in our bosque, or riparian forest. Mike and Carol expected this, considering our dry winter and spring. We also caught few or none of certain species like Bell's vireos or willow flycatchers. That isn't good, either. Mike says, "Songbirds tend to boom or bust." Carol says, "Songbirds are fragile." Songbirds live about two years, and if a population doesn't breed one year, its numbers plummet. In the Southwest, the Gila Valley has important populations of many bird species, including summer tanagers, yellow-billed cuckoos, yellow warblers, Lucy's warblers, and willow flycatchers. We don't know enough about these animals. Where do the flycatchers winter? Where do the black hawks go?

We put away our equipment for the last time this summer and talk about our favorite birds. My preferences are shallow. I like blue. I like red. I like the name of the bridled titmouse, so small and determined to escape the net. A little more selective, Carol is thrilled by yellow-billed cuckoos. She values their intelligence, the way these predators sit and watch for their largish prey: frogs, grasshoppers, and hornworms. Wintering in South America, the cuckoos arrive late in the spring and have little time to breed, so they breed fast, with the young developing six to seven days in the nest and exploding into feathers. Yellow-billed cuckoos are also called raincrows or stormcrows because their rapid, staccato calls of *kuk-kuk-kuk-kuk* and trailing *kukakakowlp-kowlp* signal the beginning of the summer rains. Cuckoos need riparian forest and can be found now in just a few concentrations west of the Continental Divide. (In the East, these birds are doing better but are still in decline.) We banded only one cuckoo this season.

Later in August, I meet with Carol and Mike and others at the Lichty Ecological Research Center for an after-dinner slide show about saving the Gila River. It seems astonishing that we need to save the Gila River, a river with its full complement of native fish species, some of which are listed as federal- and state-endangered, a river that supports unusually dense populations of birds and mammals, a river that in New Mexico still flows freely and relatively naturally. Right now, this river is rare and precious. In fifty or a hundred years, if left undisturbed, it will be of enormous scientific, biological, aesthetic, and spiritual value. Who would want to mess with this?

A surprising number of people, and for no good reason. A 2003 legal settlement of water rights in Arizona means that the four counties of southwestern New Mexico soon will be getting sixty-six million dollars for water development projects. These projects can include buying up water rights, drilling wells, or implementing conservation measures like drip irrigation. If the counties choose instead to divert water from the Gila River, they are eligible for more money from the federal government—another sixty-two million. At first glance, this incentive seems to strongly encourage building something, particularly a large pumping station to get water out of the river, a massive pipeline to move the water many miles away, and a dam or reservoir to store the water. But in fact, the cost of such a diversion would be over three times the $128 million dollars now available, and water taken from the river would be much more expensive than water gotten from other sources. The need for this water is also in doubt. Silver City, the largest town in the area, has enough groundwater to sustain its projected population for hundreds of years. Our county is actually losing people, not growing. Economically, on second glance, a diversion project does not make sense. Ecologically, in a river that floods as part of its natural process and faces the threat of global warming, diverting more water could be a disaster.

But I am sitting here at the Lichty Ecological Research Center because some people still want to do this: take water out of the Gila River. Partly, this is personal greed. There are people in state and federal agencies whose career means building things. There are people who want jobs in these agencies who are trying to curry favor. There are people in the construction business who will make a tiny bit of those millions of dollars.

Mostly, however, this is about our story of the world. Many of the people in favor of a diversion think it is wrong to let water flow wastefully down the river when we could capture and keep it here. It is wrong not to control the river, to let it flood periodically. It is wrong to let endangered fish species—tiny things like a loach minnow—dictate what we can and cannot do. It is wrong to care about the river the way these other people seem to care about it. It is wrong to get excited about a yellow-billed cuckoo.

Many of the people in favor of a diversion would call themselves Christian, and to some extent the way they feel about the Gila River is connected to a religious worldview. Although a new greener Christianity emphasizes the role of stewardship and the love of God for his Creation, the conservative Christian still sees earth as a halfway house. The plan is to go somewhere better, and what we leave behind is not so important. We are not really a part of this earth, or its forests, rivers, and mountains, in the same way we hope to be part of heaven.

The Catholic priest and historian Thomas Berry has suggested another Christian attitude toward nature: Christians are angry. In Berry's history, the Black Death of the fourteenth century and subsequent plagues had a profound effect on Western thought. So many people died so fast. A secular response was to seek greater control over the physical world, to understand natural processes and manipulate them. A religious response was to seek redemption—to find a way out of this scary, tragic world. Berry believes that the emphasis on redemption in Christianity has overshadowed the importance of creation. He speaks of "an inner rage against the conditions of earthly existence." Life should not *be* so fragile. Life should not *be* so imperfect, so terrible, so full of grief. Nature is betrayal.

Berry has a metaphor to describe our current situation. He says we are autistic. We no longer feel what we are supposed to feel toward our mother, the earth, and our father, the sun, toward our brothers and sisters and cousins, the family around us. Our human senses take in information—tracks in the sand, the movement of a leaf—but we don't know how to interpret this information. We don't know what it means. Unlike actual autism, the problem is cultural, not biological. We no longer need to survive by our instincts in the natural world, and so we no longer have the values or skills of our hunting-and-gathering ancestors. Additionally, because we are no longer animists, because we no longer see plants and animals as living, experiencing intelligences in their own right, we have been trained out of the emotions many of us still felt as young children, when the cat and dog and turtle were worthy of our love, before life was so divided into human and nonhuman.

What is our relationship to the Gila River? What do people see when they look at a river and see only a pipeline big enough to drive a truck through, a circular cement O, all the fish and trees and birds and foxes filtered out, the dreamy snake of the river picked up and carried somewhere else, dumped miles away, thoroughly dead? Who cares about a dead river? What does it mean to care?

I often walk along the dirt road to the national forest line, past the silver snake of the Gila River, and I read as I walk—Virginia Woolf, John Muir, Thomas Berry, Annie Dillard. I know that this is an odd thing to do. The rare yellow-billed cuckoo could fly right by, and I wouldn't notice. I might not notice a pterodactyl. At this moment, surely, reading diminishes my relationship to nature. Just as surely, nature is enhancing my relationship to reading. I stop every few moments. I look around. I am infused with beauty. I breathe in oxygen. I think about what Muir or Dillard is trying to say. I think about these things better when I am moving. I'm just made that way. I am listening to the voices of the dead as well as the living. We are reaching out to each other while the river dreams and the cottonwood trees glow. I think to myself: I am walking through the Mind and Body of God.

We have the same brain as our Paleolithic ancestors. Some scientists believe that the religious impulse is in the architecture of our brain, a by-product of evolution. (1) We believe in God because we are evolutionarily adapted to believe in what psychologists call an agent, something independent, purposeful, and outside ourselves that could affect us—possibly in a bad way. Humans who assume that it is a lion causing that ripple in the grass, rather than the wind, tend to survive longer. (2) We believe in God because we are evolutionarily adapted to create narratives and explanations. The tracks in the sand mean that a deer recently passed this way. A pool nearby means the deer might be thirsty, and if it moves here and I move there, I could be eating its leg for dinner. Life isn't just a matter of chance. Life is about cause and effect. (3) We believe in God because we are evolutionarily adapted, as social animals, to understand that other people have minds. We cannot see what these invisible minds are thinking or planning, but we would be wise to anticipate whether they are friendly or angry. We believe there are invisible forces in the world, invisible minds in solid bodies.

Why not, then, a mind outside the body? Why not an invisible agent involved in the story of our own life? Although such an idea mostly describes theism, the message is the same for pantheists: We are predisposed to believe in a meaningful, interconnected world, as well as in something outside and larger than ourselves. We may choose to believe in these things because such beliefs help us deal with grief and despair, motivate us to cohere socially, and are generally more fun and interesting than not.

Other scientists say that religion is less a by-product of evolution than an actual adaptation, furthering longer life and more reproduction. For example, religious belief may have allowed our ancestors to marshal the placebo effect offered by shamanistic healing. Although scientists are not sure how the human body responds to the idea of a cure and heals itself, we know that this happens on a regular basis. Ritual healing may have been particularly important when there were fewer medical options. People who inclined toward a belief in shamans, spirits, and gods—who had more of the hardwiring that promotes religious experience—better survived injury and disease and thus had a reproductive advantage.

From then to now, the hardwiring hasn't changed. We are, of course, running new software. We read. We write. We fly through the air strapped into plastic seats, drinking Diet Coke. I will never see the world the way a hunter-and-gatherer saw it. In terms of my relationship with the earth, I am sorry about that. I feel left out. I feel incompetent. But there you go. That's history, Thomas Berry would say, and by this he means that the universe is an irreversible emergent process. We are unfolding. We are moving forward along with everything else, changing and being changed. We carry with us our past and our genetic coding. We are who we were. But we can't go back either.

Tonight I sit in the Lichty Ecological Research Center, which is packed with men and women who are also coming to see a slide show about saving the Gila River. We gasp at grim photos of other pipelines diverting water from other destroyed rivers in America. We look at charts comparing the cost of a diversion to the cost of using less water by using it more wisely. We all share the same astonishment. After the presentation, we are invigorated and determined. People who do not usually go to meetings about the environment will now go to meetings about the environment. People who do not usually sign petitions will sign petitions. One woman will dress up in her version of an Apache warrior and ride her horse on the road to the national forest just as state officials are driving around looking at diversion sites. She shouts something about protecting the river. That's the Gila Valley we love, slide shows and petitions and dream catchers. There is a sense of unity. Consciousness runs in animal steps from person to person in the room.

Outside, the soft August night still smells of rain. The clay in the soil has released compounds like those found in urine, a distinct acrid odor. Walking back to my house, I hear an owl hoot, and I click off the flashlight, letting my eyes adjust to darkness. But for most of my life, I have been nearsighted, with terrible night vision. By the third grade, I was legally blind—unable to see the largest *E* on the optometrist's chart, the one as big as a toaster—and wore fashionable glasses that shaped up into sparkly triangles on each side of my head. A few years ago, I had laser surgery and now can see without glasses—*un milagro! Gracias de Dios!* But the surgery also made my night vision worse.

It is necessary to click on the flashlight again. The owl is spooked and flaps away. I walk home carefully, led by a small round circle of light. I have these autistic quirks. I'm learning to live with them.

CHAPTER 10

Make Oneness Your House

WHEN I GRADUATED from college in 1976, there seemed only one thing to do: go to India. One of my roommates was studying Sanskrit. One day, she showed me India on the map. Then I understood. You could actually fly there. Another roommate belonged to an ashram in Southern California. Before I left, he gave me ash blessed by his guru. It would protect me on my journey. By then I had read the latest translations of Eastern religious texts and the popularization of Eastern ideas by American authors. I had eaten lunch at the Golden Temple on Telegraph Avenue, looking sideways at the servers, who chanted and wore flimsy orange robes. The world is Brahmin. The Buddha's body is the world. Life is *dukka*, or suffering. Life is *lila*, or play. Life is *mara*, or delusion. This was something new, and then again, not new.

My college friend Gail and I went overland, a cheap flight to Europe and then buses and trains across Turkey, Iraq, Iran, Afghanistan, and Pakistan. (It is a comment on today that we could do that then and would not be able to do that now.) We ended up in a Hindu ashram near the town of Rishikesh in the foothills of the Himalayas. We never went further north, feeling already saturated with experience. The Himalayas represented overload. I remember thinking that I would be back. It would be good to save something for later.

The ashram was wonderful. Gail and I got up at five every day, had a yoga class from six to seven, breakfast and then, quoting from Gail's letters home (which I read twenty-five years later when she gave me copies as a Christmas gift), "a really good lecture on Hindu philosophy," lunch at eleven, yoga again from three to four, and ginger tea with our yoga teacher, Swami Krishna, who was also a cook for the ashram. We meditated from six to seven, had supper, and went to bed at nine. In between, we learned Sanskrit songs: *"Om bhur bhuvas svahe. Tat savitur varenyam"* ("Salutation to the Word, which is present in the earth, the heavens, and that which is beyond").

We visited a leper colony, where a man stroked his wife's cheek with the stubs of his fingers. She had burned herself, and he was comforting her. I had never seen anything so tender. We floated yellow marigolds in green leaf cups down the Ganges River. We looked attentive as Swami Krishna tried to teach us to cook. And we celebrated festivals, always, by eating: saffron rice, curried potatoes, dhal, papad, yoghurt curd, and hot pudding with cardamom and cashews. Gail wrote her mother, "Sharman works on her novel and I paint. It's a really good life." I wrote letters that were still trying to imitate Virginia Woolf. "The red and white, yellow and orange ashrams line the river. The turquoise-green of Mother Ganges, the flow of dark turquoise moving, and the dark shadows of carp moving beneath."

The carp were sacred. Children sold paper cones with bits of hardened wheat paste that tourists could throw into the water. The large, fat carp rose fearlessly, shouldering each other aside. Wooden stands hawked bathing towels (into that water, with those carp?) and Ganges souvenirs. Our rickshaw driver whispered to me, "Once there were many great yogis here, many great yogis! Now," he shook his head, "you have come too late." But we didn't think so. At twenty-two, in the fall of 1976, we were exactly where we were supposed to be, riding the crest of our lives like a wave. Our choices did not seem like choices but an ineluctable flow that had carried us here to the village of Rishikesh and a Hindu ashram. Almost then, I believed in the Stoic's destiny.

The earliest forms we know of Hinduism are the Vedas, or hymns, brought down by groups migrating into India from about 2000 to 500 BCE. For these Indo-Aryan tribes, a belief in multiple gods and nature deities eventually became the idea of an ultimate reality and cosmic order. Brahma, the creator, had transformed himself into all things. Brahma is also Brahman, the world spirit, and atman, the world spirit as the individual soul or self. Gods are divine manifestations of Brahman, and Hinduism is full of gods: Shiva and Kali and Krishna, forces of destruction as well as creation, destroyers as well as protectors. We can know the One through worship of the gods, or we can know it more directly through our own atman. This knowledge will require lifetimes. Most Hindus believe that each individual passes through many reincarnations before reaching the goal of liberation—liberation from the limits of human consciousness; liberation from the personal ego, which sees separation instead of One; and liberation from the yoke of fear, sin, and desire; and liberation from the cycle of rebirth and miseries of daily life.

A Hindu practicing her religion might well be a pantheist, or as likely a panentheist, believing that the Supreme-Being-World-Spirit-Brahma-Pure-Existence-Consciousness-Bliss is a divinity both immanent and transcendent, all the world and outside the world, too. She may spend her time meditating and looking inward. She may instead pay great attention to ritual and worship, a disciple of Hanuman, the monkey god, or Kali, the bloody earth mother. She may read epic stories like the Bhagavad Gita, metaphors of war and sacrifice. The Vedas themselves say, "Reality is one. Sages speak of it in different ways."

The structure of our ashram in Rishikesh was mysterious. There had been a swami or guru, recently dead, whose life-sized pictures were everywhere, sometimes cut out and pasted on cardboard and left sitting in a chair. That could be unsettling. Our cook and yoga teacher, whom we affectionately began to call Swamiji, had practiced bhakti, or unconditional love, toward this guru for most of his life, and he continued to adore the many pictures and cutout cardboard photos. I found the idea of bhakti frustrating. In bhakti, the object of your love doesn't need to deserve it. The object of your love can act badly or treat you badly. Once the Swamiji's guru had forbidden him to eat salt for a year. How arbitrary, I thought, indignant for my new friend. But Swamiji only shook his head. The important thing was your love, which became the vehicle through which you realized that you, the object of your love, and love itself were all One.

Sometimes Gail and I walked along the forest paths with Swami Shankarananda, a kind man who may have been the current head of the ashram and who called us "little mothers." (This made me feel strangely important and shy.) As the swami lectured on Hindu philosophy, the tame cows of the village came up for a pet, lowering their heads to be scratched between the horns. Once a cow ran past with a man's undershirt in its mouth, and Swami Shankarananda composed a sermon on the spot. When we left the ashram, we gave him a large, beautiful apple. He said—and Gail dutifully wrote it down—"Always remember that what you see does not exhaust Creation. You can live in this world, but now and then just glance aside. The only satisfaction in life comes from the permanent, not from the impermanent, always shifting and changing."

We went to New Delhi, then Vrindaban, the birthplace of Lord Krishna. At another Hindu ashram, we learned more Sanskrit songs and sailed more prayers of bright yellow marigolds in green leaf cups. This was something I loved to do. I loved physical prayers that were flowers. Loudspeakers played "Hare Rama, Hare Rama, Hare Rama, Rama, Rama, Hare, Hare, Hare

Krishna, Hare Krishna, Krishna, Krishna, Hare, Hare" from four in the morning until eleven at night, unless the power went off, at which point Gail and I screamed in relief. Vrindaban had peacocks—impossible birds—narrow streets, temples black with mold, and pictures everywhere of its favorite laughing blue-skinned god. Children ran barefoot in the cold. By now we were more used to poverty, skinny, skinny people with dull hair, disfigured beggars from whom we politely averted our eyes.

We befriended a family of tea-stall owners and, on Christmas Day, invited their children to the feast at the ashram, intended for schoolchildren from around town. News spread, and we stood nervously before the ashram gate with a crowd of thirteen ragged street kids. When we left Vrindaban, the tea-stall mother asked for my coat. This request took me by surprise. I smiled ignorantly and shook my head no, something I will always regret.

Predominantly Hindu, northern India also has important sites sacred to Buddhism. After Vrindaban, Gail and I went to Deer Park outside Benares, where the Buddha also went after his enlightenment. We stayed at a *dharmsala,* or hotel for Buddhist pilgrims, mostly Tibetan and Japanese. The *dharmsala* was a huge pink two-story building with a tower clock, one hand pointed forever at five. Gail and I would get up every morning when the stars were still out, the first customers at the nearest tea stall. At sunrise we went across the road through the gated entrance into Deer Park, an enclosed area perhaps a square mile with pipal trees, gravel paths, ponds and flowers, mongoose and deer.

With a glance, my friend and I parted. I went first into the temple, its walls painted with a luminous orange and yellow mural of the Buddha's life—glowing pictures of an orange infant, an orange prince, an orange monk, an orange ascetic, and an orange enlightened being with his palm upraised. Outside to the east, I walked around the stone tower, or stupa, a hundred feet high and hundred feet broad, hairy with vines and trailing leaves. Stupas are spiritual monuments that symbolize the Buddha and his teachings. By early morning, the Tibetan pilgrims would also be walking its base, round and round, chanting and fingering their prayer beads. North, I visited the archaeological ruins, geometric patterns of low brick walls with the occasional sign: "On this spot, in the third century BCE, King Ashoka . . . "

Breaking this spell of age and holiness was the Indian penchant for using bright primary colors to paint the fences and curbs that enclosed Deer Park. The park's flowerpots and trash cans and water tower were also painted red, yellow, and blue. I felt like a child among large child toys. I felt safer than I had ever felt as a child. I felt a wisdom and charity embedded in place, and this was my first experience of this: spirit and matter intertwined. I did not pray as I walked around the stupa or on the gravel paths or up to the flower gardens. Yet I found myself walking on my best behavior, trying to think my best thoughts, first to the stupa and then to the archaeological ruins, to the water tower and then the pond. I was walking where the Buddha had walked some twenty-five hundred years ago. I did not think of him as a real person—more like one of those luminous orange beings painted in the temple, a kind of friendly ghost at my side.

The Buddha probably was a real person, possibly born in the foothills of the Himalayas in the sixth century BCE during a period of social and political change. Intermittent warfare, a growing urban class, and Iron Age technology created a sense of general unease. By now, the Vedic, or early Hindu, tradition had become a conservative one dependent on ritual and an elite priestly caste. Within Hinduism, a spiritual revolution was being expressed in the new writings of the Upanishads, which emphasized the impersonal and immanent reality of Brahman and its presence in each individual as atman. The gods, the priests, the sacrifices were no longer necessary; instead, you could look inward for liberation. Outside Hinduism, people were also exploring new religious and philosophical ideas.

According to legend, Siddhartha Gautama was the son of a wealthy king. Wise men prophesied that the baby would become either an enlightened being devoted to saving humanity or a great ruler devoted to conquest. In order to prevent the former, the king kept Gautama in a "pleasure palace," where the boy had no knowledge of suffering, sickness, age, or death—where he would have no reason to develop his compassionate side. As the prince slept at night, servants swept up any withering leaves fallen from the trees. Ugly or old women were banished from sight. Musicians played only happy songs. It is a nice picture of denial. Control everything. Make delusion as comfortable as possible.

In time, the prince escaped—as he must, if he wanted to grow up—and saw that life is full of pain. Leaves fall, and women get wrinkles. Moreover, there are also terrible diseases, heart-wrenching griefs, and daily frustrations, an array of strife, disappointment, and unwelcome change. Desire something, and you have made your first mistake.

Gautama joined a community of monks who were already wandering the forests outside towns and villages, fasting and thinking about spiritual problems or walking along the road begging for food. These monks formed into groups, teachers and disciples, each promoting a different philosophy. Most were determined to find a way out of the cycle of rebirth, seeking liberation from the misery of human life.

The Jains focused on harmlessness, hardly daring to move for fear of destroying a living creature and incurring bad karma (a spiritual system of cause and effect that determined if you were born into greater or lesser suffering). Another group actually denied reincarnation and believed that human beings were simply physical bodies that decayed back into the earth. A third group questioned everything and rejected any possibility of truth.

The future Buddha was first attracted to a teacher who emphasized rational thought, something like Spinoza's intellectual love of God. Emotions were confusing and inferior. Reason best reflected the eternal spirit. Using the power of discrimination, a monk could wake to his true self, or atman, and be above the pain of the human body and mind. This philosophy also taught that the material world of nature was beneficent and holy. The universe was a friendly place designed for enlightenment, the liberation of everyone. Later, the Buddha would use some of these ideas in his own teaching. But for now, after mastering the doctrine of reason, he decided that reason alone was not enough.

Next the future Buddha tried yogic exercises. By suppressing normal physical and psychological realities, the Yogi hoped to break free from his limited consciousness or egotism. This first required a commitment to moral behavior. No one could reach this kind of control if he could not also control his baser instincts to lie, steal, drink alcohol, engage in sex, or harm other creatures. Step by step, Gautama entered the yogic states that led to Oneness. But when he came out of these trances, life rushed back in. Pettiness, desire, frustration. This enlightenment was impermanent and therefore false. Even so, Gautama had learned valuable lessons about the conscious and unconscious mind and the role of meditation.

Now the future Buddha turned to asceticism, denying his flesh as a way to rid himself of all craving. Austerity was a common practice among the forest monks, an attempt to literally starve out the personal ego to make room for the atman. Gautama had five companions who starved with him and admired him as their leader. His denials were so heroic that he almost died—which was not the liberation he had in mind. In the end, going hungry only seemed to increase his hunger. The ascetic practice was another failure.

In the stories surrounding the Buddha, Gautama now ate a handful of rice pudding, which restored him to health. His five starving companions were disgusted and left. The future Buddha sat under a pipal tree and declared he would not move from the spot until he was enlightened. It happened in a single night. *Mara,* or delusion, tried all kinds of tricks, sending images of great armies, horrible monsters, and frightening storms. Even the gods, who had come to watch, ran away in fear. In this case, there would be no divine help. All on his own, looking inward yet touching the earth at the same time, the Buddha awakened. His great insight concerned the importance of compassion and love. Almost immediately, he had to decide whether he would teach this path to enlightenment or simply sit under the tree and enjoy it. Now the god Brahma did intervene and begged the Buddha to help the rest of humanity achieve their salvation, too. So the Buddha rose the next morning to search for his five former companions.

In his first sermon at Deer Park, the Enlightened One considered his disgruntled, hungry audience and began by explaining that rice pudding. Much like the Greek philosopher Epicurus, the Buddha suggested that we not eat too little or too much. That we not be too cold or too warm. That we not deny our humanity, which was, after all, simply who we were and not an obstacle to enlightenment. This moderation between extremes was what the Buddha called the Middle Way.

Unlike Epicurus, however, the Buddha was uninterested in merely seeking pleasure and avoiding pain. His idea of tranquillity meant something much grander. He began with his four Noble Truths. Three of them were not new. (1) Other forest monks had already discovered that life is suffering, or *dukka,* also translated as "unsatisfying" or "awry." (2) The cause of suffering is desire for that which is impermanent. (3) A way out of suffering exists, called nirvana, which can be thought of as the extinction of the personal ego. (4) The way out of suffering is the Buddha's Eightfold Path.

This path was not easy. You had to have (1) right understanding of the four Noble Truths and (2) right purpose, the desire for nirvana. You needed to practice (3) right speech, (4) right conduct, and (5) right livelihood. You could not lie or steal or hurt people. A monk should also not drink alcohol or have sex. But being harmless or passive was not enough. You had to *actively* cultivate loving-kindness. You had to have (6) right effort. You had to embrace the world with compassion. Only then could you blow out the ego. To help with this, you should cultivate (7) right alertness by using the process of mindfulness, watching your thoughts but not suppressing them. Watching yourself, you saw the pathos of your self. You understood your desire. As well as mindfulness, you should practice (8) right concentration through the art of sitting and breathing. All this would allow you to achieve a focused state and the requisite feeling of love for all things, compassion for all suffering, joy for everyone, and—finally—equanimity.

The second sermon at Deer Park was about *anatta,* or no-self. Part of the Buddha's awakening had had to do with the pantheistic idea that everything in the universe is dependent on and connected to everything else. Like the no-self, everything is empty-of-its-own-being but part of the universal web of being. Nothing really exists on its own. After his enlightenment, the Buddha dismissed the idea of an eternal absolute Self, at least as something we could achieve. To think along those lines was another trick of the ego. He also denied the existence of the lowercase self. The changing ego had no fixed reality. Our sense of personality was an illusion.

Many people today think the same thing. Philosophers and anthropologists talk about who we are as a bundle of received ideas, a product of our language and social matrix. Neurobiologist Antonio Damasio adds, "The self is a repeatedly reconstructed biological state; it is not a little person, the infamous homunculus inside your brain contemplating what is going on." Psychologically and chemically, our "self" is a gestalt, a process of interdependence, in flux and change.

It was the second sermon that most convinced the Buddha's five companions to follow the Middle Way. It was the thought of no-self that seemed so liberating. In 1977, even after only a few decades of living with the illusion of Sharman, I found the idea liberating, too. I wanted something more than my self, something as big as Deer Park, maybe even bigger.

The Buddha falls short of being a pantheist. He saw the universe as an interconnected One, but he did not speak of this Oneness as sacred or divine. In truth, he wasn't much interested in metaphysics. In one story, he is asked forcefully if the world is eternal or not, infinite or not, if body and soul are identical or not, and if liberated beings exist after death or not. The Buddha likens these questions to those of a man who has been poisoned by an arrow but refuses to have the arrow taken out until he knows if it was sent by someone tall or short, pale or dusky, from a certain town or another town. All that is irrelevant.

Do you want to die from a poisoned arrow, or do you want to live free of fear, sin, and desire? Choosing the Eightfold Path—living without ego and with love and compassion—will make you happier and better equipped to deal with suffering. End of discussion.

For the Buddha, enlightenment meant that he had achieved a no-self that would last the rest of his life. It did not mean he would not experience pain and suffering but that these things could no longer possess or control him. His refuge was nirvana, an inner stillness and peace. He would live in this tranquillity until he died, and then he would attain *paranirvana,* a final rest, no longer on the wheel of rebirth. It is impossible to know or describe *paranirvana.* In texts written after his death, the Buddha says only that the enlightened being who has gone to *paranirvana* cannot be defined by speech or thought, for that being is now beyond these things.

In the generations after the Buddha's death, Buddhism spread to other countries and evolved into a variety of sects. Some elevated the Buddha into a divine being. Some were atheistic. Some were polytheistic. Some were pantheistic.

In China, the Flower Garland School is based on a sutra declaring that the cosmic Buddha is a deity who is infinite and eternal: "Buddha has Reality for his body, pure as space itself."

In Zen Buddhism, the universal Buddha-nature is unborn and indestructible. It does not belong to the category of things but transcends all limits, measures, names, and speech. In its omnipotence and glory, it could be described as divine—although it cannot really be described by ordinary human consciousness, and any such description is counterproductive. Understanding the Buddha-mind requires breaking down our usual constructs, going beyond words, beyond rational thought. Absurd puzzles and eccentric teachers can help with this, as can the discipline of meditation. Enlightenment means living fully in the present, in the perfect, spontaneous, and diverse completeness of the universe.

Nothing in particular follows after that. After enlightenment, life is ordinary again. You eat, you sleep, you haul water, you pass water. You continue to live in Sacred Reality.

At Deer Park, Gail and I did not have classes or a teacher, only the cheerful pamphlets from the Maha Bodhi Society Library down the street, religious versions of "There is no *I* in team." Day after day, we walked the paths, circled the stupa, and stood in the temple, absorbing piety as candlelight played against the walls of the yellow and orange mural. Later I would write a children's fantasy in which a young girl also visits the temple in Deer Park, enters the mural, and walks through the legend of the Buddha. One day I saw the tip of a mongoose's tail. The girl in my fantasy would speak to this animal, and he would speak back. Meanwhile Gail was writing home that we were meditating every morning, watching our breath and sitting in the lotus position, something I could do then. "In fact," Gail informed her parents, "Sharman and I shared a mystical experience, which surprised us both. We hadn't thought we were the mystical type!" It is silly, of course, and provoking that it is the mystical experience I do not recall today, just the colors and incense, flickering candles, towering stupa and brief glimpse of a mongoose's tail.

After what seemed a long time but was perhaps only a few weeks, Gail and I were asked to leave the *dharmsala*. The day before, someone had entered our room to take from Gail's backpack a hundred dollars in traveler's checks. In order to get the money reimbursed, we had to file a police report. After a number of false starts and wrong police stations, we found ourselves separated and interrogated in two different whitewashed and almost completely empty rooms.

Reluctantly, Gail said that she had seen an older man, who she thought worked for the *dharmsala,* pass by our open window earlier. The police officer suggested instead that I had stolen the traveler's checks as a scam for getting money. Another officer was saying the same thing to me about Gail. At one point, he took out his revolver, loaded it, and laid it on the desk. I looked on, mildly interested, but I was from the American West. I had seen guns before.

Suddenly, we all jumped into a big black police car. It felt like a scene from a Buster Keaton movie, with the policemen laughing uproariously and the scenery rushing by much faster than in a rickshaw. Back at the *dharmsala,* the police may have accused the old man of theft, or passed on their suspicions about us, or both. The next day, the manager of the *dharmsala* suggested we had learned enough about Buddhism for now.

We went to Calcutta to the American Express office. In this city, the poverty seemed even more brutal. For the first time, rickshaw drivers were not pedaling bicycles or using horses.

They themselves were the beast, on foot, muscles bulging, toes misshapen, straining under loads of passengers and baggage. In the garbage on the sidewalk, I thought I saw a corpse and pretended not to, as if embarrassed. Perhaps he was only sleeping. The beggars here were more numerous and missing more parts. They scooted along on callused skin or used a kind of skateboard. This was a human landscape I would never later deny, a backdrop to the rest of my life, to my children, to this yellow house, to the view even now of mountains and a hawk circling the field. It is not just me and the plants, me and the animals. It is also me and the leper, me and the rickshaw driver.

We went south and stayed in other ashrams, including one run by a Catholic priest. He waggled his fingers, each finger a religion: Christianity, Hinduism, Buddhism, Islam. They were all connected to the same hand, the priest said, the same source.

Wherever we went, India confirmed for me what I had already learned in my science and literature classes: We are an interconnected One. (The very act of reading had told me that. How else could I enter the world of someone like D. H. Lawrence and his lordly penis, or Robinson Jeffers, obsessed with stories of incest and patricide?) India showed me the sensual beauty of the religious impulse, those yellow marigolds in green leaf cups, the dusky blue of Krishna's skin, the holy beauty of the holy earth. India further explained: If we are all One, then the religious impulse is to participate in Oneness. The main obstacle to this participation is the part of our ego that experiences difference. Hindus might find their liberation from the ego through bhakti, or submission to the gods. The Buddha found his liberation through the Eightfold Path, which is not a religion so much as a strategy. The mystics of Christianity and Islam discovered another way.

Gail and I left India and went to Sri Lanka, Thailand, and Taiwan. We celebrated the Festival of the Buddha's Tooth and the Festival of the Elephants. We prayed to poisonous snakes swaying drowsily in temples. We watched movies whenever we could, charming films about Hindu gods and Buddhist heroes, bodhisattvas with magical powers, people flying through the air, ghosts and demons, and the boy getting the girl in the end. Many of these movies were subtitled in English, which for some reason didn't surprise us. We were all connected. We were all in the play of *lila,* the delusion of *mara,* the dissatisfaction of *dukka.* More and more, everything was getting mixed up together.

We ended our trip. We went to graduate school.

Almost thirty years later, I walk the Gila River Farm. In the morning, I go the loop to the pond and restored wetlands, through the bosque to the river, along the river, through the bosque again, and back by the fields. In the afternoon, I walk the road to the national forest, the river below me a silver snake slipping down from the Gila Wilderness, the canyon walls breaking off into shapes like stupas or cones or big Texas hats. Maybe I walk instead to Sacaton Mesa with its 360-degree view and greening of the land, the desert flowers, the continual celebration. I look for hawks and vermilion flycatchers. I get up at dawn and look for javelina. In September, Maria drives away to her AmeriCorps job. Our son, David, has already left to study in

Spain. My children, I understand, will always keep leaving me. On the Gila River Farm, a black bear begins to visit the orchard of apple and pears trees planted decades ago. All we see are his prints in the mud after a rain.

All my magic has been put in a box. What I hope for is a state of grace that will open into Oneness. I am walking through the Mind and Body of the Buddha. I never took the Eightfold Path, never got the hang of meditation, never trusted nirvana. I want to give up my ego—but not all of it, just the unpleasant parts. And Swami Shankarananda was right: The little mother became a mother. I remain a busy, attached person. I am also lazy. Compassion and love for everyone are hard work. Even so, despite my faults, I have been blessed. Even so, I take these walks like going to church all day long under a bright blue sky. On dirt roads now instead of gravel paths, I am once again on my best behavior, trying to think my best thoughts. Almost thirty years later, I get to return to Deer Park.

I met my husband at the University of Montana in Missoula, where I was studying for a master of fine arts in creative writing. We had mutual dreams. We wanted to root in the earth. We wanted a house made of mud. We moved to New Mexico. It didn't register at first that Peter had been a Chinese studies major as an undergraduate. But over the years, the books accumulated, shelves and piles, by the bed, under the bed, in the bathroom so he could read in the bathtub: books on Chinese history, on Chinese art, on Confucianism, on Zen Buddhism, on Taoism—especially on Taoism.

I didn't read these books myself. But I liked having them around, like low-maintenance pets, wisdom by osmosis. Now they have followed us to our house in the Gila Valley, the meditations of Chuang Tzu, a Taoist sage of the fourth century BCE, and five versions of the *Tao te Ching,* a collection of Taoist thought with over two hundred different translations and counting. These writings make up what some people call philosophical Taoism and what the *Stanford Encyclopedia of Philosophy* describes as "one of the most articulated and thoroughly pantheistic positions there is."

In the *Tao te Ching,* the Tao, or Way, is that central, mysterious, and numinous Unity that humans can revere and consider sacred. The Great Tao flows everywhere, infinite and eternal. It underlies and sustains all things. It is impersonal, nameless, and beyond words. For a man or woman, the Taoist ideal is to live a life embedded in nature, accepting what life has to offer, accepting death, in harmony with the Way. This means also accepting constant change and the unity of opposites: yin and yang, "good" and "bad," "beauty" and "ugliness." It means being compassionate, moderate, and humble.

Taoism began during the Warring States Period in China, from the fifth to third centuries BCE. Enemies were crushed, cities destroyed. Warfare progressed from unorganized masses of soldiers to fixed troop formations, lines of cavalry, standard-issue crossbows, and siege engines. Generation after generation, mother after mother saw her sons killed and daughters raped. In this period of horrific aggression, Taoism counseled nonaggression and nondominance. The Taoist text *Tao te Ching* was much concerned with promoting a public governance that achieved order without the use of force. The Taoist sage Chuang Tzu was much concerned with a private, self-actualized life inimical to the values of the conqueror and soldier, a life free of craving for wealth, recognition, and power, free of violence and self-righteousness. Instead, the Taoist valued nonconformity and a certain lighthearted sense of humor.

Chuang Tzu once dreamed he was a butterfly and later wondered: Am I now a man dreaming he is a butterfly, or a butterfly dreaming he is a man? He questioned the authority of reason to determine what is real or absolute. Sometimes logic only got in the way of intuition, as Chuang Tzu explained to a friend who was being excessively rational: "Obviously you still have a lot of underbrush in your head!"

The sage got to the heart of pantheism when he advised, "Make Oneness your house and live with what cannot be avoided." He suggested that we yield to the Tao and reflect it, that we have no other expectations: "Hold on to all that you have received from Nature but do not think you have gotten anything. Be empty, that is all. The Perfect Man uses his mind like a mirror—going after nothing, welcoming nothing, responding but not storing."

Scholars warn us not to simplify Taoism. For example, we are wrong when we try to distinguish too much between Taoism, Confucianism, and the Chinese form of Buddhism. Confucius was a sage of the sixth century BCE whose ideas of social behavior and ethics influenced later Chinese philosophy and politics. The principle ideas of Taoism arose during or after

Confucianism. Buddhism probably entered China in the first century CE. Through hundreds of years of social change and evolution, these three schools borrowed from each other, merged, flowed, and did not necessarily compete. We are left with the proverb "Every Chinese wears a Confucian cap, a Taoist robe, and Buddhist sandals."

We are also wrong when we artificially separate philosophical Taoism from religious Taoism. Philosophical Taoism is based on the *Tao te Ching* and writings of Chuang Tzu, which articulate a pantheistic Oneness—the universe-as-God, numinous and natural. Religious Taoism includes different organized schools or movements that worship a pantheon of gods. Folk or popular Taoism can also include the worship of nature deities and ancestor spirits. Despite its intellectual sophistication, philosophical Taoism can still be linked to the practice of Taoist religion, which can be linked, in turn, to Chinese alchemy, astrology, martial arts, traditional medicine, breath training, and sexual yoga. All these different approaches to the Tao are part of a living tradition. They reflect each other.

Like most everyone else, Westerners can't help themselves: Of course, we simplify other religions. We revise them for our own needs. Most recently, we like to use the Tao as a kind of exotic, all-purpose, philosophical flavoring, with a proliferation of titles like *The Tao of Baseball* or *The Tao of Knitting* or, yes, *The Tao of Pooh* and *The Te of Piglet,* the animated stuffed toys from a favorite children's story.

There is no good excuse for mangling someone else's worldview. But I find myself making excuses. The insistent desire to weave Taoist ideas into Western life is not trivial. There is just something about the Tao we really like. There is something about the Tao we really want. There is something, really, we think could help us.

And there is something to be said for flowing and merging. The American writers Emerson, Thoreau, and Whitman were all influenced by Eastern mysticism, which rippled into the work of John Muir and many others. In the last half of the twentieth century, when people began to recognize the seriousness of the environmental crisis, deep ecologists also looked to Buddhism and Taoism for a model of how humans could be at home in the world. The match with Taoism seemed especially good. Taoists reject the division between the physical and spiritual. They see humans as one thing only in the ten thousand things of creation, part of a larger whole. Their goal is to live harmoniously with nature and, by implication, frugally—the original light carbon footprint. Their desire is to be restrained, balanced, effortless, peaceful. But also fun-loving, artistic, and creative! A vision naturally rises up. A small-is-beautiful, artisan, agrarian, ecological society. People wear homespun robes and work in the garden. The older men and women look wise and mischievous. Somewhere there are computers, a recycling center, and a bus stop to the nearest green city.

Flow and merge. The deep ecology idea of self-realization or self-in-Self can be seen as a modification of the Eastern elimination of the personal ego. In this version, we are trying to enlarge rather than disappear. Deep ecologist George Sessions writes, "The deep ecology sense of self requires a further maturity and growth, an identification which goes beyond our humanity to include the nonhuman world. . . . Only in this way can we hope to attain full mature personhood and uniqueness." Mature personhood still requires mindfulness, concentration, a deep questioning process, and compassion, with the bodhisattva represented in the phrase, "No one is saved until we are all saved." Salvation extends to whales and willow flycatchers, which are equally part of the ten thousand things of creation, the totality of the Tao.

Unsurprisingly, an early Taoist text titled *One Hundred and Eighty Precepts* includes twenty ecological ones. These include (18) you should not wantonly fell trees; (19) you should not wantonly pick herbs or flowers; (36) you should not throw poisonous substances into lakes, rivers, and seas; (53) you should not dry up wet marshes; and (132) you should not disturb birds and other animals.

These Taoists were already seeing the impact of humans on their environment. But they probably could not conceive of a future in which the health of the entire planet was in our hands. The scale of the modern crisis is entirely modern. To this extent, the marriage of Taoism and deep ecology does not really answer the difficult questions we now face. What *is* the right balance between billions of human beings and the rest of nature? What is the best action to take against climate change? The Taoist ideal of *wu-wei,* also translated as "action without force" or "minimal effort with the best result," is useful in some cases. Let the current do its work. At the same time, we have a growing sense of urgency. Maybe action without force will take too long, and we will pass the tipping point of global warming. The planet will become a desert. The seas will rise. We will all die! (The Taoist might then ask if that was important.)

The assumption that a spiritual model can affect social and political change is also debatable. On a large scale, our religious or philosophical beliefs do not seem to have much influence. Despite the pacifism of Buddhism and Taoism, for example, historic China was violent toward people and nature alike, much as modern China is. Similarly, the religions of both China and India seem to value the female principle more highly than the West, but this spiritual assessment did not translate into how these cultures treated women. Perhaps there is no point in articulating new beliefs like deep ecology or returning to old ones like Taoism. Intuitively, these beliefs light the way. Realistically, they don't seem to go anywhere.

The sage Chuang Tzu might respond, "Obviously, you still have a lot of underbrush in your head."

My friend Jim Corbett was a Taoist as well as a Buddhist as well as a Quaker. When he was in his late twenties, his first marriage failed and his wife left with their three children. Buddhism and Taoism are contemplative religions that seek to create a psychic experience. Jim's experience came out of despair, as he sat in a Berkeley apartment over the course of a month and concentrated on his heartbeat. In that concentration, the stillness expanded and he felt each beat as a clutching after life. One night, as he waited with indifference for the next beat, he realized that his heart was slowing more than ever before: "The last strands of caring gave way. I let go. Out of the stillness that I thought was death, love enlivened me."

Soon after, Jim turned Quaker. He went on to use Buddhist and Taoist traditions as a context for what he called goatwalking—a way of moving through the Arizona desert as part of a goat herd, dependent mainly on goat's milk for food, going nowhere in particular, doing nothing in particular. During the day, he followed the curious, lively, highly social goats as they searched for water and browse. At night, he bedded down where they bedded down. In the morning, he wandered with them again, without a personal goal or destination. He was not always the leader, but he still had some say in group decisions. Although he often felt peaceful, he noted as well his resistance to solitude and the lack of a defined schedule or human purpose. He watched the play of his mind.

In Taoist tradition, uselessness has its own use. Chuang Tzu told the story of a worthless gnarly oak that grew tall and old because humans did not use or value its timber. What humans did value was often sacrificed for that value, and what humans valued was often arbitrary, specific only to humans. In goatwalking, Jim found new meaning in this idea. "To learn why you feel compelled to remake and consume the world," he wrote, "live alone in wilderness for at least a week. . . . To discover the uses of uselessness, you must be reborn into the present."

For Jim, goatwalking helped cultivate a detachment that was free from greed and self-centering. For society today, these self-centered cravings not only block our ability to live a meaningful life but are at the root of our destructive domination of the natural world.

Eventually Jim used goatwalking to also talk about the prophetic or biblical faith. When he worked with Sanctuary, helping illegal refugees from Guatemala and El Salvador move north through the desert, he met Catholics who showed him the living truth of their faith. He played with notions of the *cimarron,* the domesticated animal or slave that goes wild. The Hebrews had gone *cimarron* when they fled the pharaoh into the desert. The Salvadorans and Guatemalans had gone *cimarron* when they fled a repressive government and traveled to the United States. Jim and Nena and others working for Sanctuary had gone *cimarron* when they freed themselves from unjust laws.

At this point in his life, Jim became interested in the sabbath. When Moses climbed Mount Nebo to die, he looked down at his people growing fat and complacent, beset by new desires to own and use the world—and he despaired. How could they keep to their God? How could they keep to their covenant? The Lord told him how. Each seventh day, they should cease to labor and celebrate the sabbath. Each seventh week of harvest, they should feast and remember they were a *cimarron* people. Each seventh month, they should leave their homes and live in brush shelters as they had done in the desert. Each seventh year, they should stop living by agriculture.

"The sabbath is a time," Jim once told me, "to quit grabbing at the world, to rest, and rejoice in the Creation's goodness." When Jim and others formed a land trust in eastern Arizona, they thought of their 130 deeded acres by the San Pedro River and six square miles of grazing lease as a sabbatical place rather than a sabbatical time, a place where people could stop grabbing at the world, stop their incessant busy-ness, stop their selfish craving.

This late summer and early fall, I walk the Gila watershed, I walk the memory of Deer Park, and I walk my sabbatical place. I let go of some of the busy-ness and rejoice in the Creation's goodness. Flow and merge. I can wear a Quaker hat, a scientist's lab coat, a Taoist pin with a funny saying, and the running shoes of a pantheist. This is the new syncretism, which is also the old syncretism. Revelation is ongoing, and our understanding of the spirit, the atman, the Middle Way, and the Tao is not yet over.

CHAPTER 11

Holistic Science

IN THE FIRST week of October, Western New Mexico University hosts a symposium on the natural history of the Gila River. I go to a lecture by Dennis Miller, a biologist at WNMU who has been studying fish in the river for the last ten years. Like a lot of scientists, especially those who teach, he never found the time to write up his research, until some months ago when he used nearly every day of a six-month sabbatical, from 7 a.m. to 7 p.m., to record his data. At fifty-seven sites, he had collected over one hundred thousand fish. He found that 90 percent of them were not the introduced catfish or brown trout or rainbow trout or small-mouthed bass but the original native species: the spikedace, the loach minnow, the headwater chub, the Sonoran and desert suckers, and the beautifully speckled Gila trout. This is not to say that 90 percent of the biomass in the Gila River is native. A spikedace weighs about one-half gram (.017 ounce), and the introduced catfish can be a thousand grams (35 ounces). Also, in certain areas of the river—in the canyons, larger pools, and swifter channels— exotic game species seem to dominate. But especially where the river flows and spreads into the Gila Valley, in front of my house and further down, the native fish are doing well. This is important, since elsewhere in the Southwest these same species are gone or seriously declining.

I am buoyed by the news. The Gila River is special. I feel special. I remind myself, though, that research like this can be used both ways. Those people in favor of a diversion project— and they include hydrologists who work for the state of New Mexico—will now point to the river's health as proof that even more water can be taken out. Everything is fine. The fish are fine.

In fact, throughout the debate on the future of the Gila River, scientific data will be manipulated and misused. A year from now, we will pass completely through the looking glass when a spokesperson for the Interstate Stream Commission suggests publicly that the Gila River has too much water and that high flows may be causing ecological damage. He notes that the average flow of the river has increased in the last forty years, along with a decline in overall ecological conditions. He does not add that this increase in average flow is due to the severe floods of the last thirty years and therefore does not represent median flow, the amount of water in the river most of the time. He does not mention that even now, before the summer rains, the river dries out in long stretches, the fish caught in pools that shrink until the smell of rotting flesh is noticeable. He does not quote from Dennis Miller's research, which concludes that occasional high flows are partly why the Gila still has native fish.

After Dennis's lecture, I go on a field trip led by a state game-and-fish expert who works exclusively with native species. Ten of us drive to a spot twelve miles south of the Gila River Farm, following the river back into the national forest. We stop at the end of the dirt road and walk a half mile downstream. Rushing water always seems alive, an animate force sweeping around a bend, slapping the bank, and pooling against a boulder. Blue-stem willow snap my arm as we push through vegetation to reach a sandy beach where the river widens, riffles, and deepens again. The October sun is warm; the cottonwoods are still green. The game-and-fish expert and two graduate students wade right in, covered chest to feet with a rubber suit like a farmer's over-all. Each carries a shocking device, a long pole with an electric tip. The shock moves through the water, momentarily stunning fish, which float to the surface. The point is to show this group of citizens and scientists what a loach minnow or spikedace looks like close up. The graduate students joke about holes in their rubber. No one wants to get shocked.

Almost immediately, they catch a spikedace, federally listed as a threatened species in 1986. The spikedace is a flash of sil-ver that feeds on aquatic invertebrates. Breeding males be-come brilliant yellow. This particular fish is not brilliant yellow and looks like every other minnow I have seen in my life. I smile and nod.

Then they catch a loach minnow. One of the graduate stu-dents gets excited: "He has his lipstick on!" The expert agrees,

"He sure does." I think, "These people are nuts." But it turns out that breeding loach minnow males get a bright red coloration at the base of their lower fins, along some of the tail, and right under the mouth, so that they resemble drag queens who have smeared on the makeup a bit extravagantly, a bright red pucker-up. Come get me, sweetie.

The graduate student holds the two-inch loach minnow in the palm of his hand. The expert explains why native fish do so well in rivers that regularly flood. Because the introduced catfish and bass are evolutionarily bred for a big, slow river like the Mississippi, these exotics let themselves float to the edges of a flood, where they are caught high and dry as the water retreats. The native fish know better what to do and quickly swim back to the deeper pools.

We all peer at the loach minnow, admiring his genetic adaptation. The textbooks describe this fish as having an "olivaceous background blotched with darker pigments." I like the word olivaceous and am waiting for the chance to use it on someone's couch or skin color. But "blotched with darker pigments" is a disservice. This loach minnow is not blotched. He is tiger-striped—all the better to hide and pounce on aquatic invertebrates. His red coloration is also strangely virile. "I am here in the world!" the stunned loach minnow seems to say. I am something to reckon with.

The second graduate student pours water into his friend's hand, carefully moistening the skin of the fish. It is a tender moment, this hunky guy wearing big rubber boots up to his chest, delicately keeping such a little thing alive.

Two weeks later, I go out with another biologist, and when he catches a mosquito fish, a nonnative species like the bass and catfish, he tosses it into the bushes to die. This makes perfect sense to him. The mosquito fish does not belong here. The loach minnow does. I am not sentimental, and I don't want to look foolish. So I don't shriek and rush to save the mosquito fish's life. But I am a little disturbed by the casualness. I want some of the Native American spirit. Let's thank the mosquito fish for his thoughtfulness in sacrificing his place for the loach minnow. Let's reflect a bit on the sacredness of all life.

By and large, that's not how science works. Science is a method or tool used to accomplish something. Sometimes the goal is to expand our understanding of the world. Usually we have something more specific in mind: to reintroduce a native species or create a marketable drug. I was raised in the culture of science, and I read my *Science News* like a bulletin from the Holy Office in Rome, a weekly list of new miracles. I am pleased by every thing we learn about the loach minnow, from his beautiful red lips to the parasites in his digestive tract. But I am not naive. Science analyzes, divides, isolates, and often forgets to reassemble. There is something missing. As Gertrude Stein said of the American city where she grew up, "There is no there there." To be all alone on a desert island, me and science, science and me, would be a lonely exile.

Other people have noticed the problem. Holistic science is one new way of doing research that focuses on the big picture first, going "whole to parts" rather than the reverse, whether it is a mountain or the human mind. Holistic science is multidisciplinary and often concerned with the feedback loops within complex systems. The scientists know themselves to be in a relationship with their subject. There is no objective truth. There are relationships. Cognitive science, artificial intelligence, chaos theory, and complexity theory are now seen as inherently holistic. They *require* holistic science.

Fritjof Capra, author of *The Tao of Physics,* first published in 1976 and updated in 2001, would say the same of relativity and quantum theory. His version of holistic science begins with an awareness of the universe as a dynamic network, a pattern in which the parts always change and are always interconnected. The atomic parts, the subatomic parts, the particles, the waves, emptiness, not-emptiness—they all make up a cosmic Unity or Oneness or what physicists call the quantum field. Albert Einstein explained that matter—the earth or a biologist or a fish— is simply a region in space in which the quantum field is "extremely intense." Nothing exists outside the quantum field: "The field is the only reality."

This reality is mainly about process. The universe is movement. Subatomic particles move faster and faster the more they are confined. Protons and neutrons race about inside an atom's nucleus. Electrons whirl in orbit outside. Chemistry is the exchange of these electrons, and biology is chemistry. Biology is also movement. We are movement. The stars whirl, too. The galaxies. Creation and destruction. Rising and falling. Back into the quantum field.

Physicists understand that they are part of this process, an idea known as the uncertainty principle: What we see is changed by our seeing it. We cannot measure the world with certainty. Holistic scientists understand this better than other scientists. They accept approximate knowledge. We can learn enough to write a mathematical equation or design a drug to cure cancer. We can keep doing science. But the part will never know the sum.

Fritjof Capra says that the way we do science, and why we do it, must also change. We must shift our methods and values from controlling nature to cooperating with nature, from violence to nonviolence. This last point is not about science but culture. It is about ethics, or possibly survival.

Capra is famous for comparing the new physics to the principles of Eastern mysticism. He writes, "Quantum theory forces us to see the universe not as a collection of physical objects, but rather as a complicated web of relations between the various parts of a unified whole." This is the Buddha's interdependence, the Hindu Net of Indra, the enlightened experience of Tao. The new physics describe a space and time that are relative and intertwined. Mystics seem to experience this. They recognize the cosmic dance of flux and change. They see the vast spaces between the electron and its nucleus, the emptiness that makes up most of the universe. Moreover, they can grasp the beginning of the universe out of emptiness, the original vacuum fluctuation in which particles come into being spontaneously and disappear spontaneously. They get the koan of quantum theory. A Buddhist sutra says, "Form is emptiness and emptiness is form." The *Tao te Ching* says, "Being is the product of Not-being." A physicist writes, "The field exists always and everywhere; it can never be removed. It is the carrier of all material phenomena. It is the 'void' out of which the proton creates the pi-mesons."

For Capra, the alignment of science and mysticism makes perfect sense. Our scientific understanding of the world is often intuitive, and these intuitions are ancient. Similarly, Galileo looked back to the theories of Democritus and Epicurus. Charles Darwin read the pre-Socratics and saw the foreshadowing of natural selection. Capra believes that a holistic or ecological view is emerging in both science and culture. This view is based on new scientific discoveries that illumine the Oneness, interdependence, and transformations of the universe. "Ultimately," Capra writes, "such deep ecological awareness is spiritual awareness . . . and it is then not surprising that the new vision of reality is in harmony with the visions of spiritual traditions."

Stephan Harding is an ecologist and coordinator of a graduate program in holistic science at Schumacher College in England. He begins with Carl Jung's description of the four main psychological functions in a human being. Sensing is our direct observation of the world. Thinking interprets what we see. Intuition provides a sense of its deeper meaning. Feeling gives a value to it. Most of us depend consciously on one function, while the other three are less developed or only partly conscious. A healthy psychology is one that integrates and uses all four functions.

Conventional science perceives the world through sensing and interprets through thinking, while the very best scientists are strongly linked to intuition. The evaluative function of feeling, however, is almost completely ignored. The model of a human being does not apply to the field of science. But it does apply to the scientist, who even scientists agree is part of everything, too. Harding is a scientist who is retraining himself to approach science not only through sensing, thinking, and intuition but also through his feelings.

For a number of years, he has worked on issues related to the Gaia theory, the idea that life on earth—the totality of living organisms—has created a favorable atmosphere for itself, which it maintains at a favorable global temperature. This is accomplished through complex feedback loops that include the release and storage of carbon dioxide, the weathering of rock, tiny marine algae, clouds, volcanoes, and trees. Although these systems of regulation are not purposeful or sentient, they mimic the coherency of a living organism. They provide us with the image of a planet, renamed Gaia, that has to be understood holistically, a web of relationships between the animate and inanimate. Scientists who explore these relationships are impressed with their tight coupling, the way each affects the other. Gaia's ability to self-regulate is an intricate balance now being disturbed by the human production of excess carbon dioxide and the extreme changes we have made in plant communities.

Stephan Harding is distressed by the distress of Gaia. His feelings tell him that nature is not mechanistic but infused by something like Plato's idea of *anima mundi,* or soul of the world. He is particularly intrigued by the metaphor of animism, the ancient belief that all things—even mountains, even stars—are alive.

He is not abandoning conventional science. The basic principle of science is still the same: We construct models that describe nature by proposing a hypothesis, trying to disprove that hypothesis, recording the data, and integrating this work into a larger understanding of the world. Analysis and measurement are important tools. We should try to be objective. We should invite scrutiny. But at the right time and place, Harding wants to add feeling to the mix. This can lead to Fritjof Capra's greater spiritual awareness, as well as to a greater understanding of politics and social justice. Stephan Harding's feelings about global warming take him straight to the gross domestic product and the World Bank. Eventually he will end up in Guatemala.

He concludes his book *Animate Earth,* "With our reason satisfied, our intuition, seeing, and feeling are able to forge a connection so deep that we no longer need to think of it. Only when our four ways of knowing are fully engaged in this way can right action emerge—and it is only the summed effect of billions of right actions by people across the planet that may eventually lead us into a genuinely fruitful relationship with Gaia, our animate Earth."

Feelings connect science to the rest of the world. The evaluative function has long directed individual scientists to participate or not in certain kinds of research. To use experimental animals. To build weapons. To throw the mosquito fish into the bush. These decisions are not simple or obvious. I am reminded of how Spinoza concluded his book *Ethics:* "All noble things are as difficult as they are rare."

The Buddha, interestingly, believed that empathy and compassion were not simply good feelings but important ingredients in the goal of blowing out the ego. They were practical steps to a desired end. Some scientists have also found this to be true in their work. As early as the 1930s, the biologist Barbara McClintock worked with corn and developed theories as to how genes were able to turn off and on, repressing or expressing physical characteristics of the plant. Of the particular corn plants in her experimental fields, she wrote, "I know them intimately, and I find it a great pleasure to know them." Her affectionate feelings for chromosomes seemed to enhance her ability to do science: "I found that the more I worked with them, the bigger the chromosomes got. . . . I was able to see the internal parts. . . . It surprised me because I actually felt as if I were right down there and these were my friends. As you look at these things, they become part of you. And you forget yourself."

Barbara McClintock was perceived as an eccentric woman, dismissed and scorned for decades of her career. She unabashedly spoke of the Oneness of the universe, was not afraid to be called a mystic, and advised her colleagues to encourage in themselves "a feeling for the organism." In her understanding of chromosomes, she was ahead of her time. In 1981 she won the Nobel Prize for her discovery of genetic material that moved position and responded to the environment.

Ursula Goodenough is also a cell biologist and author of the best-selling textbook *Genetics* and the more personal *The Sacred Depths of Nature*. She has less to say about how we can bring our feelings and our spirituality into science—and more about how science has deepened her feelings and affected her life as a religious person. I find her ideas profoundly moving. In Quaker language, "She speaks to me."

Reverence is a given. Goodenough is filled with awe at the emergence of life from nonlife, the self-replication of RNA and DNA, the miracle of proteins and their receptors. I think of Sarah from bird banding, who once stood above a pool of hatching mayflies and almost burst into tears. I think of my sister, who works in AIDS research and got goose bumps when she first studied the immune system. I think of Mike looking at his son, Dominic: love from matter. Ursula Goodenough feels the same amazement.

But from her perspective, biological processes are also "obvious, explainable, and thermodynamically inevitable." Her science shows her how the miracles work. She knows she is thoroughly unique, the product of incalculable actions and reactions. She also knows she must die to make room for more uniqueness and the play of evolution. She accepts death as the price paid for life. She accepts her occasional experience of immanence—the pantheistic mergence into One—as a mental phenomena that is wonderful but also chemical and, again, explainable.

Even so, she is grateful for her existence. She is joyous.

Such moments come and go. Sometimes, instead, she falls into grief and resentment. Nature is betrayal. Someone she loves will be hit by a truck or get a terrible disease or drown in the ocean. The physical world is full of physical pain and suffering, and she wants more. "When my awe at how life works gives way to self-pity because it doesn't work the way I would like," Goodenough writes, "I call on assent—the age-old religious response."

Job asks, "Why me?" And then bows his head: "Thy will be done."

Assent is based on understanding. We are a part of something larger. We are a community. We spring into being like the original proton. We spring into nonbeing. Assent is based on humility. The part cannot know the sum. Truth is approximate. We bow our heads. "Assent is a dignified word," Goodenough says. "Once it is freely given, one can move fluidly within it."

One night, as a college student on a camping trip, Goodenough looked up at the stars, knowing all those impossible facts—one hundred billion galaxies, one hundred billion stars in each one—and felt overwhelmed. The universe was too big, too violent, too pointless. She wept into her pillow.

Sometime later she stopped looking for the point. She made a covenant with mystery and rested inside it. Suddenly she didn't need to find any more answers than the ones in front of her:

And so, I profess my Faith. For me, the existence of all this complexity and awareness and intent and beauty, and my ability to apprehend it, serves as the ultimate meaning and the ultimate value. The continuation of life reaches, grabs its own tail, and forms a sacred circle that requires no further justification, no Creator, no subordinate meaning of meaning, no purpose other than that the continuation continue until the sun collapses or the final meteor collides. I confess a credo of continuation.

Ursula Goodenough calls herself a religious naturalist. When I e-mail her and ask why, she explains that she finds the term more flexible than pantheist. The word religious encompasses responses that are both spiritual and moral. The word naturalist connects these responses to our scientific understanding of nature. Also, pantheism requires too much explanation of what it is and what it is not. Although she likes the idea of a word that is rooted in history, in this case, she prefers a neologism.

Goodenough is an active member of the Institute of Religion and Science (IRAS), a lovely organization with a prosaic motto: "Working for a positive and dynamic relationship between religion and science since 1954." On the IRAS Web site, you will find the names of religious figures like the priest and cultural historian Thomas Berry, who sees the new story of cosmology and evolution as our new Creation story. A primordial energy blazed forth, planets formed, life self-organized, and consciousness emerged—the universe reflecting on itself. This story is so powerful, so astonishing, and so real as to be sacred. With a sense of awe and mystery, Berry has discovered his religion in science. On the IRAS Web site, you will also find the names of people like Fritjof Capra, who can quote Chuang Tzu and the Diamond Sutra, who have gone to the great spiritual traditions and found the echo of what they do in their research and laboratories. With a sense of awe and mystery, Capra has discovered his science in religion.

And you will find many of the same names and ideas when you go to the Web site of the World Pantheist Movement, with its focus primarily on scientific pantheism. Here you will see pictures of honorary advisers like Ursula Goodenough and James Lovelock, the founder of the Gaia theory. You will see links to "Get Involved" and "Beliefs" and "Concerns" and "Practices." You may be surprised, as I was, to read this quote by Mikhail Gorbachev, the onetime head of the Russian Communist Party, who helped end the Cold War and dissolve the Soviet Union: "I believe in the cosmos. We are all linked to the cosmos. So nature is my god. To me, trees are sacred. Trees are my temples, and forests are my cathedrals." You can read other quotes from Henry David Thoreau and Sitting Bull.

At the very top of this Web page, you will be greeted with a fundamental question, the boiled-down essence of pantheism today: "Is Nature your spiritual home?" Say yes, and you can chat all day about everything from meditation to animal rights. You can link to the Unitarian Universalists and other pantheistically minded groups. You can parse for yourself the difference between atheism, humanism, and pantheism. You can learn how other pantheists celebrate the spring equinox. You can donate money to restore wetlands. Say yes, and you can join this "club of like-minded friends" for as little as ten dollars, or thirty dollars if your income is higher. Say yes, and you may—if you have, in fact, found your spiritual home—feel a little happier all day long, your four functions a little more integrated, your understanding of faith a little more clear.

I am forgetting to tell you about the food. Peter likes to cook. He finds cooking relaxing. Within a set of rules, like the prescribed syllables of a haiku or sestina, he can be creative, exchanging this ingredient for a similar one, mixing Italian into a Mexican dish, trying out a new kind of dried mushroom. He claims that cooking is meditative. You have to be in the moment. Chop, chop, chop. Watch the butter melt. Stir the onions. He likes the fact that a meal has a beginning and an end, and the end is delicious. (I do the dish washing and cleaning up.) When we pack for our long weekends in the Gila, we take along four or five cookbooks. What we are actually going to eat is usually Peter's secret. It might be lamb with tiny squash. It might be carrot soup with a sauce of roasted and blended red peppers. For lunch, he will make aioli to spread on the sandwiches. For breakfast, he mixes asparagus tips into scrambled eggs. This is all good for me, since I approach cooking with an emotional range of boredom to dislike. (The exception was feeding children, which felt primal and important.)

But Peter likes to cook, and after a week of working in town as a city planner, he needs a lot of relaxing. Chop, chop, chop. He grills and slices all weekend, and we eat these lovely, elegant meals—with a salad of local spinach and piñon nuts—and this adds to the sense that we are creating a special life in a special place. I go for walks in the Mind and Body of God. I read and grade student papers. For my graduate students who want to be writers, I edit and encourage. Good job. Nice opening. Strong ending. I am kind and supportive.

Late in October, the cottonwoods turn yellow against the blue sky, and the course of the river glows brightly. Peter and I walk together to the Nature Conservancy pond. The brilliance of these leaves! When I was pregnant with Maria and then David, I sometimes stopped what I was doing just to remind myself—that I was in the middle of a miracle. That miracles are ordinary. People grow from a cell. The caterpillar becomes a butterfly. Every fall, these colors. We are simply surrounded.

Behind us on the narrow dirt road, Mike bumps up and down the ruts in his 1996 Honda Civic. He has been checking the irrigation ditches, and we move aside to let him pass. He stops to exchange news about the sandhill cranes that have not yet arrived but that we hope will come soon. Mike takes in the scene, gestures toward the river, and smiles: "Another day in paradise."

Of course, it is not true. People here, Peter and I included, have the usual assortment of insecurities, poor health, and problems at work. There are frustrations, divorces, estrangements. General *dukka*. Here in the Gila Valley, among our friends especially, there is a lot of fear. We invite them to dinner, and they praise Peter's cooking; we have a good time, and then someone brings up the future. Mike and Carol worry about when the world runs out of oil and the economy collapses. Almost every day, Nena gets on a Web site that tells her how fast the polar ice caps are melting. Like a number of people—like the eminent scientist James Lovelock, founder of the Gaia theory—she believes we are past the tipping point in terms of climate change. We cannot prevent the coming disaster. People are afraid for their children and for themselves: We will lose this wonderful earth. The American Southwest will become a dust bowl, and the smell of rotting fish will be everywhere. Already, we are in the middle of another mass extinction, more species disappearing every day. Perhaps more to the point, this is our fault. The human race is greedy and stupid. When my non-Christian friends talk about the future, there is a strangely Christian undercurrent. We are sinners, and sinners must be punished.

No one wants now a second helping of Peter's green chilies and corn stew. Maybe more wine. We sit fearful and ashamed among the debris of our meal. Only three-year-old Dominic keeps playing happily under the table. This is not a single or singular conversation. We hear versions of it almost every weekend. We live in the constant expulsion from Eden. We live with the ghost of the brilliant nineteenth-century scholar and prophet George Perkins Marsh, like some righteous Scrooge poking his finger at the out-of-season fruit on the table, at the microwave, at the roll of paper towels. "The ravages committed by man," he intones, "subvert the relations and destroy the balance which nature has established, and she avenges herself upon the intruder by letting loose her destructive energies."

In 1999, at the close of the last century, Thomas Berry wrote a book called *The Great Work: Our Way into the Future.* Berry pointed to different cultures that in their time accomplished something significant. The Greeks began the Western humanist tradition, India had the spiritual insights of Hinduism and Buddhism, the Native Americans populated a continent with ritual and song. Today, Berry believes, modern society also has a Great Work—which is to shift our industrial civilization into a relationship that protects and lives in harmony with Gaia, the earth we live on.

Berry is clear: It won't be easy. He is honest: We aren't doing this by choice. We do not, after all, choose the moment of our birth, our parents, or our culture. "We do not," he wrote, "choose the status of spiritual insight or political or economic conditions that will be the context of our lives. We are, as it were, thrown into existence with a challenge and a role that is beyond any personal choice. The nobility of our lives, however, depends upon the manner in which we come to understand and fulfill our assigned task."

Everyone in this room, including Dominic, has been thrown into existence. Unfair as it may seem, we have an assigned task. Homework at the age of three, or fifty-two, or eighty-seven.

A number of people in the Gila Valley already know this. The alternative community makes a conscious effort to live simply and model a life of nonconsumerism and noncompliance. Next door to the Gila River Farm, a commune of some twelve people lives on eighteen acres in a scattered compound of two adobe houses, one straw-bale house, one house made of paper, one house made of stone and bottles, a teepee, and a bus. Most of them avoid driving into town. They don't buy much. They garden and eat wild foods. Meanwhile, as a city planner, Peter works on water issues and sustainable growth. It is a credit to the town of Silver City that for this job they hired someone who had been nine years with the Nature Conservancy. Our neighbors April and Merritt live half the year in Alaska, where they are active in a long list of civic and environmental organizations. They are active here, too—everywhere they go. As president of the board of the Alaska Conservation Foundation, April oversees a budget of several million. In the Gila Valley, on the board of the Upper Gila Watershed Association, she helps work with small-scale projects that protect nearby springs and promote tree thinning in the national forest. Then there are the scientists who come to study the Gila River: local biologists like Mike and Carol and Steve MacDonald and Dennis Miller, and those from further away, like Vicenc from Spain.

Mike once asked me what I thought a pantheistic community would look like. I think we would be as diverse as the paragraph above. We would each find our spiritual home in nature, which presumes a relationship with nature that is celebratory and nonviolent. We would each be involved in the Great Work—with many versions of how to do that. We would not necessarily all like each other or have the same cultural values. Here in the Gila Valley, the small-scale agriculturalist wants the river water for crops while the biologist wants the river water for wildlife. The purists limit their use of hot water and appliances and criticize the nonpurists, who buy dishwashers and fly in airplanes. The nonpurists criticize anyone who voted for Ralph Nader in 2000 instead of Al Gore.

I struggle with my own response to bad news. There is guilt and self-loathing. Peter jokes, "This food was cooked locally." But we both know we are part of the problem. We have to change. There is denial. Maybe the problem isn't as bad as we think? Maybe someone else will make it go away? There is anger and blame that too easily become a grudge, that tape loop going round and round. There is fear of that apocalyptic world where all the good things—the very sweetest things—will be taken from me and my children and their children's children. Certainly, there is sorrow for the people and animals who have already suffered, who are suffering now, and who will suffer in the future. There are all those feelings that science tries hard to avoid, and they can get mixed up and mixed together. Loud voices. Hand-wringing. What to do?

The pantheistic response would be "Hush." Calm yourself. Life is flux and change. The cost of existence is high. Think of the burning sun converting four hundred tons of hydrogen into helium every second! Think of the bill to pay for human consciousness. Stop whining. It is all on loan. Accept your life with cheerful affection. The pantheistic response would be to fall in love. Fall in love outward. Fall in love with this moment, with this earth now. In that response will be the seeds of right action or right nonaction. Fall in love and see what happens.

Thomas Berry believes in the importance of the human species. We are the universe reflecting on itself. All our four functions—sensing, thinking, intuition, and feeling—are the universe looking around. Our art is the universe doing art. Our science is the universe doing science. In this view, human consciousness becomes something to be proud of and something to protect.

I am not so sure. Life emerged from nonlife and consciousness emerged from life, and maybe this chain of events has a greater meaning, and maybe not. Maybe we have a destiny in the universe and maybe nothing in the universe is destined. The continuation of life grabs its tail and forms a sacred circle.

Meanwhile, I am making my covenant with mystery. I rest in the mystery of the future. This is what our children do, playing under the table. They give us the mystery of the future.

I rest in the mystery of the present, whirling protons I cannot see, feelings I cannot see, blue sky I see differently from a butterfly, yellow leaves dying along the river, red lipstick on a loach minnow. Sacred Reality. This little yellow house and the smell of Peter's green chilies and corn stew. From here we move forward. From here I will make the changes I am capable of making.

CHAPTER 12

Meeting for Worship

IN NOVEMBER, my father-in-law comes for an extended visit, something he does now twice a year in the fall and spring. He has just turned eighty-seven years old, with a long career in the United States military, and he still skis half the winter—downhill skiing, fast down a hill. Colonel Russell largely designed the yellow house in the Gila Valley, insisting on high ceilings and French doors and a Portuguese-style hip roof, a bit of Old Europe, where he once spent many happy years. Today he lives in Washington, D.C., and these eight hundred square feet in New Mexico have become his country home. Here, on our land near the Gila River Farm, he will plant grapes and a dozen fruit trees. He will buy a rototiller with an intimidating array of attachments. He will put up a bird feeder and plan a rose arbor. He will see all this as a memorial to Nancy, Peter's mother, who died too early of cancer at the age of seventy-two.

For these visits, Peter and I move back full time into Silver City. This November, then, I am in town on Sunday mornings. And I finally go to Quaker Meeting. We gather at what used to be a Presbyterian church, turned now into a private home and rented out to groups like us, with a sign in the front yard: The Church of What's Happening. We are what happens every Sunday at 10 a.m.

I go up the steps into the large, bright kitchen, where Elisabeth is putting down an empty bowl. She unpacks the rest of her bag, which includes winter squash to give away, newspaper clippings, and a vase of flowers. In the room next door, Polly, as clerk, has already sat down in a circle of chairs. Her job is to encourage other people to do the same, stop chatting, and join the circle of silence. Nena and Steve are not here today. There are a few people I know and some I do not. There are eleven of us altogether. Polly smiles warmly and pats the chair next to her. I have not been to Meeting for at least two years, but I feel right at home.

It is three minutes past ten. Soon we are all sitting. We are all silent.

Each time, at every Quaker Meeting, I feel the same wonder. What prompts this group of people to sit and wait so expectantly, as though we were doing something important? Do any of us pray for a visiting god? Are we all thinking about peace and love? Are we trying to levitate? Or be more like a cat?

I cannot say for sure, since I do not know everyone here. But I think we are simply trying to be silent. Like Buddhists, we hope for the still mind. We notice our thoughts and let them go. We focus on our senses, the present moment. We believe faithfully that in a moment of listening, we will hear that small inner voice. Then we won't be so lonely. We will feel a presence inside, surrounding us. We will know what we have always suspected: Eternal life is under the words.

I begin to think about pantheism. In truth, my best thinking has often been done in Quaker silence, where I have an agreement: This is not the place for work, relationships, children, sex, politics, money, or vacation plans. There is not much left to do but try to be profound or try to be still. The former is often so interesting that I forget to concentrate on my breath or the present moment.

I think of the history of pantheism, running like a river through Western thought. I am reminded of the enormous pleasure I had as a child connecting the dots in one of those simply drawn pictures in which the dots suddenly formed . . . a rooster! A pig! A birthday present with a large bow. All along, the dots had a coherence. Heraclitus and Chuang Tzu, Marcus Aurelius and Thoreau, Giordano Bruno and William Blake, Jim Corbett and Spinoza. A picture forms.

Mostly that picture will be from nature. A cow! A daisy! Nature is our spiritual home. Even in the midst of war, Marcus Aurelius paused to write about the beauty of wheat stalks or the "flecks of foam on a boar's mouth." The deep ecologist quotes Robinson Jeffers. Everyone quotes Walt Whitman. We are dazzled by the sunset, and we weep at the stars. We can't help ourselves. We come from the earth. We have a physical response.

I need that—and more. If I am to commit to pantheism, then pantheism must answer the questions all religions must answer.

The one about morality is easy. When you are part of everything, the Golden Rule is a given: Do unto others as you would do unto yourself. When everything is connected, you live in a world of relationships. You can explain human relationships, if you want, with evolutionary biology. We are social animals who need altruism to survive. As Marcus Aurelius wrote, "In a sense, people are our proper occupation." You can explain our relationship to the natural world with the science of ecology. "When we try to pick out anything by itself," John Muir wrote, "we find it hitched to everything else in the Universe." Connection is not a choice; it is Sacred Reality.

Both Hinduism and Buddhism have the further insight that the self-centered ego causes much of our suffering, our separation from the One. We can subvert the ego by filling our thoughts with compassion and loving-kindness. I have been trying to do this lately, and it seems to work. Recently, on a trip to Albuquerque, I found it effective in an airport. I looked around at all the people, impatient like me to be somewhere else, and I willed myself to love them. I was part of them. We were part of something larger. All these metal chairs, too, the carpet and windows and knickknacks in the shops. All the atoms whirling. Here, too, I found myself walking through the Mind and Body of God.

Taoism adds to the practice of pantheism by reminding us to relax. Let the current do its work. Be humble. Be simple. Laugh. Don't take yourself so seriously.

Concerning death, the Epicureans suggested we not think much about it. Why be afraid of what we will never experience? The Stoics saw death as a release back into the Unity or the

Logos. Spinoza believed that the personality disappeared but something eternal remained. Scientific pantheists find no evidence that the individual can continue without the body. For the pantheist, then, death is not a personal concern but an end to all personal concerns.

Even so, I find myself thinking now—in Quaker Meeting—about the moments before my death. I do not really count this as a premonition, but I have for whatever reason seen or imagined these moments. This is a strong visual image, modest enough to feel real. I am walking outside along a roadway, and I fall so that my cheek presses into the ground. I fall into dirt, not the road, which in any case does not have much traffic, being one of those roads that I often walk. I am alone. I have the insect's perspective. Blades of grass rise up like green swords, strange trees swaying with my breath. I see the crumbles of rock and soil, the glitter of rose quartz and silver mica. A silken white thread floats from a yellow stalk. I am grateful that I can also see blue sky, a large patch above this new horizon, the beautiful blue New Mexican sky. If I am lucky, a cloud will drift through this blue space. Although I cannot move anything but my eyes, the ground is soft and warm, and I am relatively comfortable. I know I will be here for a short while only. I am dying here, and these are the last things I will ever see.

At the moment of my death, I want to be at home in the world. I want the world to feel sacred. I want to feel special. I want to be part of something larger.

OK. Let's start over. I want to be at home right now, at Quaker Meeting where I am supposed to be waiting for the

Light and letting go of words—going under the words. I am here to drop all the questions and all the answers, too. I am here for the silence, what Quakers refer to as a practical mysticism, nothing too grand, maybe only a fleeting sense of Oneness. I remind myself of that—Stop thinking about pantheism, please—even as I look up at the round clock on the wall with its large black numbers. We sit in silence for an hour. How much time is left?

When I look up at the clock, I notice that Elisabeth is also looking up at the clock. Each time I look up and around, I see other people, some people I know and some I do not. I am grateful for them. Quakers believe that corporate worship is more powerful than individual worship. I do not know yet if this is true, but I find this circle of human beings deeply reassuring.

Elisabeth smiles wanly. I suspect she has been worrying about her sister, who is ill, or her husband, who is ninety and still ranching. Or maybe she has been thinking about her roses, which she grows in wonderful profusion in the desert and which she recently pruned and babied and bedded down for the winter. Someone coughs and coughs again. I realize I have chosen the wrong chair. This one hurts my back.

Given the depth of our struggle to reach silence, to go under the words, it seems odd that Quakers endorse what we call vocal ministry. Once a month, my Meeting has Queries, a half hour set aside for the reading and response to specific Quaker concerns. Also, at any Meeting, Quakers can rise at any time and say what is bursting to be said in their hearts and souls. Very early Quakers got their name because the emotion of hearing God's voice and seeing the Light caused them, literally, to quake. Understandably they might have imploded had they not been allowed to speak about the experience. The Quakers I know today do not quake at all, and still we continue to break silence.

Breaking silence requires a certain protocol. The desire to speak should have a sense of urgency. At the same time, there is often an inner trepidation that precedes speaking. A Quaker must be sure he or she has a legitimate message for Meeting and not simply the impulse to share a random thought or show off some insight. Convinced at last, the Quaker will rise and speak briefly. The language used is often symbolic and suggestive, the language of spirit, not fact. Very soon the Quaker sits down, letting the words sink into the center of the circle. These words do not provoke a dialogue but ripple out like the waves of a pebble thrown into a pond. In some Meetings, Quakers rise and speak fairly often. Generally, in my Meeting, they do not. At least not in the Meeting I remember.

Today, though, halfway through silence, a Friend stands and begins to protest the Iraq War. She goes on for at least five minutes. Maybe six or seven. It seems much longer. As clerk, Polly makes subtle shifts in her chair. Polly is a little annoyed. Or maybe I am projecting. Maybe only I am annoyed. This woman is giving us a lecture, a rant, not a Quaker epiphany. This is completely against protocol.

At last she stops. The room is quiet again. We are left thinking about the Iraq War, not a bad thing to think about, surely. We are left with images of suffering.

Pantheism is weak on suffering. The pain of burnt five-year-olds and women ripped apart by bombs and men tortured in secret rooms is not its strong point. There is little comfort in the idea that this is all God, too. But then, I would say that none of the religions deal well with a burnt five-year-old—not theism or polytheism, atheism or animism or any of the rest. The pain of a human being is about being human in a particular body and mind. (The same is true for the pain of a dog.) We seem to be talking about different levels of reality. There is the screaming child, and then there are the stars. There is the screaming, weeping child and the glory of a loving personal God or the spirit in the trees or the egolessness of nirvana. To use an analogy, different parts of physics also don't make sense side by side. Everything is One, but the scientists can't put it all together yet, and neither can I.

Now a man in our Quaker Meeting also stands. He is off on a different topic. He wants to talk about sustainability and global warming and that apocalyptic future where all the sweetest things will be taken from us and our children and our children's children. Metaphorically, he wrings his hands. He froths. He despairs. By now it is clear to you and to me that this is not a circle of Taoist sages. We are not of the still mind. We are flawed and restless, some more than others. This time I do not feel annoyed. I am caught up in the theater, this man on the stage of Quaker worship, and I find myself moved by his heartfelt emotion. I am glad the silence is broken. I want to hear what this man has to say.

Why is silence so hard to bear? Even in Quaker Meeting, especially in Quaker Meeting, we can't stop thinking and talking. We can't be quiet enough to listen. In her essay "A Field of Silence," the writer Annie Dillard (a descendant, surely, of the transcendentalists) describes the silence of matter, the nonhuman world, as holy and terrifying:

> I lived there once and I have seen, from behind the barn, the long roadside pastures heaped with silence. Behind the rooster, suddenly, I saw the silence heaped on the fields like trays. That day the green hayfields supported silence evenly sown; the fields bent just so under the even pressure of silence, bearing it, palming it aloft; cleared fields, part of a land, a planet, that did not buckle beneath the heel of silence, nor split up scattered to bits, but instead lay secret, disguised as time and matter, as though that were nothing, ordinary—disguised as fields like those which bear the silence only because they are spread, and the silence spreads over them, great in size.

"I do not want," she concludes, "ever to see such a sight again."

Later in the essay, Annie Dillard decides that this field of silence was in fact a field of angels. "If pressed I would say they were three or four feet from the ground. Only their motion was clear (clockwise if you insist); that, and their beauty unspeakable."

Oh, Annie, you and me. The silence of matter is also one I cannot easily hear or understand. The silence of matter is holy and terrifying. Angels are a story I might tell, if pressed. Pantheism is another. I sit in Quaker Meeting in the silence of the Universe-that-is-God, and I long to hear that silence. Then again, apparently, I do not.

The man who wants to talk about global warming sits down. I am thinking about Annie Dillard. I am thinking I should have brought a pillow for my back. I am thinking—because of this man—that once I believed I was at the cutting edge of Thomas Berry's Great Work, that living as a back-to-the-lander and finding my personal connection to nature was the larger work of our industrial society. I was young then and lived more simply, having much less money. Since then, for various reasons, I have been coopted into a consumptive and rapacious middle class. Since then, I suspect, I have been moved into an eddy, a backwater of the Great Work, which is now in the cities where most people live and in the metasystems of government and law and commerce. I believe this in my more hopeless moments: that I have nothing to contribute. Then I reverse my opinion. Pantheism would say, "Hush." Everyone is important. Every place is important. We are all part of everything.

I look up to see Polly looking at the clock. Some clerks, I notice, end silence a few minutes before the hour, and some end a few minutes after the hour, and some end exactly on time. Polly will end exactly on time.

Straightening in her chair, she seems to gather energy. "Good morning, Friends," she says, and we all stand and reach for each other's hands and form a circle. We are happy and relieved. Silence is over.

A few weeks later, I am walking around the Nature Conservancy pond with my friend Patty. I have been to Quaker Meeting every Sunday this month, and I will go again later in May, when my father-in-law returns for his spring visit. It is a strange kind of Quakerism, two months of the year. Maybe I need to rethink this. Or maybe I just need to relax. Take each Sunday as it comes. The Mondays, too, Wednesdays and Fridays.

Today is Thursday, and Patty and I have come out to the Gila Valley for a Silver Consolidated School Board Meeting. We do this twice a year at the small rural school down the road that is also part of our district in town. Patty and I are prematurely nostalgic because I am leaving the school board soon, after eight years, and she is staying on. We have sat together through some tumultuous meetings, often about sports—crowds of people who want a coach fired or crowds of people who don't want a coach fired—but also about our health insurance policy for domestic partners or how to fund the arts or what kind of food to put in the vending machines. We have suffered through the No Child Left Behind Act, which we also call the No Child Is Unique Act. We have listened courteously to beliefs we strenuously disagree with. We have saluted the American and New Mexican flags countless times, at the beginning of every meeting. Each time, I have been impressed by myself, on the school board. What could be more grown-up? This is how public service makes me feel. Like a grown-up.

By now, most of the yellow cottonwood leaves have dropped to the ground. The trees are bare again, and the sandhill cranes have come back to the fields. Just moments ago, Patty and I passed twenty cranes poking through the soil. We stopped to watch one land. In the air, the long legs of these birds usually trail straight behind, the long neck pointing forward—amazing flying sticks. But on landing, the legs drop, a sudden weight directed down. The crane cups her wings and spreads her tail, falling like a parachute and flapping quickly at the last moment.

We stop again and I show Patty two more cranes at the edge of the Conservancy's newly recovered wetlands, a second pond fifty yards away. I have brought my binoculars for this purpose, to show off my wonderful life. One of the cranes jumps into the air, flapping his wings. Facing her partner, the second crane also jumps into the air, flapping her wings. I exclaim too loudly, but the birds do not care. These cranes are dancing.

As I pass the binoculars to Patty, I explain that this is very exciting. It is a privilege to see a crane dance, especially in the winter past the mating season. I have been waiting a long time for this. The first crane jumps, his neck stretched out. The second crane jumps, her neck stretched out. Then the first crane. Then the second crane. Patty catches my enthusiasm. Soon I notice that Patty is actually more enthusiastic than I am, which is interesting and a little surprising. Later that night she will tell the school superintendent, "The most amazing thing happened today!" and her face will light up with happiness.

We continue our walk around the pond, to the river, and back to my house. I am wondering whether I should use these cranes in the book I am writing. It is awfully pat. Will my readers believe me? A year ago, I hoped to see the dance of the greater sandhill cranes. Now they have danced for me as a kind of literary conclusion. The shape of a story. I wonder if people will understand how often this happens in my line of work, how often truth is shaped like a story.

And why don't I feel that divine rush of pleasure and awe? Why is Patty more excited about the sandhill cranes than I am?

What do I feel anyway?

Calm, I think. Serene.

As we approach my little yellow house—the color so inviting, the wraparound porch, the hip roof—I realize that for a long time now I have known I would see the cranes dance. I have had faith. After all, I live here. This fact is finally beginning to sink in. I live here, and when you live in a place, eventually you will see all its wonders.

ACKNOWLEDGMENTS

In particular, I would like to thank a circle of friends and fellow writers who looked over this manuscript as it was being written: Sarah Johnson, Carol and Mike Fugagli, Kate Storm Guthrie, Nena MacDonald, April Crosby, Gail Stamler, Polly Walker, Elisabeth Simon, Patty Reed, Kate Haake, and Peter Russell. Their encouragement was invaluable. Special thanks must go to my husband, Peter, and to my daughter, Maria—who helped me in many ways, not least with her understanding of Eastern religions and her beautifully drawn timelines.

I am also grateful to a wonderful group of bird banders, some of whom overlap with my writing friends: Sarah Johnson, Carol and Mike Fugagli, Nena MacDonald, Peter Russell, Eleanor and Tom Wooten, and Patricia Tabor. In addition, Shirley Pevarnik was a good lunch companion who re-introduced me to Thomas Berry.

As usual, my editors at Perseus Books Group were also supportive. Meg Hustad originally accepted the proposal, and Lara Heimert shepherded the project to final publication. Lara's enthusiasm and intelligence contributed enormously to the manuscript.

My colleagues at Western New Mexico University were help-ful as well, particularly the scientists in the Biology Department: Dennis Miller, Bill Norris, and Randy Jennings. As always, I must thank the staff at the Interlibrary Loan Department in the WNMU Miller Library. I sometimes wonder what they must think of my peculiar tastes and range of reading material. They never comment. They just get me the books I need.

SELECTED REFERENCES
AND NOTES

Introductory Note and Chapter 1: Standing in the Light

The quote from Marcus Aurelius can be found in Marcus Aurelius, *Meditations* (New York: Modern Library, 2002), wonderfully translated by Gregory Hays. More information on how Quakers view the Light is in Howard H. Brinton, *Friends for 300 Years* (Wallinford, Pa.: PendleHill, 1947). Information on Universalist Quakers can be found specifically in *The Quaker Universalist Reader, Number 1* (Landerberg, Pa.: 1986), and Patricia A. Williams, ed., *Universalism and Religions* (Columbia, Md.: Quaker Universalist Fellowship, 2007). The Web sites www.universalistfriends.org and www.qug.org.uk have a number of quotes and material on this aspect of Quakerism.

An important source of information about pantheism is Paul Harrison, *Elements of Pantheism* (Coral Springs, Fla.: Llumina Press, 2004). Harrison gives a good overview of the history of pantheism, along with various definitions, core beliefs, ethics, ceremonies, and controversies. He is the founder of the World Pantheist Movement and creator of two Web sites on the subject. Go to www.pantheism.org.

I am also indebted to Michael P. Levine, *Pantheism: A Non-theistic Concept of Deity* (London: Routledge, 1994), and Michael Levine, "Pantheism," *Stanford Encyclopedia of Philosophy* at http://plato.stanford.edu/entries/pantheism. Levine's online article in the *Stanford Encyclopedia of Philosophy* is particularly insightful and comprehensive.

The comment on "sexed-up atheism" is from Richard Dawkins, *The God Delusion* (Boston: Houghton Mifflin, 2006).

The quotes from Walt Whitman are from the poem "Walt Whitman," later and more familiarly called "Song of Myself," in Walt Whitman, *Leaves of Grass* (Brooklyn, N.Y.: Whitman, Rome Bros., 1855). I also used the early edition Walt Whitman, *Leaves of Grass* (Philadelphia: David McCay, Washington Square, 1900). The statement by Robinson Jeffers is from a letter he wrote in 1934, which I found quoted in George Session, "Spinoza and Jeffers on Man in Nature," *Inquiry: An Interdisciplinary Journal of Philosophy and the Social Sciences,* vol. 20, no. 4, Winter 1977. Frank Lloyd Wright is quoted from Harrison's *The Elements of Pantheism.* Albert Einstein's quote can be found in Albert Einstein, *Ideas and Opinions* (New York: Crown, 1954), edited by Carl Seelig and translated by Sonja Bargmann.

Some scholars would not label the Greek and Roman Stoics as pantheists. I would argue, with others, that their beliefs were clearly pantheistic and that Spinoza's ideas of how to live in the world as a pantheist were strikingly Stoical.

The curse by which Spinoza's Jewish community exiled him is from a translation of the Portuguese original by Frederick Pollock in 1880. I found it in Antonio Damasio, *Looking for Spinoza: Joy, Sorrow, and the Feeling Brain* (Orlando, Fla.: Harcourt Books, 2003), and in Steven Nadler, *Spinoza: A Life* (Cambridge, England: Cambridge University Press, 1999), which is the source I used for this translation. Other sources for Spinoza's life and philosophy included Stuart Hampshire, *Spinoza* (New York: Penguin Books, 1951); Steven Nadler, *Spinoza: A Life* (Cambridge, England: Cambridge University Press, 1999); and Steven Nadler, "Baruch Spinoza," *Stanford Encyclopedia of Philosophy,* http://plato.stanford.edu/entries/spinoza.

More information on John Toland can be found at the World Pantheist Movement Web site. The quotes from Toland come from John Toland, *Pantheisticon* (New York: Garland, 1976). This is also the source for his description of secret pantheistic clubs and their rituals.

Harrison's theory on the numbers of pantheists in the world is found in *The Elements of Pantheism.* More information on the Institute of Religion in the Age of Science (IRAS) can be found at its Web site, www.iras.org. The quote from the *Stanford Encyclopedia of Philosophy* is from the article by Michael Levine.

Thoreau's quote is from his earlier journals—the italics are mine. I found this statement in Frank Stewart, *A Natural History of Nature Writing* (Washington, D.C.: Island Press, 1995). Stewart's work is an excellent overview of nature writing.

Here and later, I talk about the hardwiring of the religious impulse. My thoughts have been influenced by a range of reading that covers many years. Most recently, I have enjoyed Pascal Boyer, *Religion Explained* (New York: Basic Books, 2001); Scott Atran, *In Gods We Trust: The Evolutionary Landscape of Religion* (Oxford, England, and New York: Oxford University Press, 2002); Loyal Rue, *Religion Is Not about God* (New Brunswick, N.J.: Rutgers University Press, 2005); and Daniel C. Dennet, *Breaking the Spell: Religion as a Natural Phenomenon* (New York: Viking, 2006). A good summary of current thought is Robin Marantz Henig, "Darwin's God," *New York Times Magazine,* March 4, 2007.

Chapter 2: The Early Greeks

For much of my natural history of cranes, I used Paul A. Johnsgard, *Crane Music: A Natural History of American Cranes* (Washington, D.C.: Smithsonian Institution Press, 1991), and Peter Matthiessen, *The Birds of Heaven: Travels with Cranes* (New York: North Point Press, 2001). For some of the cultural information, I relied on Alice Lindsay Price, *Cranes: The Noblest Flyers* (Albuquerque, N.M.: La Alameda Press, 2001). I also enjoyed Susan Tweit, *The San Luis Valley: Sand Dunes and Sandhill Cranes* (Tucson: University of Arizona Press, 2005).

The quotes from Aldo Leopold are from Aldo Leopold, *Sand County Almanac* (New York: Oxford University Press, 1949).

A great source of information on the pre-Socratics is Anthony Gottlieb, *The Dream of Reason: A History of Philosophy from the Greeks to the Renaissance* (New York: Norton, 2000). This is an engaging and stimulating book. I also read W. H. Auden, *The Portable Greek Reader* (New York: Penguin Books, 1948); Charles H. Kahn, *The Art and Thought of Heraclitus* (Cambridge, England, and London: Cambridge University Press, 1979); G. S. Kirk, J. E. Raven, and M. Schofield, *The Presocratic Philosophers* (Cambridge, England, and London: Cambridge University Press, 1957); Whitney J. Oates, *The Stoic and Epicurean Philosophers: The Complete Extant Writings of Epicurus, Epictetus, Lucretius, Marcus Aurelius* (New York: Modern Library, 1957); John Burnet, *Greek Philosophy, Thales to Plato* (New York: St Martin's Press, 1961); and Ava Chitwood, *Death by Philosophy: The Biographical Tradition in the Life and Death of the Archaic Philosophers Empedocles, Heraclitus, and Democritus* (Ann Arbor: University of Michigan Press, 2004).

The quotes from Heraclitus are from the translation in *The Presocratic Philosophers.*

It has to be emphasized that what we know about the pre-Socratics is through the filter of later historians, who range from Aristotle, a few hundred years later, to Diogenes Laertius, from the third century CE. This information is often conjecture and speculation. Particularly what we know of Heraclitus is based on a few remaining fragments and the perceptions of later philosophers who mostly didn't like him.

The wag is John Bigelow, who is quoted in Dirk Baltzly, "Stoic Pantheism," *Sophia,* vol. 42, no. 2, October 2003.

The Roman philosopher Lucretius is the Epicurean who spoke of how atoms come together in all manner of ways to form the world we know.

The quotes from Epicurus, the quotes from Lucretius, and the quote by Epictetus concerning giving back what you have been lent are from *The Stoic and Epicurean Philosophers: The Complete Extant Writings of Epicurus, Epictetus, Lucretius, Marcus Aurelius.*

The article about the grieving parents is Rusty Pafford, "She Is the Circling Hawk, the Butterfly," *Pan Magazine,* Winter 2005/Spring 2006. The quote from Carlos Fuentes is in Deborah Solomon, "Questions for Carlos Fuentes," *New York Times Magazine,* April 30, 2006. I do not mean to imply that Carlos Fuentes is a pantheist, only that his technique for grief is one that a pantheist might use.

Chapter 3: Ruler of Everything

Although I read a number of translations of the *Meditations,* I am most indebted to Marcus Aurelius, *Meditations* (New York: Modern Library, 2002), translated by Gregory Hays. Most of the quotes by Marcus Aurelius are from this work.

The long letter to Fronto, however, as well as other comments to Fronto are from C. R. Haines, trans. and ed., *The Correspondence of Marcus Cornelius Fronto with Marcus Aurelius, Antonius Pius, and Various Friends* (Cambridge, Mass.: Harvard University Press, 1919).

For biographical information, I relied on Anthony Birley, *Marcus Aurelius: A Biography* (New Haven, Conn.: Yale University Press, 1987), as well as Henry Dwight Sedgwick, *Marcus Aurelius* (New Haven, Conn.: Yale University Press, 1921), and Alan K. Bowman, Peter Garnsey, and Dominic Rathbone, eds., *The*

Cambridge Ancient History, 2nd ed., vol. 11, *The High Empire, A.D. 70–192* (Cambridge, England, and London: Cambridge University Press, 2000).

In my thoughts on Stoic reason and analysis, I referred to and found helpful a discussion of the three Stoic disciplines—action, desire, and perception—in Pierre Hadot, *The Inner Citadel: The Meditations of Marcus Aurelius* (Cambridge, Mass.: Harvard University Press, 1998). Here Peter Hadot writes, "Ordinary people are content to think in an old way, to act haphazardly, and to undergo grudgingly whatever befalls them. The good man, however, will try, insofar as he is able, to act justly in the service of other people, to accept serenely those events which do not depend on him, and to think with rectitude and veracity."

Information about Commodus comes from *The Cambridge Ancient History,* vol. 11, where I found the quote by Cassius Dio. I also read Martin M. Winkler, *Gladiator: Film and History* (Oxford, England: Blackwell, 2004).

I am always reading popular books by physicists on physics and trying to understand them, with little real success. A good summary of vacuum fluctuations is Brad Lemley, "Guth's Grand Guess," *Discover,* April 2002.

Chapter 4: The Gila River

A further clarification of Peter's jobs would be that he worked as a high school teacher, an outfitter in the Gila Wilderness, Main Street director for Silver City, city planner for Silver City (1992–1996), field director for the Nature Conservancy in Grant County (1996–2005), and city planner for Silver City again (2005–present). He was involved in buying the Gila River Farm for the Nature Conservancy. We bought our adjoining property, however, at a price considerably above market value. No special deals!

Dr. Vicenc Acuna was the Fulbright scholar. Kathy Whiteman was the graduate student tapping water from junipers. Mary Harner worked on studying tree roots and the ecology of cottonwoods and sent me pictures of root systems. Teresa Tibbets was another graduate student doing work in the valley. One study that discusses the history of human modifications in the valley is Ellen Soles, "Where the River Meets the Ditch: Human and Natural Impacts on the Gila River, New Mexico, 1880–2000," submitted for her masters of arts degree in rural geography at Northern Arizona University. The biology professor at WNMU is Dr. Bill Norris. The herpetologist doing the reptile survey, also from WNMU, is Dr. Randy Jennings. Peter Jacobsen is a hydrologist who did important earlier work in the Gila as a Nature Conservancy Fellow at the Lichty Ecological Research Center. Guy McPherson, author and range scientist, also stayed at the Lichty Ecological Research Center and is now returning to live in the Gila Valley as a neighbor.

More information on the Monitoring Avian Productivity and Survivorship program (MAPS) is on the Web site for the Institute of Bird Populations, www.birdpop.org.

Mike's quote from Thoreau comes from Henry David Thoreau, *The Maine Woods* (Boston: Ticknor & Fields, 1864).

Since I have some Cherokee ancestry, the mythical woman who made this pot is genetically related to me, too, but that's not the point of this paragraph.

The information about nanny javelinas comes from Christian R. Schmidt, "Peccaries," *Grzimek's Encyclopedia of Mammals,* vol. 5 (New York: McGraw-Hill, 1989).

Chapter 5: A Renaissance Magician

For the philosophy and biography of Bruno Giordano, I read a number of books, including Paul Henri Michel, *The Cosmology of Giordano Bruno* (Ithaca, N.Y.: Cornell University Press, 1973); Frances A. Yates, *Giordano Bruno and the Hermetic Tradition* (Chicago: University of Chicago Press, 1964); Giordano Bruno, *The Expulsion of the Triumphant Beast,* trans. by Arthur D. Imerti (Lincoln: University of Nebraska Press, 1964); Hilary Gatti, *Giordano Bruno and Renaissance Science* (Ithaca, N.Y.: Cornell University Press, 1999); and Hilary Gatti, ed., *Giordano Bruno: Philosopher of the Renaissance* (Burlington, Vt.: Ashgate, 2002).

Frances A. Yates is the eminent scholar who originally placed Bruno within the Hermetic tradition, referring to him repeatedly as a Renaissance magician. As she wrote in *Giordano Bruno and the Hermetic Tradition,* "By using magical or talismanic images as memory images, the Magus hoped to acquire universal knowledge, and also powers, obtaining through the magical organization of the imagination a magically powerful personality, tuned in, as it were, to the powers of the cosmos."

Scholars continue to have different interpretations of Bruno. Some, like Hilary Gatti, emphasize his role in the early development of science in the late Renaissance rather than his relationship to magic. I enjoyed following this debate in their books.

The quote by Bruno about his childhood is from *The Cosmology of Giordano Bruno*. The quote by the unnamed theologian on Christianity and magic can be found in *The Dream of Reason*. I took the long quote about the Egyptian Reflection of the Universe in the Mind from *Giordano and the Hermetic Tradition,* which is also the source for the other listed images by Bruno. The quote by Bruno about the Oxford faculty is from *The Expulsion of the Triumphant Beast;* the reply is from *Giordano and the Hermetic Tradition*. The quote by Bruno about animals and plants is from *The Expulsion of the Triumphant Beast*. The scholar who noted how Bruno used metaphor is Paul Henry Michel in *The Cosmology of Giordano Bruno*.

Information on the continued biography and trial of Bruno came from all of the above sources, but I am particularly indebted to the foreword by Arthur D. Imerti in *The Expulsion of the Triumphant Beast* and to Maurice A. Finocchiaro, "Philosophy versus Religion and Science versus Religion: The Trials of Bruno and Galileo," in *Giordano Bruno: Philosopher of the Renaissance*. Bruno's quotes from that trial are taken from *The Expulsion of the Triumphant Beast*.

The account of spikes being used at Bruno's trial comes from Michael White, *The Pope and the Heretic* (New York: HarperCollins, 2002). From this book, I also took the quote by Bruno, "To think is to speculate with images."

More information on the Iron Knot Ranch can be found at its Web site, which is www.ironknot.org, and which is the source of quotes concerning its mission.

The quote about the definition of magic and the accompanying story is in Margot Adler, *Drawing Down the Moon* (New York: Penguin Books, 1986). The quote about the ecological function of magic is in David Abram, *The Spell of the Sensuous* (New York: Vintage Press, 1996).

Chapter 6: Baruch Spinoza

Sources for Spinoza's life and philosophy included Antonio Damasio, *Looking for Spinoza: Joy, Sorrow, and the Feeling Brain* (Orlando, Fla.: Harcourt Books, 2003); Stuart Hampshire, *Spinoza* (New York: Penguin Books, 1951); Jonathan Israel, *Radical Enlightenment: Philosophy and the Making of Modernity 1650–1750* (Oxford, England: Oxford University Press, 2001); Steven Nadler, *Spinoza: A Life* (Cambridge, England: Cambridge University Press, 1999); Steven Nadler, "Baruch Spinoza," *Stanford Encyclopedia of Philosophy,* http://plato.stanford.edu/entries/spinoza; and Matthew Stewart, *The Courtier and the Heretic* (New York: W. W. Norton, 2006.)

In particular, Nadler's excellent *Spinoza: A Life* includes material on Spinoza's excommunication, the report by Brother Thomas, and Spinoza's relationship with Quakers.

The material concerning Spinoza's meeting with a Quaker leader in Amsterdam is from Richard H. Popkins and Michael S. Signer, eds., *Spinoza's Earliest Publication? The Hebrew Translation of Margaret Fell's "A Loving Salutation to the Seed of Abraham among the Jews, wherever they are scattered up and down the Face of the Earth"* (Wolfeboro, N.H.: Van Gorcum, 1987). The letter from the Quaker leader William Ames is from the Introduction to this book. This book also discusses Spinoza and Quakerism, as well as Spinoza's influence on Peter Balling, the author of *The Light on the Candlestick*. Balling's work is also discussed in "Sources of Universalism in Quaker Thought," *The Quaker Universalist Reader, Number 1* (Landenberg, Pa.: Quaker Universalist Fellowship, 1986), and in Israel's *Radical Enlightenment*. The quote from *The Light on the Candlestick* was found in Israel's book.

More information on early Quakerism can be found in Howard H. Brinton, *Friends for 300 Years* (Wallinford, Pa.: PendleHill, 1947). A wonderful fictionalized account of the first Quakers is Jan de Hartog, *The Peaceable Kingdom* (New York: Atheneum, 1971).

The quote by Spinoza concerning everlasting happiness is from his *Treatise on the Emendation of the Intellect,* which I found quoted in *The Courtier and the Heretic* and which can also be found in Baruch Spinoza, *The Ethics, Treatise on the Emendation of the Intellect, Selected Letters,* trans. Samuel Shirley (Indianapolis, Ind.: Hackett, 1992). This translation uses the word joy instead of happiness. Stewart also discusses the three rules of life from this treatise. I also found in Stewart the quote concerning Thales.

The three rules as taken from Shirley's translation of *Treatise on the Emendation of the Intellect* are

1. To speak to the understanding of the multitude and to engage in all those activities that do not hinder the attainment of our aim. For we can gain no little advantage from the multitude, provided that we accommodate ourselves as far as possible to their level of understanding. Furthermore, in this way they will give a little more favorable hearing to the truth. 2. To enjoy pleasures just so far as suffices to preserve health. 3. Finally, to seek as much money or any other goods as are sufficient for sustaining life and health and for conforming with those social customs that do not conflict with our aim.

For my purposes in discussing these rules, I changed the order of the last two. The quotes by Spinoza are taken from Benedict De Spinoza, *Ethics,* trans. by James Gutmann (New York: Hafner, 1957).

The quote on Spinoza's insight is in *Looking for Spinoza.*

The information about cowbirds and the yellow warbler is from Kenn Kaufman, *Lives of North American Birds* (Boston: Houghton Mifflin, 1996).

Damasio discusses the legacy of Spinoza in his book *Looking for Spinoza.* In *Radical Enlightenment,* Jonathan Israel lays out in detail the influence Spinoza had on the Enlightenment, believing that the philosopher "fundamentally and decisively shaped a tradition of radical thinking which eventually spanned the whole continent, exerted an immense influence over successive generations, and shook western civilization to its foundation."

The quote by Einstein is from Ronald W. Clark, *The Life and Times of Albert Einstein* (New York: World, 1971).

Harrison's book *The Elements of Pantheism* includes a nice chapter on the history of pantheism and its expression in nineteenth-century poets and philosophers. I also read Nicholas Boyle, *Goethe: The Poet and the Age* (Oxford, England: Clarendon Press, 1991), and other writers. The quote from Goethe concerning the *Ethics* is in his autobiography, quoted in Damasio's *Looking for Spinoza.* The few lines of poetry from Goethe were translated by Paul Harrison and can be found on his Web site, http://members.aol.com/Heraklit1/poets.htm. The fragments of Coleridge's poetry are from "The Eolian Harp" and "Frost at Midnight" in Elisabeth Schneider, ed., *Samuel Taylor Coleridge, Selected Poetry and Prose* (New York: Rinehart Press, 1971). Wordsworth's lines of poetry are from "Lines Composed a Few Miles above Tintern Abbey," in Geoffrey Hartman, ed., *William Wordsworth, Selected Poetry and Prose* (New York: New American Library, 1970). A discussion of Wordsworth's pantheism, the accusations against him, and his vague replies is in Raymond Dexter Havens, *The Mind of a Poet,* vol. 1 (Baltimore; Md.: Johns Hopkins University Press, 1941). The brief quotes from Blake, Hegel, and Schelling can be found Harrison's *Elements of Pantheism* and elsewhere.

Chapter 7: The Peaceable Kingdom

My sources on Quaker history include some twenty years of reading. One classic reference is Howard H. Brinton, *Friends for 300 Years* (Wallinford, Pa.: PendleHill, 1947).

An account of Sanctuary can be found in Jim Corbett, *Goatwalking: A Guide to Wildland Living and a Quest for the Peaceable Kingdom* (New York: Viking, 1991). This book also includes material about Jim and Nena's trial and the Juniper-Saguaro Land Association. I also recommend Jim Corbett, *Sanctuary for All Life,* ed. by Pat Corbett (Berthoud, Colo.: Howling Dog Press, 2005), and Elna Otter and Dorothy Pine, *The Sanctuary Experience* (San Diego, Calif.: Aventine Press, 2004).

The quote about possessing the earth is from Sharman Apt Russell, *Kill the Cowboy: A Battle of Mythology in the New West* (Reading, Mass.: Addison-Wesley, 1993). Some of the material about Steve and Nena and their work with ranchers was first published in this book.

In my readings on Guatemala, I must include the Guatemalan Human Rights Commission and their regular newsletters. Their Web site is www .ghrc-usa.org.

Chapter 8: Walt Whitman

For the transcendentalists, I enjoyed reading a number of scholarly Web sites, as well as Richard Geldard, ed., *The Essential Transcendentalists* (New York: Jeremy P. Tarcher, 2005), and other books. Ian Frederick Finseth's master's thesis, "Liquid Fire within Me: Language, Self, and Society in Transcendentalism and Early Evangelicalism, 1820–1860," is excerpted on the Web site http://thoreau.eserver.org and mentions the influence of the romantic poets. This is also the source of the 1838 quote from the early transcendentalist Orestes Brownson. The essay by Harold W. Wood, Jr., "Pantheist Prophet: Henry David Thoreau," on the same Web site is the source of the quote by Horace Greeley when he reviewed Thoreau's first book and commented on its pantheistic egotism. Martin Bickman, "An Overview of American Transcendentalism," www.vcu.edu/engweb/transcendentalism, has a good discussion of the influence of the transcendentalists. This is also the source for the story about Dickens and the quote by Poe. The quote from James Freeman Clarke, a member of this elite club, can be found at www.themystica.com/mystica/articles/t/transcendentalism.

The quotes by Thoreau are from Bradley P. Dean, ed., Henry David Thoreau, *Letters to a Spiritual Seeker* (New York: W. W. Norton, 2004).

The quotes from Walt Whitman are from the poem "Walt Whitman," later and more familiarly called "Song of Myself," in Walt Whitman, *Leaves of Grass*

(Brooklyn, N.Y.: Whitman, Rome Bros., 1855). I also used the early edition Walt Whitman, *Leaves of Grass* (Philadelphia: David McCay, Washington Square, 1900). At times, I deliberately mix fragments of Whitman's poetry into a paragraph, trusting that such famous phrases as "The damp of the night drives deeper" will be recognized.

I first wrote about clouds in Sharman Apt Russell, "The Language of Clouds," *Onearth Magazine*, Fall 2003. I also recommend Gavin Pretor-Pinney, *The Cloudspotter's Guide* (New York: Berkeley, 2006).

For the life and times of Walt Whitman, I read a number of sources, including Gay Wilson Allen, *The Solitary Singer: A Critical Biography of Walt Whitman* (New York: Macmillan, 1955); Philip Callow, *From Noon to Starry Night* (Chicago: Ivan R. Lee, 1992); David S. Reynolds, *Walt Whitman's America: A Cultural Biography* (New York: Knopf, 1996); J. R. Masters and Donald D. Krummings, eds., *Walt Whitman: An Encyclopedia* (New York: Garland, 1998); and Roy Morris, Jr., *The Better Angel* (Oxford, England: Oxford University Press, 2000). I also enjoyed Martha C. Nussbaum, *Upheavals of Thought: The Intelligence of Emotion* (Cambridge, England: Cambridge University Press, 2001), and the chapter "Democratic Desire: Walt Whitman."

Information on Walt Whitman's Quaker background can be found under *Q* in *Walt Whitman: An Encyclopedia*. Whitman himself wrote a biography of Elias Hicks, which can be found in Floyd Stovall, ed., *Walt Whitman, Prose Works 1892*, vol. 11. Here Whitman describes the history of Quakerism, its schisms and beliefs, as well as the life, beliefs, and sermons of Hicks. Here, too, is the story of Hicks's comments about the blood of Christ and canes thumping. Whitman's account of listening to Hicks's last sermon is told in a number of biographies, including *The Solitary Singer*.

Whitman's quote on how to live a good life can be found in his 1855 preface to *Leaves of Grass* and in Floyd Stovall, ed., *Walt Whitman, Prose Works 1892*, vol. 11.

The quotes from critics of *Leaves of Grass* are in *Upheavals of Thought*. Whitman's quote "Perhaps I do not know what it all means" is from a correspondence with John Addington Symonds and is also quoted in *Upheavals of Thought*.

The story about Whitman's alleged sexual conduct with teenage boys is controversial. It can be found in *Walt Whitman's America*. Reynolds won a Pulitzer Prize for this biography and discusses the research in an interview on www.booknotes.org.

A good discussion on Whitman in the Civil War is *The Better Angel*. The quote from Whitman on diarrhea is from this book. Concerning the use of calomel, I also read Martha Saxton, *Louisa May: A Modern Biography of Louisa May Alcott* (Boston: Houghton Mifflin, 1977).

Information on West Nile virus and global warming can be found in a number of sources, including Doug Struck, "Climate Change Drives Disease to New Territory," *Washington Post,* May 5, 2006.

A good discussion on Whitman's attitude toward technology is in *Walt Whitman's America* in Chapter 15, "The Burden of Atlas: The New America." Reynolds writes that Whitman saw in technology "an almost transcendental significance."

The quote from George Perkins Marsh can be found in Frank Stewart, *A Natural History of Nature Writing*. This is also the source for the statistics on cars in the early twentieth century and the revival of nature writing.

Chapter 9: The Mind and Body of God

The quotes from Lawrence's character Connie are in D. H. Lawrence, *Lady Chatterley's Lover* (New York: Grove Press, 1962). The quote by Lawrence about the pine tree is in "The Death of Pan" by D. H. Lawrence in Edward D. McDonald, *Phoenix: The Posthumous Papers of D. H. Lawrence* (New York: Viking, 1936).

The quote from Mr. Bentley is in Virginia Woolf, *Mrs. Dalloway* (New York: Harcourt, Brace & World, 1953).

The statement by Robinson Jeffers is from a letter he wrote in 1934, which I found quoted in George Session, "Spinoza and Jeffers on Man in Nature," *Inquiry: An Interdisciplinary Journal of Philosophy and the Social Sciences,* vol. 20, no. 4, Winter 1977.

I have been reading about deep ecology since college. For this book, I depended mainly on Bill Duval and George Sessions, *Deep Ecology* (Salt Lake City, Utah: Peregrine Smith Books, 1985), and George Session, "Spinoza and Jeffers on Man in Nature," *Inquiry: An Interdisciplinary Journal of Philosophy and the Social Sciences,* vol. 20, no. 4, Winter 1977. The quote from Sessions comes from this article.

Berry's theory of the plague can be found in Thomas Berry, *The Dream of the Earth*. This is also the source of his quote on rage and his metaphor of autism.

My thoughts on the hardwiring of the religious impulse have been influenced by a range of reading that covers many years. Most recently, I have enjoyed Pascal Boyer, *Religion Explained* (New York: Basic Books, 2001); Scott Atran, *In Gods We Trust: The Evolutionary Landscape of Religion* (Oxford, England, and New York: Oxford University Press, 2002); Loyal Rue, *Religion Is Not about God* (New Brunswick, N.J.: Rutgers University Press, 2005); and Daniel C. Dennet, *Breaking the Spell: Religion as a Natural Phenomenon* (New York: Viking, 2006). A good summary of current thought is Robin Marantz Henig, "Darwin's God," *New York Times Magazine,* March 4, 2007. Dennet specifically discusses the role of shamanistic healing.

Chapter 10: Make Oneness Your House

For Hinduism and Buddhism, I read many sources, including Kenneth W. Morgan, ed., *The Religion of the Hindus, Interpreted by Hindus* (New York: Ronald Press, 1953); E. A. Burtt, ed., *The Teachings of the Compassionate Buddha* (New York: New American Library, 1955), a book that I bought in India in 1977 for ninety-five cents; Alan W. Watts, *The Way of Zen* (New York: Vintage Books, 1957); David J. Kalupahana, *A History of Buddhist Philosophy* (Honolulu: University of Hawaii Press, 1992); Livia Kohn and Michael Lafargue, *Lao-tze and the Tao-te-ching* (New York: State University of New York Press, 1998); Huston Smith and Philip Novak, *Buddhism: A Concise Introduction* (San Francisco: HarperSanFrancisco, 2003); and Loyal Rue, *Religion Is Not about God* (New Brunswick, N.J.: Rutgers University Press, 2005). For the story of the Buddha's life, my favorite source is Karen Armstrong, *Buddha* (New York: Viking Penguin, 2001). This is a great book. I also enjoyed Karen Armstrong, *The Great Transformation: The Beginning of Our Religious Traditions* (New York: Knopf, 2006).

The quote about the self as a repeatedly reconstructed biological state is from Antonio Damasio, *Descartes' Error: Emotion, Reason, and the Human Brain* (New York: Putnam, 1994).

An important source on Taoism and its assimilation in the West is J. J. Clarke, *The Tao of the West* (London: Routledge, 2000). This book also contains interesting material on Taoism and the new physics and Taoism and deep ecology.

Material on the Warring States Period is from Roger T. Ames and David L. Hall, *A Philosophical Translation, Dao de Jing* (New York: Ballantine Books, 2003).

The quotes from Chuang Tzu come from Burton Watson, trans., *Chuang Tzu* (New York: Columbia University Press, 1964). I also read Arthur Waley, trans. and ed., *The Way and Its Power: Lao Tzu's Tao de Ching and Its Place in Chinese Thought* (New York: Grove Press, 1958), and Lao Tzu, *Tao te Ching*, trans. Richard Wilhelm (New York: Penguin Books, 1990).

For the discussion on Taoism and deep ecology, I particularly read Bill Duval and George Sessions, *Deep Ecology* (Salt Lake City, Utah: Peregrine Smith Books, 1985), and N. J. Giradot, James Miller, and Liu Xiaogan, eds., *Daoism and Ecology: Ways within a Cosmic Landscape* (Cambridge, Mass.: Harvard University Press, 2001).

The quote from George Sessions is from *Deep Ecology*.

The precepts from the early Taoist texts come from Kristofer Schipper, "Daoist Ecology: The Inner Transformation, A Study of the Precepts of the Early Daoist Ecclesia," in *Daoism and Ecology*. Also in this book, the essay by Liu Xiaogon, "Non-Action and the Environment Today: A Conceptual and Applied Study of Laozi's Philosophy," has a good discussion on the use of nonaction.

The quote by Jim about love is from Jim Corbett, *Goatwalking: A Guide to Wildland Living and a Quest for the Peaceable Kingdom* (New York: Viking, 1991). This is also the source of his quote on uselessness.

Chapter 11: Holistic Science

Dennis Miller's research is in John N. Rinne and Dennis Miller, "Hydrology, Geomorphology, and Management: Implications for Sustainability of Southwestern Fishes," *Proceedings of the 2003 Arid Land Symposium*, Tucson, Ariz.

The material about the relationship of quantum physics and Eastern religion is from Fritjof Capra, *The Tao of Physics* (Boston: Shambhala Press, 2000). The quote by Einstein is also in this book, as is the quote from the physicist on pi-mesons and Capra's quote about deep ecological awareness.

More information about Gaia and Harding's theories can be found in Stephan Harding, *Animate Earth: Science, Intuition, and Gaia* (White River Junction, Vt.: Chelsea Green, 2006). Of course, I also recommend any books by James Lovelock, the founder of the Gaia theory.

For material on Barbara McClintock, I read Evelyn Fox Keller, *A Feeling for the Organism: The Life and Work of Barbara McClintock* (New York: W. H. Freeman, 1983). The quote about a feeling for the organism is from this book.

I also read Linda Jean Shepherd, "The Feminine Face of Science," *Resurgence Magazine,* www.resurgence.or/resurgence/articles/shepherd.htm. This article quotes McClintock's ideas about working with chromosomes.

I am a great fan of Ursula Goodenough, *The Sacred Depths of Nature* (Oxford, England: Oxford University Press, 1998). The quotes on assent and on her credo are from this book.

More information on the Institute of Religion in the Age of Science (IRAS) can be found at its Web site, www.iras.org. More information on the World Pantheist Movement is at its Web site, www.pantheism.org.

The quote on the Great Work is from Thomas Berry, *The Great Work: Our Way into the Future* (New York: Harmony/Bell Tower, 2000).

Chapter 12: Meeting for Worship

The brief quotes from Marcus Aurelius are from the *Meditations.*

The quote about silence is from Dillard's essay "The Field of Silence" in Annie Dillard, *Teaching a Stone to Talk* (New York: Harper & Row, 1982).

INDEX